GRACE
AND
SOCIAL
ETHICS

GRACE AND SOCIAL ETHICS

Gift as the Foundation of Our Life Together

ANGELA CARPENTER

Baker Academic
a division of Baker Publishing Group
Grand Rapids, Michigan

Published by Baker Academic
a division of Baker Publishing Group
Grand Rapids, Michigan
BakerAcademic.com

Printed in the United States of America

Library of Congress Cataloging-in-Publication Data
Names: Carpenter, Angela D., author.
Title: Grace and social ethics : gift as the foundation of our life together / Angela Carpenter.
Description: Grand Rapids, Michigan : Baker Academic, a division of Baker Publishing Group, [2024] | Includes bibliographical references and index.
Identifiers: LCCN 2024019822 | ISBN 9781540961815 (paperback) | ISBN 9781540968258 (casebound) | ISBN 9781493447381 (ebook) | ISBN 9781493447398 (pdf)
Subjects: LCSH: Gifts, Spiritual. | Social ethics.
Classification: LCC BT767.3 .C36 2024 | DDC 241—dc23/eng/20240531
LC record available at https://lccn.loc.gov/2024019822

Cover design by Gayle Raymer

Baker Publishing Group publications use paper produced from sustainable forestry practices and postconsumer waste whenever possible.

24   25   26   27   28   29   30   7   6   5   4   3   2   1

For Rob,
with gratitude for the gift
of a life shared with you

CONTENTS

ACKNOWLEDGMENTS

The idea for this book first took root in 2016, while I was a postdoctoral scholar funded by a John Templeton Foundation grant at the University of Notre Dame. It was, the reader may recall, an election year and a time of considerable social and political upheaval, and I was gifted the opportunity to reflect on the events of the day and their intersection with Christian belief and practice. Fast-forward a few years, and I was once again given an opportunity, this time to write the book before you as part of the John Templeton Foundation grant called Collaborative Inquiries in Christian Theological Anthropology. In addition to the John Templeton Foundation, I am grateful to the principal investigator of this grant, Jesse Couenhoven, and co-investigators Gerald McKenny and Neil Arner for convening a group of scholars who were interested in bringing together theological and scientific explorations of the human person and for enabling us to do so in ways that were rigorous and responsible. Jesse, Jerry, and Neil worked intentionally to foster a sense of community among our group (even during a global pandemic and, in many cases, over Zoom) that would outlive the grant itself and would support scholarly collaboration and conversations for years to come. I offer special thanks to Catherine Ricketts, who worked with such care and thoughtfulness in organizing our gatherings. It was a joy to be a part of this project.

My writing mentor, Jennifer Herdt, and writing-group member Kevin Hector faithfully read and incisively commented on drafts of several chapters and offered steady encouragement that this book was worth bringing to fruition. I am grateful to our other grant fellows and mentors, including Elizabeth Agnew Cochran, Emily Dumler-Winckler, Chris Jones, Christina McRorie, Paul Scherz, Patrick Smith, Jonathan Tran, Christiana Zenner, Willa Swenson-Lengyel, Dylan Belton, John Bowlin, and Stephen Pope, for reading portions of this manuscript and for participating in ongoing conversations with me and others. Special thanks are due to Gerald McKenny and Jennifer Herdt, who continued to comment on drafts even after the grant period ended. My science consultants—Agustín Fuentes in anthropology, Benjamin Meagher in social psychology, and Steven McMullen in economics—have guided me to relevant research in their discipline and assisted my understanding of it. Their expertise was invaluable, and any errors are, of course, entirely my own.

I would also like to thank many others who contributed in their own ways to this project. My department chair, Jeff Tyler, and my former dean, Sandra Visser, supported my request for research leave a mere three years into my time at Hope College. My current administrators, Dean Steven Maiullo and Provost Gerald Griffin, graciously granted a semester sabbatical in fall 2023, during which I completed this manuscript. Colleagues at Hope College and Western Theological Seminary listened to and commented on portions of chapter 4 at our regular theology workshop. Several friends and colleagues, including Han-luen Kantzer Komline, Todd Billings, Janna Hunter-Bowman, and Brian Hamilton, read and commented on various portions of this project.

Finally, none of my work would have been possible without the unflagging support of my family. My parents, Ken and Becky Fairbanks, and my sister, Jennifer, have encouraged me throughout the writing process and remained keenly interested in my progress. My daughters, Rilla and Lucy, have shared my time and attention and even attended a presentation to an adult Sunday school class so they could "hear what Mom has been working on." I am especially grateful to my husband, Rob, who has been unfailingly supportive and proud of my work. It is no exaggeration to say that without him, this book would never have been written. In a book that focuses on our foundational human interdependence and on the gifts we are to one another, it is all the more appropriate that I take the opportunity to acknowledge the deep joy I experience in these relationships.

INTRODUCTION

"What do you have that you did not receive?" In his first letter to the church at Corinth, the apostle Paul asks this deceptively simple, yet probing question. With a few words he forces the reader to acknowledge the thread of grace that runs through the whole of Christian thought. When one follows the question to its logical conclusion, the response, of course, is "nothing." We have received everything, even our very existence, as a gift. While this is true, for Christians the concept of grace generally refers to that which we receive through Jesus and the Holy Spirit—forgiveness of sins and the gift of God's own presence with humanity. In this more specific formulation, human beings were made for God, but we could not, even in a state of Adamic innocence, accomplish this for ourselves.[1] We could only ever receive it as a gift. God comes to humanity. Humanity cannot go to God. In Jesus, God has definitively come to humanity and is with humanity. At its core the Christian story is one of dependence and gift.

On the surface, such claims seem lofty and otherworldly, and we are often perfectly content to relegate them to categories like "personal spirituality" or "human salvation" (understood as a matter pertaining to ultimate human destiny after death). Both categories seem divorced from the messy, practical matters of human societies. In this book I will contest such an impression. The fundamental concept of God's grace is not only crucial to thinking about our lives as individuals or to the eschatological hope of beatific vision; it also has

---

1. This notion is contested by federalist theology. Theologians in this tradition theorize a "covenant of works" with Adam in which he had the capacity to obey God's commandments and continue in a blessed state.

profound implications for how we understand human nature and, by extension, for how we should think about human societies.

Christian theological commitment to God's grace is expansive, bearing on
every point of doctrine, from creation to Christology to soteriology. Human
beings are not self-sufficient but are instead dependent on God for our existence, our sustenance, and our rescue from sin and death. Such a degree of
dependency might, in some circumstances, seem like an affront to human
dignity. Being dependent on another person can mean that one is subject to
manipulation and control, to being used as a means to that person's desired
ends. By saying that humans are dependent on God's gift or grace, however,
Christian theology has sought to avoid such implications. Because God offers a gift and invites a response of love and gratitude, God is not seeking
to control human beings or to achieve some private good. Receiving from
outside ourselves—being dependent—is, therefore, not a contradiction or
denigration of our action or agency. Rather, human dependence on God
is the foundation and source of action at every moment. Human agency is
always "acting in dependency" agency. Dependency, whether on God or others, is not something to be overcome and thrown aside, even though modern
Westerners do tend to find it uncomfortable or intolerable.[2] In fact, rejecting
or avoiding this truth about ourselves leads to all sorts of destructive behaviors that Christians have traditionally called sin. Crucial to the claims of this
book will be the idea that we are this same creature, with the same nature
and agency, whether this agency is being expressed in relationship to God
or in relationship to other human beings. Our dependence on God's grace
is primary and fundamental (not to mention asymmetrical; God, after all, is
not dependent on us), but this dynamic of grace and a fundamentally dependent agency is reflected in our bodily existence. Indeed, Jewish and Christian
thought has looked to our bodily dependence—on food or shelter or human
love—to understand our deeper dependence on God's gifts. What does all
of this mean for flourishing human community? At the very least it should
make us suspicious of the assumption that humans should be self-sufficient
and of the notion that we should not need one another, that needing others
is a sign of weakness and failure.

Thus far I have been referring to Christian teaching on grace in the most
general terms, ones that could be embraced broadly by Christians of many
persuasions. But this book will also examine a Reformation account of grace

2. Even in Alasdair MacIntyre's recognition of human dependency, e.g., he portrays "independent practical reasoners" as the *telos*, or goal, of human formation in dependency. See MacIntyre,
Dependent Rational Animals: Why Human Beings Need the Virtues (Chicago: Open Court, 1999),
81.

as affording unique insight.[3] In both Martin Luther and John Calvin one finds not simply a commitment to grace, instantiated in claims of *sola gratia*, but also a *psychology* of grace. The Reformers contrast those individuals who think they can earn or deserve God's approval with those who know God's acceptance and forgiveness are accomplished by Christ and are a gift. For the latter, a different kind of agency and relationship to God are possible. These people can relate to God the way they would relate to a loving parent or friend rather than someone from whom they must secure that which is desperately needed and in danger of being withheld. And furthermore, their actions can be freely undertaken—not for the sake of earning approval but because of the goodness and desirability of the actions themselves.[4] This important strand of Reformation thought has by no means been uncontroversial or unproblematic. Luther at times conflates grace itself with this psychological awareness of it, or at least he so closely connects them that one cannot be the recipient of grace if one is not fully aware and certain of this fact. But despite the difficulties that ensue from this problematic articulation, Luther is right to claim that awareness of grace makes possible something that is otherwise not.

Here again one might ask how such a claim could have implications for human society. An answer to the question will unfold throughout the book, but a few points may be distilled here. First, we might imagine different forms of social organization if we recognize that no one's status or worth arises from their actions, abilities, or accomplishments and if, instead, we see that our actions arise from prior gifts. Second, awareness of grace as a source of worth—both for oneself and for others—enables a different approach to human sociality. Relationships are different if one seeks to encounter and discover the value of another person as opposed to requiring that others establish their own worth. Finally, a different perspective on human sociality prompts a different kind of action toward others, one that might be described as care rather than competition or exploitation. When we believe that we must establish our own worth and provide for ourselves, there is a temptation to see others as opponents whose worth we must surpass or as tools we can use to secure what we need. In other words, how a society chooses to attribute value to human beings shapes the kinds of relationships and actions it cultivates between its members.

3. This is a "Reformation" rather than Reformed account, as it begins with Luther and remains a feature of both Lutheran and Reformed theology.
4. While I take this analysis to be, in some important sense, indebted to the Reformers, it is not exclusively Protestant. I have found one of the more powerful recent expositions to be that of Gustavo Gutiérrez, which makes no reference to the Reformation. Gutiérrez, *On Job: God-Talk and the Suffering of the Innocent* (Maryknoll, NY: Orbis Books, 1987).

The basic argument of this book, then, goes as follows. The kind of creature we are is one whose dependence on God's gifts goes all the way down. From God we receive every good gift, most especially, in Christ, the gift of fellowship or union with God. Furthermore, we are meant to recognize and welcome this truth about ourselves, to let it determine our own self-understanding. We should not, therefore, expect that in our relationships with others we will be somehow fundamentally different creatures. If dependence on the good gifts of God goes all the way down, we should expect this dependence to be reflected or expressed in intrahuman society. This book will explore precisely how grace might be reflected in intrahuman society and how understanding ourselves and others as receivers of gifts can shape our lives together.

Locating the Argument

This book's argument will take shape with respect to three different frames of reference and conversations occurring within them. First, it will fit within a set of intra-Christian conversations regarding the relationship of grace to human action, especially to human morality. Does grace mean that good action does not matter? These conversations have occurred throughout Christian history and, indeed, are evident in the New Testament itself, especially in the Pauline corpus. Most recently, they have focused on the concern that grace as a means of personal salvation does not simply discourage good action in general but especially undermines the political and social dimensions of the gospel. These anxieties have taken slightly different shapes throughout the centuries, but they never seem very far from the surface in any particular era of Christian history. Notable instances have been the controversy between Augustine and Pelagius, Reformation-era debates regarding *sola gratia* and *sola fide*, Walter Rauschenbusch's promotion of the social gospel, and, most recently, debates between American Protestants who identify the Christian faith with social justice and those who are suspicious that such an emphasis threatens the integrity of the gospel. In contemporary academic scholarship, one can see traces of these debates in multiple disciplines. Biblical scholars have sought to recover the social and political implications of Jesus's kingdom language in the Gospels and to relocate a Pauline theology of grace in the context of early Christian debates between Jewish and gentile Christians. Within the field of Christian ethics, scholars like Stanley Hauerwas and his students have developed a more robust ecclesiology to provide an account of Christian character formation and to argue that the gospel is inherently social and political.[5] Jennifer Herdt has traced the historical development of habituation into virtue to better understand certain readings of an Augustinian doctrine of grace and also to critique them from within the tradition itself.[6]

While I will not directly engage each of these avenues of conversation, the very existence of this history does serve to underscore the significance of the topic. Christians across the centuries, it would seem, find that they need to ask and answer anew a very similar set of questions about how grace relates to human action. Rather than viewing this issue as tired or unresolvable, we should perhaps see it as both timeless and generative, prompting reflection on important themes that need to be heard and reformulated again and again. At the same time, certain moments in this history will feature more prominently than others. Writing as a Protestant theologian in the Reformed tradition, I will give special attention to the way these issues were formulated by the magisterial Reformers, especially Luther and Calvin. The point of this engagement, however, is not to invest in specific debates regarding Reformation-era accounts of grace or to defend these accounts directly. Rather, I will take a back-door approach to defending a Reformed account of grace by suggesting that it has something unique to offer. This approach is somewhat unusual in the contemporary landscape in that it offers both a robust doctrine of grace expressed in terms of personal salvation and a sustained concern with what might be broadly characterized as social ethics. I will argue that the *sola gratia* and *sola fide* of the Reformation imply an ethic, a way of being in the world in community with God and neighbor.

All this is not to say that beginning with theologies of grace is the only way or even the best way to think about Christian social ethics. While I will argue that grace can offer a distinctive emphasis—one that is particularly helpful at this time and place—as well as unique insights that might not be as evident otherwise, I will happily concede that there are multiple paths for thinking theologically about human social flourishing. One should expect that those who begin with Christology or with the kingdom of God or some other theological locus would come to similar conclusions, perhaps each with their own distinctive contributions. The decision to do social ethics from the standpoint of grace is a strategic one related to the current state of Protestant Christianity. On the one hand, many American Protestants find a theology of *sola gratia* and *sola fide* to be central to the gospel as they understand it but do not see any particularly compelling reason for Christians to be invested in social justice.

5. Stanley Hauerwas, *A Community of Character: Toward a Constructive Christian Social Ethic* (South Bend, IN: University of Notre Dame Press, 1991).

6. Jennifer Herdt, *Putting on Virtue: The Legacy of the Splendid Vices* (Chicago: University of Chicago Press, 2008).

For these Christians, the central gospel message is personal and spiritual, not social or political. On the other hand, Protestants wishing to emphasize social concerns often accept the same framing—that these are irrelevant to traditional beliefs like *sola gratia*—and they respond by deemphasizing traditional doctrines. In other words, it is precisely because so many Protestants do not see any connection between a core aspect of their tradition—personal salvation that is the result of grace alone—and Christian social ethics that I find it critical that Protestant theology at this moment in time pursue such a connection. The alternative would seem to be Protestants abandoning the project of Christian social ethics or abandoning a distinctively Protestant theology.

The second frame of reference for this book is what seems to be a prominent cultural concern with earning, deserving, or meriting.[7] For example, in early 2019, when the Green New Deal was the subject of considerable public discussion, Ivanka Trump responded to its proposed job and wage guarantee by claiming, "I don't think most Americans, in their heart, want to be given something. I have spent a lot of time traveling around this country over the last four years. People want to work for what they get."[8] Many commentators seized on the irony of a woman who was born into substantial wealth insisting that people want to earn their own way. And yet the very fact that Trump did not recognize this irony, that in her own perception she is instead a self-made woman, is indicative of the reality that, on one level, she is quite right. Human beings, and perhaps particularly Americans, want to see themselves as *deserving*. We want to accomplish things and be appropriately recognized for our accomplishments. We want to see what we have as something we have earned. Furthermore, we tend to view this dynamic in exclusively positive terms.

Examples of this phenomenon abound. I once attended a lecture on Christianity and socialism where the speaker casually claimed that to receive something one has not earned is an affront to human dignity. It struck me as a rather odd claim for a Christian to make. More publicly, Ken Cuccinelli, the director of Citizenship and Immigration Services in the Trump administration, suggested that the poem on the Statue of Liberty would be better if amended to say, "Give me your tired and your poor who can stand on their own two

---

7. This cultural tendency is observed and critiqued in a number of recent books on the failure or weaknesses of meritocracy. See, e.g., Michael J. Sandel, *The Tyranny of Merit: What's Become of the Common Good?* (New York: Farrar, Straus & Giroux, 2020); Daniel Markovits, *The Meritocracy Trap: How America's Foundational Myth Feeds Inequality, Dismantles the Middle Class, and Devours the Elite* (New York: Penguin Press, 2019).

8. Quoted in David Von Drehle, "No, Ivanka Trump. People Don't Want to Work for the Sake of Work," *Washington Post*, February 26, 2019, https://www.washingtonpost.com/opinions/no-ivanka-trump-people-dont-want-to-work-for-the-sake-of-work/2019/02/26/a1b0cf94-3a01-11e9-aaae-69364b2ed137_story.html.

feet and who will not become a public charge."[9] But the point here is not to marshal anecdotal evidence. Rather, the intent is to investigate and analyze social structures and institutions, being especially attentive to how human worth is conceived and recognized. There is now, for instance, a substantial body of research on middle- to upper-class adolescents detailing a profound increase in social pressures to achieve and to portray a façade of perfection to an ever-observant world. Studies of the US criminal-justice system suggest that it is structured less with goals of justice in mind than with the function of distinguishing "good" from "bad" people and dehumanizing those convicted of crimes. Are these social circumstances consistent with a Christian belief that human value is a gift of God that, quite simply, cannot be earned? Does the tension between a society's stated commitment to human dignity and its emphasis on human earning and deserving bear any relation to ongoing Christian discussion about grace and its relationship to action or agency?

Such questions bring us to the third frame of reference: scientific investigation of the human person, including human identity, agency, and sociality. As we consider what it means when we say of human nature that we were made to live by God's grace, we will also examine scientific study of humans. It is not my position here that all theological work within the field of theological anthropology must be interdisciplinary or that theological claims stand or fall with the findings of science. Indeed, scientific discovery is ongoing, and one cannot claim that science offers a definitive source of knowledge about humanity. What, then, does interdisciplinary dialogue have to offer here? Broadly speaking, the engagement with evolutionary anthropology and social psychology will serve three purposes in advancing the argument of the book. First, widespread and cross-disciplinary consensus in the human sciences can offer confirmation of a theological anthropology. It should go without saying that within the discipline of theology there is not simply one anthropology. Even within the boundaries of creedal orthodoxy, we have multiple options for thinking about human beings. It seems perfectly reasonable that, to some extent, empirical evidence—or one might simply say our experience of ourselves as human beings—can provide some guidance, though, naturally, theological arguments will also be a crucial factor. In this book I will argue that the most sound theological arguments and the empirical evidence are actually in agreement and work together in depicting a consistent anthropology. This convergence will end up being fairly significant because a crucial part of my

9. Devan Cole and Caroline Kelly, "Cuccinelli Rewrites Statue of Liberty Poem to Make Case for Limiting Immigration," CNN Politics, August 13, 2019, https://www.cnn.com/2019/08/13/politics /ken-cuccinelli-statue-of-liberty/index.html.

argument is that the humanity we experience in ourselves and encounter in others is a unified one—the nature expressed in intrahuman community is the same one that exists in relationship to God.

The second function of an interdisciplinary engagement with science is to provide a thicker and more specific account of our embodied humanity—especially our capacities for action in relationship to God and to one another. As I will argue, God's grace is primary and fundamental to understanding who we are as human beings, but at the same time we become creatures who are open to the divine and have the capacities for divine-human relationship in and through our embodied humanity. One widely accepted insight along these lines is the oft-observed connection between a person's experience of earthly parents and their understanding of God as father. As we reflect on what makes for a flourishing humanity in all of our relationships, we should be armed with the best information possible, even as we acknowledge that all forms of science are an ongoing inquiry and that future changes in scientific theory might prompt us to revisit our analysis. If such vulnerability makes us uncomfortable, we would do well to situate it within the context of our broader limitations as historically located and finite (not to mention sinful) reasoners—whether we are engaging scientific disciplines or not. Do we not now read with revulsion expressions of anti-Judaism in theological works from throughout the ages? Given the argument of this book, it should behoove us all the more to recognize that anything of lasting value here is always due to the grace of God.

The third area in which a dialogue with the human sciences will prove helpful is in establishing common ground in a pluralist setting. This book, broadly speaking, is a work of theological social ethics. That is, it speaks from a theological perspective to the ethics of how human beings arrange their lives together in society. Since it is a *theological* project, several questions immediately arise. Is the vision that I will develop in these pages one that could apply only to a society composed exclusively of Christians? Such would seem to be the approach of the prominent Hauerwasian strand of Christian ethics, with its focus on the church. Or is this a vision of human society that could apply to a broader swath of humanity, even if the mode of argument is explicitly Christian? Throughout the book I will argue along the lines of the second approach. This book is an effort to think theologically about human community in the form in which Christians today almost exclusively live it: diverse, pluralistic societies.[10] My core argument is that Reformation-era ac-

---

10. In previous eras—e.g., the time in which much of the New Testament was written—there would have been very little purpose to this kind of analysis. Christians by and large had little say in the organization of society. Today's democratic institutions, however, presuppose a government by the people, making social and political reflection a legitimate and crucial task for theology.

counts of grace and salvation have profound implications for how we think about flourishing communities and, by extension, social ethics. As such, it is very much an explicitly Christian vision of human society. Yet this theological vision is intelligible to the non-Christian because it deploys an anthropology that is, to some extent, visible in empirical and scientific investigations of human nature. While scientific study can help establish common ground, it cannot, on its own, provide a robust foundation for social ethics without some other system of value. We Christians may find that as we articulate a Christian vision for human society and seek to marshal empirical evidence that at least partially supports this vision, other parties find they can share aspects of it, albeit on diverse theoretical or ideological grounds.

Each of these three points speaks to the purpose of dialogue with the human sciences, but I would be very remiss if I did not also discuss the method in which theology can undertake this task. Engaging with another discipline without formal training in that field should naturally be undertaken with considerable humility, but a proper intellectual humility is not synonymous with deference to an external authority, whereby theology simply accepts as established fact the claims about human nature made in the name of science.

In the first place, these disciplines have their own internal disagreements, and the theories of one discipline may or may not be consistent with those of another. It thus makes sense to read broadly within a discipline and, if applicable, consider the same set of questions from multiple disciplinary perspectives. In this project we will look at the social dimensions of human agency in both anthropology (with a primary focus on evolutionary anthropology) and social psychology. As one reads broadly, it is crucial to consider the primary scholarship (academic journal articles and published experiments) and not just look at distillations of the literature for a popular audience. Not all studies are equal, and it is possible, even for an outsider, to learn enough about a discipline to be discerning of quality, to evaluate experimental design, to assess the strength and reliability of findings, and so forth. Humanists are not generally experts in the sciences, but we do have valuable critical ability that we can put to use, such as an eye for conceptual clarity and rigor. In making use of scientific research, preference should be given to findings that are broadly shared throughout a discipline and substantiated by multiple and replicated studies. If these claims are substantiated by evidence in another discipline, that is a further point in their favor.

There is more to say along these lines, specifically about research in psychology, given the replication crisis of the last decade. The crisis first entered public consciousness in 2015, when psychologist Brian Nosek and his colleagues attempted to replicate one hundred major psychology studies and found that only thirty-six of them were successfully reproduced.[11] While some of these findings were later challenged by other scholars, the question of reproducibility in psychology remains a challenge for the field as a whole.[12] Many psychologists, especially early-career researchers, are working to develop better standards for data analysis and transparency, but it remains an open question as to how much confidence one should have in psychology research from the past several decades. In this project I have been attentive to criteria that psychologists use in identifying questionable versus more reliable research, and I will occasionally make reference to some of these criteria specifically.

A theologian participating in dialogue with the human sciences must be attentive to and critically assess the assumptions that undergird particular scientific theories or lines of empirical research. Even though scientists value objectivity and proceed, ideally, on the basis of empirical evidence, there is no such thing as a value-neutral or completely objective science. The questions one chooses to investigate and the hypotheses one develops might be prompted by any number of concerns that are completely separate from empirical evidence. It is possible that a scientific starting point might, with no sound empirical reason, even be hostile to theological concerns. The careful reader of scientific literature will consider how research trajectories are established and shaped by a variety of unspoken commitments, and the theological reader will be especially attentive when these assumptions presume a world closed off from the divine and from God's grace.

The Progression of the Book

The arguments of this book will unfold in two parts. In part 1, I will examine the theological and scientific resources for articulating a vision of the human person as constituted by gift or grace. Then, in part 2, I will draw on this graced anthropology to analyze three contemporary social issues. My own starting point and theological commitments will be explicitly stated and analyzed in chapter 1, where I will explore the anthropological implications of grace in Christian theology, with particular attention to what I will call the Reformation psychology of grace. I will provide a brief history of Christian reflection

11. Brian A. Nosek, "Estimating the Reproducibility of Psychological Science," *Science* 349, no. 6251 (August 28, 2015): aac4716.

12. For more information on the crisis and the efforts within psychology to respond to it, see Marcus Munafo et al., "A Manifesto for Reproducible Science," *Nature Human Behaviour* 1, article 21 (2017); Joseph P. Simmons et al., "False-Positive Psychology: Undisclosed Flexibility in Data Collection and Analysis Allows Presenting Anything as Significant," *Psychological Science* 22 (2011): 1359–66.

on grace, both to better understand this central Christian commitment in its complexity and to provide context for the particular version of it that appears in the sixteenth century. Then I will turn to Martin Luther and John Calvin and examine their teaching on justification by faith. I will argue that the emphasis on one's knowledge or awareness of grace is critical to these Reformers' thinking. This distinctive aspect has much to offer Christian theology, especially in its grasp of human dependence and the psychological dynamics of loving relationships, but unfortunately the same theological commitments that provide substantial insight into human nature are also the source of the Reformers' greatest theological vulnerabilities. I will conclude the chapter by arguing that the broader Christian tradition can benefit from these insights without necessarily repeating the Reformers' theological errors.

Next, I will turn to the scientific study of nature, particularly of human social capacities and relationships. In chapter 2, I will examine the recent turn to the theme of cooperation in the study of human evolution. Contradicting old stereotypes of violent male hunters providing for a nuclear family, recent work on evolutionary anthropology explores a variety of evolutionary pressures that suggest a fundamental vulnerability of early humans and an increasing reliance on cooperation in small communities. To the extent that these theories are correct, they suggest that humans evolved in an environment that selected for cooperative social traits, including emotional and social intelligence. Various forms of paleoanthropological evidence indicate that this trajectory of human evolution extends deep into our evolutionary history, with the corresponding implication that the resulting suite of social capacities are firmly entrenched in human biology. Furthermore, while competition among individuals is certainly a part of the human lineage, these theories suggest a fundamental primacy of membership. They suggest that belonging in a community and mutual inter-dependence among its members is of greater significance than the competition for status and power within it. Equally important, however, is the flexible character of human social relationships and social organization. Both cooperation and competition are important in the human lineage, and there are myriad ways in which individual societies have negotiated these conflicting impulses.

In chapter 3, I will explore two social motivations that are prominent in the field of social psychology: the need to belong and the need for self-worth or self-esteem. Both of these drives motivate social interaction and facilitate cooperation. The literature on the need to belong reveals that persons who have stable and loving interpersonal relationships experience many physical and psychological benefits. Such individuals are paradoxically enabled in their agency as individuals, as displayed in traits such as initiative, resilience, authenticity, and compassion. In the language of this book, belonging can be a gift that facilitates flourishing. In addition to needing to belong, human beings also display a strong desire to feel a sense of self-worth, so much so that they will even deceive themselves about their abilities, successes, and failures. This desire to feel worthy can motivate actions that are valued by the broader social group, but failure to establish a sense of worth as a person can lead to depression or be incapacitating. Understanding the role of self-esteem in human sociality will help set the stage for a theological grounding of worth as the beloved child of God, a worth that is given prior to and apart from any action.

I will conclude the theoretical analysis of grace and theological anthropology in part 1 with a theological discussion of grace and human community. Why should a human dependence on God's grace have implications for our lives together? Here I will argue that if we are to be consistently the same creature, then our social lives must also reflect our origin in gift. It is in our lives together that we learn the humility and gratitude that are appropriate responses to God's grace, and it is when human social existence reflects the overflowing love of God that it sacramentally reflects divine being. This connection between grace and social existence is not a new argument but one that is present in the Pauline corpus and in the economic analyses of Luther and Calvin. Drawing on this theology and on the scientific study of human nature in the previous chapters, this chapter will offer concluding guidelines regarding how an anthropology of grace can be foundational for human social thought in other contexts.

In part 2, we will turn our attention to several specific social issues. These topics have been selected not only for their contemporary salience but also because they afford opportunities to examine the significance of different aspects of Christian grace—specifically creation, redemption, and eschatological hope. The argument in the second half of the book is that the graced anthropology developed in part 1 can function as a tool for analyzing existing social structures and for assessing the extent to which they are consistent with human beings existing and living by grace.

Chapter 5 will consider questions of human agency and human value through an analysis of work in the contemporary American context. In Christian thought, work has traditionally been construed as a way for individuals to contribute to the common good and as an ascetic practice to discipline desire and instill virtue. In this chapter I will argue that cultural and economic shifts call for a different analysis. In the US context, work has become a means of establishing identity and self-worth and of assigning social value to others. Many of the poorest Americans work in low-skilled jobs in which they are treated as expendable rather than as creatures with the calling to live in fellowship with God and neighbor. Meanwhile, highly educated professionals devote more and more of themselves to work as a way to establish their own identity and value instead of receiving these things as gifts. Here I will argue that a theology of grace prompts cultural shifts in the meaning and value of work and structural changes in how work is connected to the distribution of the gifts of creation.

Chapter 6 will take on the question of grace as it relates to sin and redemption through an analysis of the US criminal justice system. While crime and sin are not synonymous, many serious crimes would also fall within the Christian category of sin. In this chapter I will undertake a more thorough discussion of sin and original sin, including the universal need for grace, to argue that the predominant American Christian approaches to crime have been too quick to assume that the full responsibility for crime lies with the perpetrators. Rather, the doctrine of original sin provides a complex account of human agency in which people are responsible for their sin, but sinful dispositions (and sometimes even sinful behaviors) are not something individuals consciously choose for themselves. Furthermore, in keeping with the interdependence of a humanity constituted by and for grace, each person plays a role in reproducing sin in the broader social context. As such, we should think about crime not in terms of individual sin and punishment, but rather in terms of communal sin and the work of God's grace to produce repentance and restoration. The current model of punitive mass incarceration, with its routine degradation of the human person, stands in stark contradiction to the Christian commitment to grace and hope for transformation.

Chapter 7 will consider God's eschatological promises in the context of human finitude and vulnerability. Fear and anxiety are pervasive responses to finitude, especially in our current cultural context. Our vulnerabilities lead us to turn inward protectively, to reject the call to love our neighbor, and to despair at the impotence of finite human agency in the face of profound social problems. I will argue that eschatological grace opposes a life thus determined by fear. The confidence that Christ meets the person at the frontier of death should interrupt the anxious preoccupation with one's own needs and open the person up to a broader concern for human community and love of neighbor. Furthermore, God's ultimate responsibility for the restoration of creation can mitigate the temptation to despair at human limitations. I will explore these dynamics in relation to the contemporary epidemic of gun violence—an epidemic that includes not only the terror of mass shootings but also the everyday reality of gun homicide and suicide. In a cultural context where Christians are particularly inclined to rely on guns for a sense of security and safety, God's promise to act on our behalf should enable Christian gun owners and Christian gun-control activists to refocus the conversation on gun violence away from individual vulnerabilities and toward communal flourishing.

PART 1

AN ANTHROPOLOGY OF GRACE

CHAPTER 1

CHRISTIAN GRACE AND THE REFORMATION PSYCHOLOGY

There is, for Christians, literally nothing that does not have its origin in God and is not, at the most basic level, a gift. God creates *ex nihilo*, out of nothing, which means that existence itself derives from God, as do creatures' particular abilities and characteristics. The necessities for ongoing sustenance, like food or rain, are likewise gifts of God. When contemporary Christians think of grace, however, they are typically thinking more specifically of the person and action of Jesus, especially the incarnation, death, and resurrection of Jesus and the subsequent giving of the Holy Spirit.

What does it mean to say that in *Jesus* grace is given to humanity? In one early Christian account, that of Athanasius in *On the Incarnation*, Jesus restored God to humanity and joined human nature to God. According to Athanasius, God initially created human beings with a special gift, the image of God, which was a participation or creaturely sharing in the divine life. When this image was corrupted through sin, humanity lost its share in the divine nature and was subject to natural decay and corruption. In the incarnation, Jesus restored this divine image to human nature and enabled humanity to share once again in the divine life and to know God.[1] Athanasius also discusses a second sense in which God extended grace to humanity: by undergoing, on

---

1. Athanasius, *On the Incarnation* ¶¶3–5, 11–13.

humanity's behalf, the death that results from sin. When humanity fell into sin, the consequence of disobedience was that humanity would know "the corruption of death according to nature."[2] To rescue humanity from this fate, Christ offered his own body "as a substitute for all" and, through the grace of the resurrection, restored life to human beings.[3]

In general, Catholic thought about grace tends to contrast it with nature: grace is what is given to human beings beyond their created nature, like Athanasius's interpretation of the image of God or the gift of the Spirit in baptism, to bring them into communion with God. Protestant thought, by contrast, tends to focus on sin: grace is focused on Jesus's death and resurrection, which he endured for the forgiveness of sin and defeat of death.[4] In this work by Athanasius, we see each of the two senses of grace. We see grace as that which is given in addition to nature—the participation in the divine life that is depicted by the language of the image of God. And we see grace that is a counterpoint to sin, canceling out sin's consequence of death. In both cases, the objective of God's grace is to bring to fruition God's purpose of humanity being in union or communion with God. Of knowing God.

I begin with Athanasius's account of God's grace in Christ because it depicts both the stereotypically Catholic and the stereotypically Protestant framings of grace. In the account of grace that I develop in this book, both perspectives are present, and both will be important in thinking about social ethics. Because the tension between grace and ethics has, however, typically been a Protestant tension, I am particularly interested in the formulation of grace that emerges in the Reformation. We are, mercifully, in an era in which Christians are seeking to reconcile these ancient divisions, as the Catholic-Lutheran *Joint Declaration on the Doctrine of Justification*, which has now been affirmed by the Reformed communion, illustrates. In such an era of reconciliation, I have little interest in a full-throated defense of Luther's or Calvin's doctrine of grace. The Reformers were not always right, and much that was said then was appropriate to a very distinctive moment and is perhaps less helpful now. Instead, I wish to ask, What does the Reformation account of grace have to offer that is distinctive? What does it contribute?

One answer, I think, is that the Reformers and those who follow them offer us extended reflection on why it is important for human beings to grasp God's grace thoroughly and to live life suffused with this recognition. In other

2. Athanasius, *On the Incarnation* ¶3, trans. John Behr, Popular Patristics Series 44A (Yonkers, NY: St. Vladimir's Seminary Press, 2011), 52.
3. Athanasius, *On the Incarnation* ¶9, 58.
4. See Karen Kilby, "Paradox and Paul: Catholic and Protestant Theologies of Grace," *International Journal of Systematic Theology* 22, no. 1 (January 2020): 77–82.

words, the Reformation account of grace offers us a lengthy meditation on a distinctive psychology. The primary objective of this chapter is to understand this distinctive Reformation emphasis and locate it in relation to the broader history of Christian reflection on grace. A second objective will be to assess this Reformation emphasis, analyzing its strengths and weaknesses. The final objective, which is woven throughout the chapter, is anthropological. What does the broader Christian teaching on grace, both Catholic and Protestant, mean for our understanding of human nature? This theological understanding of human persons will provide the foundation for my reflection throughout the rest of the book about the flourishing of human communities.

A Brief History of Grace

Before we look specifically at the contributions of the early Reformers, it is helpful to have a broader sense of some of the ways Christians have understood grace throughout the centuries. This survey will be unavoidably brief, but the goal is not to have a comprehensive grasp of the development of the related doctrines. Rather, I will seek to understand the continuity in Christian teaching about grace—what it has at least minimally meant throughout the centuries—and to provide some context for recognizing what is distinctive about Luther and those who follow him.

Athanasius's discussion of Christ is broadly consistent with the patristic pattern. Grace describes the actions of Jesus on behalf of human beings, and there is a particular emphasis on the elevation of humanity to life with God. The death and resurrection of Jesus also result in the forgiveness of sin, though this is sometimes only for sins committed before baptism, as indicated by the frequent decision to delay baptism until one's deathbed. In his *Commentary on the Epistle to the Romans*, for instance, Origen puts particular emphasis on the apostle Paul's comment that God "had passed over the sins previously committed" (Rom. 3:25). For Origen, this comment suggests that the forgiveness of sins through Christ's death applies only to sins committed before a person came to faith.[5] Origen anticipated an ongoing purgation of subsequent sin through suffering, both in and after this life, that would ultimately result in the salvation of all. Given Origen's universalism, it makes more sense to interpret this suffering or punishment for sins committed after baptism as a means of grace rather than a contradiction of grace. And in general, the moral rigorism of the early centuries of Christianity was understood to be compatible with

5. Origen, *Commentary on the Epistle to the Romans* 3.9.4.

God's grace. For instance, in the late second-century account of the martyrdom of Perpetua and Felicitas, the great actions of the martyrs are simultaneously their own victories and the result of divine grace. The editor of Perpetua's narrative attributes them to "extraordinary graces" and claims that "God always achieves what he promises."[6] While grace is thus robustly affirmed in the first four centuries, one finds little theorization about grace as an abstract concept, a fact that is hardly surprising given that the primary theological controversies of the earliest centuries focused on the person of Christ. This changed in the fifth century with the debates about sin and grace that centered on the teaching of Pelagius.[7]

Prior to his disagreements with Augustine, the British monk and theologian Pelagius was busy defending the goodness of creation, and especially of humanity, in the face of Manichaean claims that matter was inherently evil.[8] It makes sense that Pelagius would be particularly sensitive to suggestions that human nature might be morally corrupt. Pelagius denied neither human sinfulness nor God's grace, but his way of understanding each of these things emphasized the freedom of the will. Regarding sin, Pelagius maintained that it came about through the imitation of the evil example of others, initially Adam and Eve, and eventually consolidated into a pattern and habit of sinfulness. While Pelagius believed a person could freely choose a sinless life, he thought it would be extremely rare and difficult and did not claim sinlessness for himself. The grace that rescued human beings from sin included forgiveness through Christ's death, but much more important for Pelagius was the virtuous example of Jesus. Since sin had its origin in the imitation of sinners, salvation came primarily, though not exclusively, from imitating the perfect example of the incarnate Christ.[9]

In his debates with Pelagius, Augustine insisted that the consequences of Adam and Eve's actions were much more severe for human nature than the simple setting of a bad example that others imitated. Much, of course, has been said about Augustine's account of sin, but for our purposes the crucial features are sin's pervasive impact on all of human nature and its effect on the

---

6. *Martyrdom of Perpetua and Felicitas* ¶1, in *After the New Testament: A Reader in Early Christianity*, ed. Bart D. Ehrman (New York: Oxford University Press, 1999), 43.

7. While Augustine is often portrayed as breaking new ground in his theology of grace, he stands in greater continuity to earlier approaches than is typically acknowledged. See Han-luen Kantzer Komline, "Grace, Free Will, and the Lord's Prayer: Cyprian's Importance for the 'Augustinian' Doctrine of Grace," *Augustinian Studies* 45, no. 2 (2014): 247–79.

8. This account of Pelagius's theology is drawn from Stuart Squires, *The Pelagian Controversy: An Introduction to the Enemies of Grace and the Conspiracy of Lost Souls* (Eugene, OR: Pickwick, 2019), 183–93.

9. Squires, *Pelagian Controversy*, 189–90.

will. Adam's sin changed not just Adam but all of his descendants for ill. This change in human nature consisted in a defect of the will, an inward bent that denied the human need for God and replaced it with self-reliance and selfishness. Because this defect affected everyone from birth, and because it involved the will, Augustine believed it was insufficient to say that grace could consist in something external, like the law or the example of Christ. Even if people outwardly obeyed the law, which they might do through fear of punishment, they would still be sinning by not genuinely loving God.[10] Rather, grace involved an internal transformation through the indwelling Holy Spirit. Grace was interior, and it was prior to and enabled good human action.[11] In practice this meant that a person should try to obey the law and should also pray for the grace to do what the commandment required.[12] With Augustine we see a complexity to theological anthropology. Human nature is not static in salvation history. The initial, created nature of Adam and Eve was good but had a potential for disobedience to or rejection of God. Since the fall, human nature has been universally corrupt and under the influence of sin. With Christ, however, human nature not only is restored by grace, so that it is possible for a person to do good, but eventually, in the life to come, surpasses the original created goodness by being unable to sin.[13]

The Pelagian controversy resulted in official condemnation of many of Pelagius's teachings on sin and grace, while the Augustinian emphases in the doctrine of grace would remain prominent in Christian reflection in the West and gain greater specificity and technical clarity in the medieval period. Thomas Aquinas, for instance, maintained a robustly Augustinian doctrine of grace whereby virtue—the theological virtues of faith, hope, and love as well as the cardinal virtues—was infused in the Christian. For Aquinas, the need for grace within a person was not only about overcoming sinfulness but was also, perhaps even more prominently, about elevating human nature so that it could experience communion with God. Grace was necessary to accomplish something that human nature, even in an unfallen state, could not do for itself.

10. This argument becomes crucial for Luther as well. See Phillip Cary, "The Lutheran Codicil: From Augustine's Grace to Luther's Gospel," *Logia* 20, no. 4 (2011): 5–9.

11. See Jesse Couenhoven, *Predestination: A Guide for the Perplexed* (London: T&T Clark, 2018), 24.

12. On holding together the tension between trying to obey and asking for grace, see Han-luen Kantzer Komline, "Preaching on God's Grace and Our Willing," in *Cambridge Companion to Augustine's Sermons*, ed. David V. Meconi and Andrew Hofer, forthcoming.

13. On the complexities of Augustine's use of this classic fourfold understanding of human nature, see Han-luen Kantzer Komline, *Augustine on the Will: A Theological Account* (New York: Oxford University Press, 2020), 11.

The late medieval era was marked by more intense scrutiny of the human role in salvation, with some influential theological factions shifting their teaching in the direction of Pelagianism.[14] The theological movement that scholars now refer to as the *via moderna* (modern way) speculated that if people did what they were capable of doing, even though these efforts fell far short of perfection, such people would then merit the infusion of grace.[15] This *pactum*, or agreement, between God and humanity is indicative of a broader late medieval anxiety surrounding salvation, one that can be seen in the increasing prominence of the sacrament of penance and the sale of indulgences. Martin Luther began his theological career very much in this milieu. The early Luther, who adhered to the *via moderna*, agonized over the question of whether he had, in fact, done that which he was capable of doing, and he frequently availed himself of the sacrament of penance. He became increasingly convinced that he could never be sufficiently confident in his own efforts to do enough, and his thinking on the subject underwent a (literally) revolutionary change through his fresh encounter with the writings of Paul.

As a religion centered on God coming to humanity rather than human beings going to God, Christian theology has always, to one extent or another, been a theology of grace. As such, it has also been about human dependence on God, not just for the biological necessities of life or the continuation of bodily and spiritual existence but even for human agency. As this brief history illustrates, grace involved the transformation of life and action, and this transformation was understood to be the work of Christ and the Spirit. Human agency was genuine and free but also dependent. For Augustine and those after him, human beings were capable of fellowship with God because God transformed them internally. God gave the love with which the person loved God and by which the person could eventually be reconciled and restored to God.

Luther and the Reformation Psychology of Grace

Luther and subsequent Protestant Reformers introduced one very significant shift in how the grace of Christ was understood. Prior to the Reformation, a person's standing before God as righteous (or "justification," in technical theological terminology) was based on Christ's forgiveness of sins and on transforming grace ("sanctification," in technical terms), which was the love poured into the soul that Augustine insisted was necessary for a human nature that

14. Stephen J. Duffy, *The Dynamics of Grace* (Eugene, OR: Wipf & Stock, 1993), 173–74.
15. Duffy, *Dynamics of Grace*, 174–77. See also Alister McGrath, *Iustitia Dei: A History of the Doctrine of Justification*, 2nd ed. (Cambridge: Cambridge University Press, 1998), 170–72.

was internally warped and incapable of loving God. Unlike those before him, Luther conceptually separated these two aspects of salvation.[16] For Luther, a person's status before God as righteous was based solely on the forgiveness that came through faith in Christ and did not depend on any actions the person might take, even those that arose from faith and were the work of the Spirit. Luther asserted that a person of faith was *simul justus et pecator*, "simultaneously righteous and a sinner." Since the resolution of the Pelagian controversy, theologians throughout church history had claimed, in one way or another, that people were righteous because God, by grace, transformed them internally so that they were capable of acting rightly. Although the *via moderna* theologians stretched this claim to the breaking point, they still technically maintained that it was God's grace that made a person truly righteous. In contrast to the *via moderna*, according to which the person first needed to do everything within their capacity to merit God's grace, Luther wanted to claim, with no room for ambiguity, that a person's acceptance before God (justification) was not the result of their actions, even righteous actions that had been made possible by the Spirit (sanctification).

Luther's claims about justification understandably raised questions about the significance of morally good action—"good works" in the theological language of the time. A surface reading of Luther might suggest that because good works did not contribute to a person's status before God, they were, therefore, superfluous. Luther, however, did not believe this was the case. Instead of good works contributing to one's status before God, one's status as accepted by God supported and enabled the doing of good works. Through faith, itself the work of the Holy Spirit, a person would begin to exhibit the "active righteousness" of love of God and neighbor. Luther referred to justification and sanctification as "two kinds of righteousness"—the alien righteousness from Christ that was given to the person who repented in faith and the active righteousness that resulted from the reception of Christ's righteousness.[17] This basic description might give the impression that the primary feature distinguishing Luther from those who came before him was a technicality, the proper ordering of what took place in human salvation. But we do not see the full picture of what is unique about Luther, and why this order matters to him, until we examine what I call the distinctive Reformation psychology of grace.

This psychology of grace appears clearly and forcefully in Luther's early writings as a Reformer, particularly *On the Freedom of a Christian* and the *Treatise*

---

16. McGrath, *Iustitia Dei*, 209.

17. See Gifford Grobien, "Righteousness, Mystical Union, and Moral Formation in Christian Worship," *Concordia Theological Quarterly* 77 (2013): 144–46.

on Good Works, both written in 1520. Here Luther distinguishes between those people who do good works in order to secure God's approval and those who "live by faith," trusting that God already loves and forgives them. The former, who have not learned of God's grace in Christ, really only worship a God of their own imagination, a God who, they assume, hates sin and is pleased by good works. In their fierce desire to gain God's approval, they even invent good works. These moral agents are idolatrous, using their own actions to control and manipulate a God of their own invention. For Luther, such individuals act "as if God were in our service or debt and we were his liege lords."[18] Luther also sees many of these individuals as "weighed down by all this to the point of despair" and "miserable with anxiety."[19] Even if certain individuals are somewhat successful in keeping their own high standards, their posture toward such a God cannot be one of love but only of fear. Nor can they glorify God, for their good works are their own accomplishment over and against the God who demands them.[20]

By contrast, those who live by faith are transformed through the knowledge of grace and by the Word of God, which tells them first that they are sinful and then that they are forgiven. This knowledge produces several effects. First, their conscience is no longer crushed by the burden of unending works, especially, for Luther, those "many and useless" ones that have not been commanded by God.[21] Next, the knowledge that they are sinners and cannot keep the law means that the glory of human salvation is exclusively God's.[22] God commands, but God also fulfills through faith what is commanded, leaving no space for human self-congratulation.[23] Finally, and most significantly for our purposes, when people choose to do good works from a position of faith, those works are genuine and "free." Previously, good works—especially, for Luther, ceremonial works—were of ambiguous value because the agent's objective was not love or worship of God but, rather, establishing their own good reputation and being able to make a legitimate claim with God. For Luther, however, faith implies absolute trust in God and therefore makes people "genuine and lively children of God."[24] Any works such as fasting or religious observance undertaken in the context of such faith will thus also be sincere worship.

18. Martin Luther, *The Large Catechism,* trans. Robert H. Fischer (Philadelphia: Fortress, 1959), 11.

19. Martin Luther, *Treatise on Good Works,* trans. Scott H. Hendrix (Minneapolis: Fortress, 2012), 23.

20. For a thorough exposition of this psychology, see Randall Zachman, *The Assurance of Faith* (Louisville: Westminster John Knox, 2005).

21. Martin Luther, *The Freedom of a Christian,* in *Martin Luther's Basic Theological Writings,* ed. Timothy F. Lull (Minneapolis: Fortress, 1989), 601.

22. Luther, *Freedom of a Christian,* 601, 603, 615.

23. Luther, *Freedom of a Christian,* 601. See also Zachman, *Assurance of Faith,* 41.

24. Luther, *Treatise on Good Works,* 30.

This sincerity of human action means that the works are "free," though not in the sense that people can do good works or omit them according to their choosing. Antinomianism might be a perennial risk in Protestant thought, but it is explicitly not Luther's intention. In *The Freedom of a Christian*, he repeatedly states that Christians should do good works.[25] When Luther says that individuals are free, he means that they are not compelled to act in order to secure something for themselves or to look good to God and others.[26] God's grace has ruled out these motivations by preemptively granting all that anyone ultimately needs, including God's love, forgiveness, and acceptance. Thus, the works are free because they can be undertaken for the sake of the work itself—in other words, out of love for God and neighbor. As Luther writes, "From now on I need nothing except faith which believes that this is true. Why should I not therefore freely, joyfully, with all my heart, and with an eager will do all things which I know are pleasing and acceptable to such a Father who has overwhelmed me with his inestimable riches."[27] Here the gratitude that one feels toward God because of God's grace evokes a genuine and joyful response. In describing these works that please God, Luther does not simply mean works of a religious nature; he includes ordinary daily activities such as "walking or standing still, eating, drinking, sleeping, or engaging in any activity that sustains the body or promotes the common good."[28]

The psychology I am describing here is no doubt familiar to most readers of Reformation theology. What is particularly important to underscore is that this is not simply a cognitive knowledge but is, rather, more similar to what contemporary psychology calls a self-concept. It has to do with a core understanding of oneself, whether explicit or implicit, which provides the foundation for action in a social world. We will examine the psychology literature on self-concept in chapter 3, but for now it is sufficient to see that Luther is describing a self-understanding that is constitutive of a person and that Luther believes can and should be cultivated and strengthened. This distinction comes out most clearly when he speaks of the "inner man" or the "heart." He criticizes those who would preach of Christ's life and teaching as "historical facts, as if the knowledge of these would suffice for the conduct of life."[29] Rather, Luther is after a much more intimate connection that is transformational, "that he may not only be Christ, but be Christ for you and me, and that what is said

25. Luther, *Freedom of a Christian*, 610–12, 621, 624–25, 628.
26. Luther, *Freedom of a Christian*, 615.
27. Luther, *Freedom of a Christian*, 619.
28. Luther, *Treatise on Good Works*, 20.
29. Luther, *Freedom of a Christian*, 609.

of him . . . may be effectual in us."[30] When this takes place, Christians learn that they are "kings and priests and therefore lords of all."[31] On the basis of this realization about the self who is united to Christ, one will, in turn, react differently in the world:

> What man is there whose heart, upon hearing these things, will not rejoice to its depth, and when receiving such comfort will not grow tender so that he will love Christ as he never could by means of any laws or works? Who would have the power to harm or frighten such a heart? If the knowledge of sin or the fear of death should break in upon it, it is ready to hope in the Lord. It does not grow afraid when it hears tidings of evil. It is not disturbed when it sees its enemies. This is so because it believes that the righteousness of Christ is its own and that its sin is not its own, but Christ's, and that all sin is swallowed up by the righteousness of Christ.[32]

Here it is not only knowledge of Christ, but an understanding of who the person is in relation to Christ, that is crucial for human agency. As Gifford Grobien notes, Luther's anthropology is fundamentally relational and dependent, and he is very attuned to the ways in which humans look to society for approval and worth.[33] For Luther, all such efforts are ultimately doomed to failure because God is the only true source of worth or value. It is when such faith or trust in Christ is "strong and substantial" that believers are able to bear the knowledge of other truths about themselves, such as the sinfulness and inadequacy of their actions.[34] Luther further emphasizes the psychological component when he insists that God's mercy must be "forever before my eyes" and that an "awareness of your grace through faith" will make the heart glad.[35] He also repeatedly speaks of faith in terms of confidence in God's favor and as an attitude that can be practiced: the Christian is "learning constantly to do everything with that trust."[36] This confidence is most especially strengthened by beholding Christ. It is not manufactured but, rather, "must bubble up and flow from the blood, wounds, and death of Christ."[37]

For Luther, the sense of self as accepted by God because of Christ is at odds with what people can observe about their own ability to keep God's

---

30. Luther, *Freedom of a Christian*, 609.
31. Luther, *Freedom of a Christian*, 609.
32. Luther, *Freedom of a Christian*, 609.
33. Gifford Grobien, *Christian Character Formation: Lutheran Studies of the Law, Anthropology, Worship and Virtue* (Oxford: Oxford University Press, 2019), 126–29.
34. Luther, *Treatise on Good Works*, 36.
35. Luther, *Treatise on Good Works*, 36.
36. Luther, *Treatise on Good Works*, 31.
37. Luther, *Treatise on Good Works*, 37.

law.[38] Experience tells them about their sin, failure, and inadequacy and can only confirm their condemnation. What is more, Luther has rather robust thinking about the role of the devil in a person's inner life. Satan, the accuser, is constantly seeking to sow seeds of doubt about a person's identity. As Heiko Oberman puts it, "For Luther, the conscience is so clearly the Devil's prize that the Devil appears, boring into us and gnawing us when we go to bed at night and look back on the day's events. . . . The Devil is not only an exterior power, hidden under avarice and sexual lust. He reaches right into the *center* of the human soul and employs the voice of conscience for his own purposes."[39] This language of the devil can be somewhat jarring to the modern reader, for whom talk of the devil is comparatively rare. It is worth observing here that this is the precise area where modern people still use the metaphor of the demonic. We "face our personal demons" in the torturous questions of what to believe about ourselves when we are confronted with empirical evidence showing we are not the person we wish we were and when we experience our most profound feelings of failure and inadequacy.

The Psychology of Grace in Calvin

As Alister McGrath notes, the Protestant Reformation was not exclusively, or even primarily, about the doctrine of justification, even though it was clearly a preoccupation for Luther.[40] Some significant later Reformed figures, like the Puritan Jonathan Edwards, even explicitly rejected the psychology laid out by Luther.[41] Such cannot be said of John Calvin, who in this respect agreed wholeheartedly with Luther while also making substantive contributions of his own.[42] References to the psychological character and effects of faith abounded in Calvin's *Institutes of the Christian Religion*. Faith involved knowledge "that God is our merciful father, because of reconciliation effected through Christ."[43]

38. Zachman, *Assurance of Faith*, 58.

39. Heiko Oberman, *The Reformation: Roots and Ramifications* (Grand Rapids: Eerdmans, 1994), 66 (emphasis original).

40. McGrath, *Iustitia Dei*, 208–9.

41. Jonathan Edwards argues that love of God resulting only from gratitude for what God has done for the person cannot be genuine love of God because the true object of love in this case is the self, not the goodness or excellence of God. See Edwards, *The Religious Affections* (1746; repr. Edinburgh: Banner of Truth Trust, 1997), 165–73.

42. I provide a more thorough analysis of this psychological dynamic in Calvin's thought in Angela Carpenter, *Responsive Becoming: Moral Formation in Theological, Evolutionary, and Developmental Perspective* (London: T&T Clark, 2019), 13–44.

43. John Calvin, *Institutes of the Christian Religion* 3.2.2, ed. John T. McNeill, trans. Ford Lewis Battles (Philadelphia: Westminster, 1960), 545.

This was especially important to Calvin because if Christians did not realize that God wills their good, their conscience could only "tremble and be afraid" or "shun the God whom it dreads."[44] It was, Calvin said, "upon grace alone that the heart of man can rest."[45] When individuals recognized that God was gracious to them, they could then obey God joyfully, knowing that God was indulgent of their faults, just as a loving parent was with children.[46]

One distinctive feature of the way Calvin deployed the psychology of grace was his use of the metaphor of God as a loving father. He thought that people could not approach God in peace and without fear unless they first understood God to be a father who loved them, cared for them, and sought only their good. This realization was so foundational, not merely to faith but also to the transformation from sinfulness to holiness, that Calvin insisted it was "the first step toward godliness."[47] Like Luther, Calvin employed a relational anthropology, and changes in one's relationships precipitated psychological transformations that were then naturally expressed in action.[48]

Despite Calvin's fundamental agreement with Luther on this point, he and the Reformed tradition more generally were also more sensitive to the suspicions of others, especially their Roman Catholic interlocutors, that this approach to grace and justification would discourage good works. Because of this, Calvin had a more pronounced doctrine of sanctification, which even preceded his account of justification in the *Institutes*. Calvin understood justification and sanctification to be a "double grace," gifts that are received simultaneously when a person is united to Christ in faith. Given this emphasis on sanctification, Calvin was also more comfortable than Luther with speaking of a positive use of the law. The law did not merely show people their sins and drive them to Christ but also provided positive moral guidance for them in obeying God in the life of faith.

Barth and the Continuation of a Reformation Psychology

While it is not necessary, for our purposes, to have a comprehensive picture of the psychology of grace in the Lutheran and Reformed traditions, one later figure has been especially influential and will prove to be helpful as we draw connections between the theological anthropology of the Reformers and con-

44. Calvin, *Institutes of the Christian Religion* 3.2.7, p. 550.
45. Calvin, *Institutes of the Christian Religion* 3.2.7, p. 550.
46. Calvin, *Institutes of the Christian Religion* 3.19.5.
47. Calvin, *Institutes of the Christian Religion* 2.6.4, p. 347.
48. See Brian Gerrish, *Grace and Gratitude: The Eucharistic Theology of John Calvin* (Minneapolis: Fortress, 1993), 87–102.

temporary social concerns: the giant of twentieth-century Protestant theology, Karl Barth. A significant feature of Barth's version of the psychology of grace is that he shows how the categories of the Reformation account are applicable in a modern context, in which most people do not experience Luther's constant anxiety about their status before God. For Barth, even if modern people are not consciously thinking about how to earn divine approval, they are still burdened by limitless moral demands that come at them from every direction. Every person experiences such demands—from governing authorities but also from friends or family or social convention. There is seemingly no limit to the demands that can be placed on a person and to the sense of obligation that the human hunger for approval can create. Barth even portrays the internal conflict in violent terms: these demands are constantly "assaulting him, grasping him, forcing him in different directions and detaining him at different points."[49] In other words, for Barth, modern humans who are not particularly concerned with divine approval are still worried about status and still feel that they must create their own worth or value. Even if people deny all social demands in order to live only by their own choices regarding the good, the sense of being overwhelmed by demands does not disappear, for they are then haunted by all the various paths they could have chosen.[50] This human preoccupation with establishing oneself also comes at the cost of a genuine relationship with God. When humans are convinced they must be for themselves, they cannot trust God to be for them and, therefore, cannot enjoy the form of existence for which they were created: fellowship with the God who has determined from eternity to be with and for humanity. With this sort of language, Barth shows how the logic Luther used in analyzing the sixteenth-century preoccupation with one's eternal destiny can also apply to a twentieth-century spiritual malaise or ennui.

As with Luther and Calvin, the solution to this intolerable anxiety and alienation from God is the psychology of grace.[51] In his exposition of this theme, however, Barth seeks to avoid what he takes to be fatal instabilities in the thought of the Reformers. First, Barth believes that the Reformation approach to sanctification—that it is dependent on and flows from justification, as in Luther's two kinds of righteousness or Calvin's double grace—ultimately

49. Karl Barth, *Church Dogmatics* II/2, *The Doctrine of God*, ed. Thomas F. Torrance, trans. Geoffrey William Bromiley (Edinburgh: T&T Clark, 1956), 586.

50. Barth, *Church Dogmatics* II/2, 596.

51. For a more robust defense of the claim that Barth also employs this psychology, see Angela Carpenter, "To Live by Grace: The Role of a Distinctive Reformation Psychology in Barth's Ethics," in *The Ethics of Grace: Engaging Gerald McKenny*, ed. Paul Martens and Michael Mawson (London: T&T Clark, 2023), 19–33.

returns human beings to their own actions and re-creates the very anxieties the Reformers wished to avoid. For Barth, the way to avoid this problem is to insist that sanctification is already accomplished in Christ, that Jesus has fully realized the truly good human life in such a manner that other human agents can in no way contribute to or take away from it.[52] A second instability that Barth seeks to correct occurs in the doctrine of election, which leaves individuals in a perpetual state of doubt about whether they are chosen by God. For Barth, Jesus is the elect human being, and because of this, humanity is chosen in Christ for fellowship with God. On both of these points Barth, like Luther and Calvin, emphasizes a psychological component. People must be *aware* that God has, in Christ, elected humanity for fellowship with God. They must *recognize* that Christ has also realized this fellowship in its perfect form, such that their own actions are not needed for it to be completed. This psychological language of awareness, recognition, acknowledgment, affirmation, understanding, and assent permeates Barth's anthropology.[53] People who are given such knowledge and awareness are thereby enabled to live lives of gratitude and joy in response to what God has graciously accomplished. In the account of grace and human nature that I will develop in this book, I will follow Barth in applying the psychology of grace more broadly to contemporary anxieties regarding self-worth and status.[54]

Assessing the Psychology of Grace

Barth's broad application of the Reformation psychology suggests that it is more than just a component of a technical debate regarding the "how" of salvation. Reformation psychology has implications for how these theologians understand the human person before God. This anthropological significance is particularly apparent in Luther's analysis of the first commandment to have no other gods. In his discussion of the ten commandments Luther argues that to have a god is to look to someone or something as the source of all good and to trust in that object with all one's heart. So, for example, Luther observes that some people

52. For an exposition of this theme, see Gerald McKenny, *The Analogy of Grace: Karl Barth's Moral Theology* (Oxford: Oxford University Press, 2010), 68–72; McKenny, "Karl Barth and the Plight of Protestant Ethics," in *The Freedom of a Christian Ethicist: The Future of a Reformation Legacy*, ed. Brian Brock and Michael Mawson (London: T&T Clark, 2018), 17–37.

53. See esp. Barth's discussion of gratitude in *Church Dogmatics* III/2, *The Doctrine of Creation*, ed. Thomas F. Torrance, trans. Geoffrey William Bromiley (Edinburgh: T&T Clark, 1956), 164–79.

54. I also presume that something like Barth's reformulation of election is necessary if Reformed thought is to avoid the kinds of preoccupations that have warped human psychology in previous generations. I am not committed, however, to Barth's reworking of sanctification.

trust absolutely in money and are either assured or despairing, depending on how much they possess. Crucially, he notes that the one who trusts in wealth "cares for no one."[55] Such people cannot ultimately care for others when they must at all costs protect their own wealth. However, to have the true God as one's god is to understand "that it is God alone . . . from whom we receive all that is good and by whom we are delivered from all evil," and to be willing to live as those who receive all good from God instead of seeking the good elsewhere or grasping it for ourselves.[56] Luther extends this analysis to what he terms "false worship"—the human attempt to do good works and thus control one's own salvation rather than receive it as a gift.[57] Here we find in Luther a vision of authentic humanity as one that recognizes and willingly lives in a deep dependence on God. From this perspective, faith—the absolute trust in God as the gracious giver of all good—is not simply the path to forgiveness of sin but is itself the antithesis of sin. This psychological aspect, the recognition of grace, is thus part of what salvation actually means, and it is both one of the Reformation's most profound theological insights and a recurring vulnerability.

Why is this notion both a profound insight and a recurring vulnerability? To see the positive contribution of the Reformation tradition on this point, we need to take a step back and think about the human capacity to love. While there are multiple typologies for understanding love in the Christian tradition,[58] I draw here on Jonathan Edwards to distinguish two forms that love can take. The first is the attraction to what is beautiful. We encounter an object, find it beautiful or lovely, and are drawn to it and captivated by it. We delight in it. We love it. The second form that love takes is the love of care or self-gift. Regardless of whether we find a person beautiful or not, we might care about them and give of ourselves in some way to meet their needs.[59] This kind of love is possible for humans precisely because we are finite and dependent creatures. If we had no need or lack, we would not be able to give and receive this sort of love to one another. In fact, we will discover in chapter 2 that this very finitude and vulnerability has been crucial to the biological underpinnings and evolution of human love. Technically speaking, humans cannot directly love God in this way because God has no lack. However, because God has created and loves a contingent creation, in a way we can express love to God

55. Luther, *Large Catechism*, 9.
56. Luther, *Large Catechism*, 12.
57. Luther, *Large Catechism*, 11.
58. See, e.g., C. S. Lewis, *The Four Loves* (New York: Harcourt, Brace, 1960).
59. Jonathan Edwards calls these two forms of love "benevolence" (the love of care or acting for the good of another) and "complacency" (the love of beauty). See Edwards, *Ethical Writings*, ed. Paul Ramsey, vol. 8 of *The Works of Jonathan Edwards* (New Haven: Yale University Press, 1957), 541–43.

through these actions when we care for others, especially the "least of these" (Matt. 25:40), the vulnerable people Jesus associates with himself. Although these two forms of love can be separate, in general we desire both of them in our most meaningful and intimate human relationships. We want others to find us beautiful and to care for us through gifts of themselves, and we want to find others beautiful and give of ourselves.[60] It is also worth noting that there is some conceptual overlap between these two forms of love. Often what we find beautiful about someone else is precisely this willingness to give, to sacrifice of themselves for others. And this is especially true for God, who is eternal, overflowing, self-offering love. This is revealed to us in Jesus and is beautiful and attractive.

While the fact that humans are finite and dependent creates a possibility of expressing love through giving, this same reality of finitude also raises several questions about human love. If our relationships consist in giving and receiving care and addressing the needs and vulnerability of others, how do we know our motive is really love? Are we not just using one another because we are vulnerable? Would my spouse still love me if, perhaps through severe illness, I was no longer able to give the same things or in the same way? The attraction to beauty is also not immune to questions raised by our finitude, although these may have more to do with whether we accept and are at peace with finitude rather than finitude itself. When we encounter that which attracts us, will we admire and love its beauty? Or will we try to possess it, thinking it can somehow fulfill a lack or a need? Will we truly admire and love the attractive qualities in our friend, or will jealousy subtly corrupt our love over time as we lament that we do not possess the same kind of beauty? Will our friendships give way to competition for superiority? Will we isolate ourselves from love because all we see is our need or lack and we do not believe anyone could find us lovable?

As these questions indicate, the challenges of human finitude are closely related to the theological category of sin, but it is crucial to underscore that the concepts are distinct and that finitude on its own is not sinful. Rather, traditional theological accounts of sin that portray it as human attempts to be like God or to reject limits through disobedience can also be formulated in terms of *rejecting* finitude. In this account, humans are finite creatures intended to live in communion with God, depending on the gifts of God. Rejecting God also means acting as if we are not finite, as if we are self-sufficient and the source of our own value and worth. In other words, it means denying we need God's gifts or grace. Of course, when we deny our finitude, our experi-

---

60. For Edwards, the love of benevolence is the primary component of virtuous love, and we express both forms of love to God. Edwards, *Ethical Writings*, 543, 551.

ence in a dangerous world challenges this impression of ourselves. We become uncomfortable with our experience of vulnerability and respond by trying to gain power and control over others. We constantly feel the need to prove our superiority over others and demonstrate our value. We cling desperately to what we have and are unable to care for or respect our neighbors properly. Sin, in other words, entails denying our finitude but also rejecting the proper way in which we are meant to live with it and find it bearable: through trust in God and through mutually caring relationships with others. As Norman Wirzba puts it, "For many people, the creaturely world of finitude, impotence, and vulnerability but also membership and gift is too hard to bear. And so we feel compelled to construct and flee to the more controlled, convenient, and comfortable worlds of our own making."[61]

Philosophers and theologians have reflected on these dynamics for millennia. The book of Job, for example, asks how one can truly know God and love God when we all simultaneously need or want things from God and when we think we can secure them from God through our good action.[62] Much of Christian reflection about idolatry is not really about images made to look like a deity. It is about how our attraction to the beautiful becomes corrupted and we seek to possess and manipulate created things for our advantage rather than allow the beauty of creation to direct us to its source in God. Augustine, in his account of sin and grace, is particularly concerned with these questions. Regarding human love for God expressed in obedience to God's law, Augustine observes that if a person would disobey God if they knew they would not be punished, then their obedience was really out of fear of punishment and showed no true love of God.[63] If loving God is the ultimate purpose of human life, then how, in the face of human finitude and sin, can it be possible?

It is at this point that the Reformers take a slightly different approach than the rest of the Augustinian tradition, and it is this approach that, as I said earlier, offers an important insight but also produces a vulnerability. Faced with humanity's inability to love God, Augustine encourages Christians to pray for grace. He argues that God, by giving the Holy Spirit, pours the love of God into the heart so that a person could love God. The solution to the dilemma of love in the midst of our finitude is that God gives the love that human beings lack. In this respect Augustine's account of justification fits perfectly within the theology of the Council of Trent. God, by the Spirit, gives the love with

61. Norman Wirzba, *Food and Faith: A Theology of Eating*, 2nd ed. (Cambridge: Cambridge University Press, 2019), 122.

62. See Gustavo Gutiérrez, *On Job: God-Talk and the Suffering of the Innocent*, trans. Matthew J. O'Connell (Maryknoll, NY: Orbis Books, 1987).

63. Cary, "Lutheran Codicil," 6.

which the human person loves God. And on the basis of this sanctification, the person is made righteous or justified.

Luther agrees with Augustine but only up to a point. Luther, as we have seen, says that people will undertake all kinds of obedience to commandments, and even invent new commandments, to assuage their fear or to secure something from God, and he agrees that this is not genuine love for God. Furthermore, he agrees that what a person absolutely needs is grace. But for Luther, the resolution to this anxiety is not God's gift of the love God requires. Instead, the Christian's anxiety is lifted because God says to the person, in essence, "I love you first. I want your absolute and ultimate good; you don't have to accomplish that for yourself, because I, in Christ, have already accomplished it. You need only receive this gift."[64] The difference here is sometimes described in terms of "imputed" versus "imparted" righteousness.

For Augustine, righteousness is imparted—the love of God is poured into the heart by the giving of the Holy Spirit. For Luther and Calvin, and the Lutheran and Reformed traditions as a whole, righteousness is imputed—people are considered righteous because of Jesus. What people receive, according to Luther, is the promise that, because of Christ, God loves and forgives and welcomes them, that before God they are already righteous. For Luther, and for Calvin and Barth after him, it is crucial that human beings know this and trust it—the psychology of grace. Why? Because it is this very recognition of grace, the awareness of the love of God that precedes human action, that creates the possibility for human communion with God and authentic love of God. Those human beings who do not know God precisely as the God of grace—a revelation that is given through the work of Christ and the Spirit—are alienated from God in one of several ways that mirror the problems of love and finitude. Such people might recognize their vulnerability and need and might fear that they are not good enough for God to meet those needs. The end result is despair or denial of God. On the flip side, a person might think that pleasing God is within their power and might seek to meet what they take to be the divine demands, ultimately thinking that God owes them something and that, in essence, they can control God through their own actions.[65] Such a "relationship" to God is a mirage, not simply because human sin will inevitably make this effort unsuccessful but also because the dynamics of earning

64. Augustine, of course, also insists that God loves the person first and that God acts before any human action. What is different with Luther is that justification is distinct from and does not depend on God's work of sanctification.

65. Federalist versions of Reformed theology, which posit a pre-fall covenant of works with Adam, seem to miss this point. Here Adam is promised eternal life if he obeys God's commands, a scenario that seems to imply some external reward, rather than love of God, as the motive for good action.

and deserving in a relationship are different from those of love and gift. Love is not the sort of thing that can be earned, and those who attempt to do so do not truly know God, because the God revealed in Jesus is fundamentally a God of grace.

When, however, people believe that they are forgiven in Christ, they recognize their dependence on God. The act of trusting in Christ, which is itself a gift, is a renunciation of a false independence, with all the desperate grasping for power and control that goes along with this mindset. The recognition of grace is also an insight into who God is. In Jesus, people learn that God is overflowing love, and they are drawn into relationship with this God. All of this means that instead of God infusing the love with which they can love God—though all these thinkers would strongly affirm the indwelling by the Spirit—the promise that in Christ one is forgiven neutralizes the difficulties that human finitude presents so that, with the Spirit's help, people can, in turn, love God with their human capacities. Because God has achieved their ultimate good, such people do not have to seek this good for themselves or try to use God or others to achieve it. Luther and Calvin do not put it quite in these terms, but in my reading of their theology, one crucial function of grace is to solve the problems of love and human finitude. When one's action is not the cause of their status before God as righteous, then the person is able to love God without it being for the sake of God's approval in return. But this is the case only if the person recognizes and trusts that God loves and accepts them.

This psychology of grace does not just shape a person's relationship to God. It also provides grounding for a way of being in the world with others. The realization that we did not create ourselves, with our particular traits and abilities, as well as the recognition that all humans are in a common condition of sin and alienation from God, has a leveling effect. Awareness of God's grace from creation through redemption cultivates a posture toward others that is understanding of the human condition, compassionate, and willing to forgive. It does not seek to exploit or control for personal gain, because those who trust that God intends only their good and freely gives all good things do not need to employ such methods. They can even be unsparing in care and generosity toward others, knowing that God cares for them far more than for the birds of the air. The more people trust God with the ordinary vulnerabilities of finite life, the less these vulnerabilities need to be decisive for how they act in the world. Christians are able to genuinely rejoice in the successes of others and not be devastated by their own failures, knowing that these failures do not alter their fundamental worth and that all such accomplishments are the result of God's gifts.

These insights, of course, are not the exclusive property of the Reformers. Dependence on God was crucial to Augustine's theology of grace, and the late medieval mystical tradition, in particular, emphasized an existential recognition of grace.[66] What was unique about the Reformation approach was thus, in part, rhetorical—the psychology of grace was spelled out more clearly and assumed a prominence it had not previously held. But the difference was also technical, as Luther and Calvin insisted that good action (sanctification) was only ever the result, and not the cause, of a person's justification, of their status before God as righteous, a status that could be attributed only to the work of Christ.

This insistence would prove to be a source of persistent vulnerability in Protestant theology. For the opponents of the Reformers, the notion that justification or status before God must precede human action raised obvious questions about the status of that action. Did morally good action even matter? Could people simply commit grave sin if they so desired, confident that God would forgive them?[67] Luther and Calvin took great pains to deny this notion, with Calvin even asserting that sanctification was the purpose of justification. While blatant antinomianism never truly gained a foothold, more subtle forms of passivity have proven more difficult to deny. Does moral effort, habituation, or socialization into virtue threaten the integrity of grace? If one tries to be morally upright, does that person thereby risk a false self-assertion that seeks to earn God's approval? It is not at all difficult to find statements in Luther or even Calvin that encourage such suspicions.[68]

Further vulnerability comes from the fact that the Protestant notion that one must be certain, and not merely aware, of God's grace in Christ has the potential to instill a new kind of anxiety that rivals the pursuit of good works and the complete confession of sin that so plagued Luther in the sixteenth century.[69] The insistence on certainty stemmed, in part, from the broader anxiety about salvation and damnation that is somewhat foreign to the twenty-first-century reader. Luther's and Calvin's affirmation of the doctrine of predestination only heightened the stakes. If God chose to save only some by bestowing faith in

66. Teresa of Ávila, e.g., explores the themes of self and dignity given by God and discusses how people try to control God through their good actions. See Teresa of Ávila, *The Interior Castle*, trans. Kieran Kavanaugh and Otilio Rodriguez, Classics of Western Spirituality (Mahwah, NJ: Paulist Press, 1979).

67. These concerns were not new in the Reformation. In the New Testament, Paul refers to similar criticisms of his theology, and Augustine faced these questions as well.

68. Luther, e.g., rejects habituation with his metaphor of a good builder building good houses and with his insistence that one must be internally transformed into a good person before performing good actions (*The Freedom of a Christian*, 613). The metaphor itself, however, seems to support the opposing argument. Surely, good builders have learned over time through emulating those who are experienced, acquiring much practice and perhaps even making some bad houses before becoming good builders.

69. Jennifer Herdt, *Putting on Virtue: The Legacy of the Splendid Vices* (Chicago: University of Chicago Press, 2008), 192–96.

Christ on them, then ordinary people would desperately want to ascertain their status. But how could they be certain of faith? And what were they to do if they were uncertain or doubting? In the Reformed tradition these questions led to a new form of moral rigorism, where one's actions could provide evidence or confirmation of faith.[70] These anxieties could also have the contrary effect of encouraging passivity. People might assume that they should direct their attention first and foremost to the inner life and faith and never arrive at action.

These are difficult questions with a long history, and my objective in this book is not to rehash Reformation-era debates about grace. Nevertheless, if we are to pursue the positive contribution of the psychology of grace and its implications for human communities, we must at least consider how such concerns might be addressed.[71] I will present some initial thoughts here and return to the issue of grace and its effect on moral motivation in the epilogue. It is worth noting that extreme anxieties about predestination have largely receded from our collective consciousness. Along with this cultural trend, one finds very little reflection, even among churches that embrace a Reformed identity, on moral goodness as a confirmation of one's status as elect. One might assume that substantial rethinking of the doctrine of election, along with speculation about the possibility of universal salvation, have likewise encouraged this shift.[72] I have suggested elsewhere that Calvin's use of the metaphor of parental love gives us a framework for imagining and articulating a more nuanced account of the human awareness of, and response to, the divine love offered in Jesus.[73] In relationships between parents and children, we observe that the child's awareness of the parent's love and the child's trust of the parent begin gradually, without the child even being conscious of this awareness and trust. Even without conscious reflection, however, children are still responding to the parent's love and care. Modern psychology helps us see how this sort of knowledge can be genuine and exert a profound influence on one's agency without necessarily being the subject of explicit reflection. In other words, the psychological dynamics related to grace that I have described here rely on a kind of knowledge and awareness and likely benefit from a deepening of knowledge and a habituation of response, but they do not depend on certainty.

70. Zachman carefully parses this dynamic in both Luther and Calvin. See Zachman, *Assurance of Faith*, esp. 244–48.

71. I have elsewhere addressed these issues in much greater detail. See Carpenter, *Responsive Becoming*, 149–73.

72. See Suzanne McDonald, *Re-Imaging Election: Divine Election as Representing God to Others and Others to God* (Grand Rapids: Eerdmans, 2010); David Bentley Hart, *That All Shall Be Saved: Heaven, Hell, and Universal Salvation* (New Haven: Yale University Press, 2019).

73. Carpenter, *Responsive Becoming*, 156–65.

Reflecting on moral effort in a relational context also helps us begin to address the concerns of passivity. As any child psychologist will readily affirm, it is absolutely critical for social and emotional health that children know that their parents love them unconditionally. This dynamic is a human analogue of the psychology of grace. At the same time, however, it would be rather odd, not to mention dysfunctional, for children to obsess over whether they themselves were sufficiently confident of that love. "Does my mother love me?" is an ordinary, though heartbreaking, question. "Do I sufficiently believe that my mother loves me?" is just bizarre. To the extent that Luther and Calvin encourage the latter sort of second-order reflection, something has gone wrong. The difficulty occurs whenever the Reformers imply that it is somehow up to each individual to be certain that they are acting from a knowledge of grace, as if the knowledge of divine love were somehow something they could control. Rather, just as it is largely the parents' role to assure children of their love and act in such a way that children can be confident they are loved, it is God who instills the knowledge of divine love in Christ. Each child's role is to respond in the loving relationship, and their confidence in their parents' love and their own capacity to respond grows through living in this relationship. If we are able to conceive of faith in Christ in terms of degrees, with varying levels of conscious awareness and reflection, then it is also possible to say that faith can grow and deepen as a person lives responsively in fellowship with Christ. The truth is that, at times, we almost certainly will think that God's love is the sort of thing we could earn or deserve. Our insecurities run deep, and trust does not come easily. The Reformers are right to remind their readers that a person's status before God comes from Christ and not from themselves. But they are wrong when their rhetoric suggests that individual believers should not act at all unless they are certain of God's love or when they encourage believers to suppose they can manufacture that sort of confidence for themselves.

But what if the tension between grace and a return action runs even deeper than this, such that any expectation of a response to God's gift in Christ is, by its very nature, bound to undermine the gratuity of grace? This is the line of reasoning developed in the twentieth-century philosophical discourse on the nature of the "gift."[74] In this analysis, any kind of reciprocity or return brings the exchange out of the realm of gift and into an economic dimension where the value of the gift is canceled out by the response. While this analysis provides much insight—we can certainly recognize how our patterns of giving can be

74. For a summary of the relevant literature as it relates to a Pauline doctrine of grace, see John Barclay, *Paul and the Gift* (Grand Rapids: Eerdmans, 2015), 11–65. See also J. Todd Billings, *Calvin, Participation, and the Gift: The Activity of Believers in Union with Christ* (Oxford: Oxford University Press, 2009).

used to control others or be a source of burden rather than joy—it also has some limitations, and once again, the context of a loving human relationship is indispensable to our understanding. The whole point of gifts, at least the best sort of gifts, is that they are expressions of love. Delighting in giving and receiving is part of what we do when we enjoy intimate relationships constituted by mutual care, affection, admiration, and so forth. In this context, what is the point of giving if it can go in only one direction, if it cannot be shared? To insist that the purest form of gift is one-directional is to elevate an ideal of the perfect gift above the love that gifts are meant to express. But acknowledging the possibility of return does not then mean that gifts, and, therefore, also love, are conditional on some kind of reciprocity. Rather, if someone wants to receive a gift but never offers any kind of return, what they are actually doing is refusing a relationship and thus, in a sense, rejecting the true gift. This is especially the case with God's grace, as the gift quite literally is the relationship. If we think we can receive it and then go live an independent existence without God, we are fundamentally mistaken about what the gift is. In this instance would we then say that God stops giving and that grace is conditional? No, but we might say that God's unconditional love could take a different form.

Conclusion

In this chapter we have seen some of the ways of understanding dependence on God's grace that have taken root in Christian theology over the centuries. In Christian thought, human existence, knowledge of God, forgiveness of sin, and friendship or union with God are all entirely up to God in the sense that our capacity for each of these aspects of human life does not originate with us. We are at every moment, and especially in the most important aspects of our humanity, thoroughly dependent on a God who loves us and seeks only our good and who, in Christ, has achieved our good. Even our good action, our love for God and for one another, is mysteriously our own but also not our own. This chapter has also attempted to argue that a Reformation approach to grace makes a distinctive contribution to understanding the dynamics of grace and agency. In this line of thinking it is important not only that we receive grace but also that we are aware of grace. When we realize that God simply loves us in Christ, that we cannot earn that status through our action, we are opened up to a different kind of relationship with God and with one another. Our love of God, in the language of Gustavo Gutiérrez, is "disinterested."[75] It is simply

75. Gutiérrez, *On Job*, 3–6.

love, not instrumental action for the sake of some other good that God might give us, as if there could be, for us, some good other than God.

As with Augustine, the picture of human nature we find in the Reformation account is a complex one shaped by salvation history. Human nature is not static but is created good, then is fallen, and ultimately is redeemed. At each moment, however, the theological anthropology of this tradition is shaped by the relationship of the person to God's grace. The goodness of created nature is, in Barth's terminology, suitable or adapted for a covenant partnership with God.[76] One objective of our scientific engagement in chapters 2 and 3 will be to ask whether such a suitability is visible in empirical studies of human beings. Sinful nature, in this account, is explicitly defined as opposition to God's grace. Sinful people, in rejecting God, believe they can accomplish their own good. In seeking to do so, they make God, other human beings, and creation as a whole into means of achieving their good and are unable to love them for themselves. It is only in recognizing grace—in trusting in Christ, who has definitively accomplished their good—that they can truly love God and others.

In chapter 4, we will look quite closely at what these anthropological claims might mean for how we relate to one another and, more specifically, for how we structure human societies. For now I will simply observe that it would be a profound and ultimately disastrous inconsistency if we were to claim that in their relationships with God human beings receive all that is good as a gift, but that somehow in their relationships with one another they must earn acceptance and manufacture their worth. This is not to say that any language of earning or having rights is, therefore, entirely suspect, but we will need to ask first how this basic reality of dependency and gift can be recognized in our humanity as that humanity is expressed on a horizontal plane, in relationships with one another.

In chapters 2 and 3, the human sciences will be our companion as we seek to understand personhood and agency on this horizontal plane. In chapter 2, evolutionary anthropology will help us understand the biological connections between dependency and finitude, on the one hand, and the capacity for love, on the other. We will discover that we human beings love *because* we are dependent, and membership is our primary evolutionary strategy for coping with our profound vulnerabilities. Then, in chapter 3, we will turn our attention to social psychology to investigate the mechanisms we have for attributing value and worth to one another and the way these attributions of worth affect human agency.

---

76. Barth, *Church Dogmatics* III/2, 224.

CHAPTER 2

HUMAN EVOLUTION AND THE MYTH OF SELF-SUFFICIENCY

In their provocatively titled book *Man the Hunted*, evolutionary anthropologists Donna Hart and Robert Sussman conclude their survey of the literature on the predation of early human species with an imaginative reconstruction of life in an *Australopithecus* community.[1] The bipedal apes spend their day in a close-knit community, playing, grooming, and foraging together while they scan the horizon for predators. When they are attacked by a group of large hyenas, they run for the protection of denser woodland, with the larger males running in opposite directions to divert attention from the vulnerable females with offspring. While there is strength in numbers—extra eyes to watch for threats and large males to fight or distract predators—a few in the group still succumb to the attack. After the reader's initial visceral shock of imagining one's early ancestors, and perhaps by extension oneself, being torn limb from limb as food for a prehistoric hyena, what stands out the most about this account is the physical intimacy of the imagined relationships. Hart and Sussman depict creatures who so need one another—not for any particular skill sets but for simple physical membership in a group—that the

---

1. Donna Hart and Robert W. Sussman, *Man the Hunted: Primates, Predators, and Human Evolution* (New York: Westview, 2005), 248–50.

experience of being alone, if it ever occurred, would seem disorienting and eerily threatening.

In this chapter we will examine recent literature on human origins in order to better understand this basic need to belong and to matter to the social group. The objective is not to provide a comprehensive perspective on human evolution that considers human nature broadly construed. Instead, it is to ask if we can discern patterns of gift in the emergence of humanity. The vision of the human person that I am advancing theologically is one in which all creatures depend on God and on other people—on gift and not merely what we achieve for ourselves. In this chapter and in chapter 3, we will explore whether this vision is consistent with empirical study of humanity and human community. Can we see, in our evolutionary history, glimmers of the human person as one grounded in gift? A constant theme of this material will be interdependence. The earliest humans needed one another and survived by belonging to and working with a social group. According to much theoretical work of the last two decades, it is because ancient humans needed one another that they evolved the cognitive, social, and emotional capacities to care about one another and to work together to survive. But this interdependence is not the full story. A second and related theme is the immense variety with which these capacities are expressed in human communities. This study of human evolution will provide insight into how humans might value one another, but it will not depict any single pattern or social arrangement as natural or inevitable. Instead, it is part of the human pattern to express these capacities in different ways and even to evaluate and seek to change these forms of expression.

This use of human evolution in theology may seem perplexing to some readers who are skeptical of some or all aspects of evolutionary theory. It is not my intent here to wade into these debates or to discuss potential challenges to Christian belief. Many other books do this quite well.[2] Rather, I am operating with the assumption that evolutionary theory on the whole offers a highly persuasive account of the development of life on the planet. Further, because all truth is God's truth, Christians should assume that a deeper understanding of our best science can be illuminating and productive for theological reflection. That being said, the overall argument I am making theologically throughout this book does not stand or fall with evolutionary theory. Readers who are skeptical of evolution can proceed to chapter 3 and still follow the main contours of the book.

2. See, e.g., Gijsbert van den Brink, *Reformed Theology and Evolutionary Theory* (Grand Rapids: Eerdmans, 2020).

Why and How Do We Study Human Evolution?

Before we get to the literature itself, it is worth asking both *why*, beyond simple curiosity, humans might be interested in their evolutionary history and *how* it is possible to examine these ancient origins. There are many scientific disciplines that we humans use to study ourselves. Why consider our evolutionary history, especially when these origins are remote, and the physical evidence is relatively sparse? To begin, it is worth noting that understanding human beings is quite an intellectual challenge from any discipline. The human brain, for instance, is still very much a mystery, and despite a public fascination with neuroscience, the discipline is currently limited in what it can actually tell us about our emotions, thought patterns, and actions.[3] Similarly, we mapped the human genome, and yet after this monumental achievement we found ourselves shocked at what it still could not tell us. If so much of our genetic material is identical to our nearest relatives, why are we so very different? And while we are on the subject of difference, how can we even uphold humanity as a meaningful category when we are so different from one another? When cultural anthropology displays so many variations, can we say anything about a common nature?

To the extent that we can learn about our evolutionary history, it provides a few advantages over other disciplines. First, human evolution is, at the most basic level, what we share as a species. It thus provides one, albeit limited, response to the question of human essentialism: What are we at our core? We are creatures who evolved in *this* way, with *these* particular traits that have enabled us to survive in virtually any habitat. Evolution cannot tell us what we might become, either as individuals or as a species, but by helping us understand how we got here, it can enable us to see something of who we are. Second, the study of evolution can help us consider how deeply rooted some aspects of our experience are. We might not be able to identify how a desire to belong in a social group functions at the level of neuroscience or what aspects of the genome it could be associated with, but if we understand how that capacity might have enabled ancient humans to survive in the dramatically fluctuating climate a million years ago, perhaps we can begin to grasp how it continues to function in our day-to-day lives. We must, of course, exercise great caution here. Over the years, evolutionary biologists have made grandiose claims about human nature that have simply been wrong and even dangerous.[4] It cannot be the sole source of our knowledge or the only consideration in making decisions

---

3. See Joel Paris, *Psychotherapy in an Age of Neuroscience* (Oxford: Oxford University Press, 2017).
4. For a brief history of some of these claims, see Penny Spikins, *How Compassion Made Us Human: The Evolutionary Origins of Tenderness, Trust and Morality* (Barnsley, UK: Pen & Sword, 2015), 18–37.

about our lives and our communities. It can, however, be one tool, one source of insight that we consider in conjunction with others.

But how can we begin to gain insight deep into our evolutionary past and understand these creatures who lived one million or two million years ago? The scientific work is painstaking and multidisciplinary, beginning with the most direct evidence—the archeological remains of ancient humans and their artifacts. Discoveries of ancient human (pre–*Homo sapiens*) remains are rare and tremendously exciting events. The partial bone fragments may not look like much, but careful study can yield a surprising quantity of information. Brain size and shape, for instance, can be indicative of the caloric content of food that a species consumed or of their cognitive capacities. Bones might reveal injury or illness or tell us whether the individual was a victim of violence or predation. Tools and other artifacts might likewise initially seem unimpressive, but they have profound implications regarding the lives and capacities of those who made them. What does it say about an individual of a million years ago that this early human was concerned with the aesthetics of a tool and its symmetry, not just its function? What does it say of early humans that 2.5 million years ago one of them saved a small pebble resembling the face of an infant and carried it hundreds of miles from its point of origin?[5] Studying archeological remains of ancient peoples calls for great care and precision but also imagination, awe, and wonder.

Anthropologists are aided in their quest by reconstructions of the history of climate and geography. How much did temperatures and rain fluctuate on the African savannas during the Pleistocene (2.5 million–11,700 years ago)? What kinds of predators threatened early humans, and what food sources were available? As we will see, there is good reason to think that a rapidly fluctuating climate, coupled with ongoing risks of predation for bipedal apes, would have presented unique challenges and evolutionary pressures. Again, thinking through the implications requires both knowledge and imagination.

Because access to ancient human remains is so rare, evolutionary anthropologists turn to a few other disciplines to gain insight into the past. One such source is the study of other contemporary primates. While contemporary chimpanzees and bonobos are our closest living relatives, they are not our evolutionary ancestors. At least seven million years of evolutionary history separates the genus *Pan* from *Homo*, and both genera have been evolving during this time frame. Although we cannot take chimpanzees or bonobos as models for our ancestors, we can learn from them by observing commonalities among primates or, more specifically, among great apes. These commonalities might

5. Spikins, *How Compassion Made Us Human*, 61.

tell us something about our common ancestors and thus the evolutionary starting point for our species. We can also look for differences in capacities and try to understand how these differences are suited to our respective forms of life. For instance, both chimpanzees and humans generally have one offspring at a time, but chimp mothers are very protective of infants and rarely allow others to have access to them. Human mothers, however, welcome assistance from a variety of sources. Reflecting on why the two species are different in this regard might tell us something rather significant about human evolution.

Finally, cultural anthropology can help us gain distance from the forms of social organization and cooperation that are prominent in Western industrial societies and help us grasp the immense variety of expression of human communal life. Within these ethnographies, much attention has been given to contemporary societies where people live in small mobile bands and survive primarily through hunting and foraging food. (Typically, these people are referred to as foragers or hunter-gatherers.) These societies have been of particular interest to evolutionary theorists because it is widely thought that the ancestors of *Homo sapiens*, as well as *sapiens* individuals living before the advent of agriculture twelve thousand years ago, lived in much the same manner. Great care must be exercised, however, in how evolutionary theorists use this literature. Contemporary foragers, just like contemporary chimpanzees, are not our ancestors and cannot be seen as models for early humans. They are fully modern human societies, with their own language, culture, and technology. These societies occupy a different climate and face different environmental and social pressures than did our ancestors of a million or five hundred thousand years ago. Furthermore, among contemporary foragers we find substantial variety in ways of life and social organization. At the same time, some theorists do argue that broadly studying common aspects of foraging life across multiple societies can help us understand and imagine what foraging life might have been like in our evolutionary history.[6]

The study of human evolution, like any science, trades not in certain knowledge but in the continual refinement of theory based on empirical evidence. Attention to the quality of the empirical evidence is important, but perhaps a greater risk than poor methodology is uncritical selectivity, becoming attached to a particular theoretical standpoint and attending, whether consciously or not, mainly to evidence that supports that theory. This is a particular risk when studying humanity because we are both student and object. We want to believe

6. For more on this debate, see Robert L. Kelly, *The Foraging Spectrum: Diversity in Hunter-Gatherer Lifeways* (Washington, DC: Smithsonian Institution Press, 1995); Frank W. Marlowe, "Hunter-Gatherers and Human Evolution," *Evolutionary Anthropology* 14 (2005): 54–67; Christopher Boehm, *Moral Origins: The Evolution of Virtue, Altruism, and Shame* (New York: Basic Books, 2012), 76–82.

certain things about ourselves, and due to our own cultural context we possess assumptions about human nature that cannot, in fact, be universalized. With this chapter I have sought to minimize these risks by reading broadly in the literature, especially seeking out areas of debate, and by engaging, wherever possible, the study of non-Western, nonindustrial cultures. At the same time, I will privilege one particular narrative of human evolution, a narrative that focuses on the role of cooperation. In my judgment this trend in evolutionary anthropology is where the momentum in the discussion currently lies and best accounts for the variety of empirical evidence.[7]

Human Cooperation and Interdependence

Despite the popular impression that evolution is primarily about competition between organisms and "survival of the fittest," research of the last few decades has uncovered the important role of cooperation in evolution, which goes all the way down to the cellular level.[8] With respect to human evolution, this shift in the literature has been quite dramatic. In the mid-twentieth century, theories of human evolution centered on the paradigm of a killer ape who competed directly and violently with members of his own species. At the core of human nature, far back in humanity's evolutionary lineage, was an inherent aggression. This "killer" depiction was then surpassed by a "hunter" depiction, with its paradigm of male hunting and female homemaking. Male power and aggression were still a central aspect of human evolution, and rational self-interest was the primary lens for understanding the behavior of ancient hominins.[9] Since the late twentieth century, however, this paradigm has undergone a radical overhaul, beginning with a focus on human social capacities.

Evolutionary biologists can say little about the last common ancestor between humans and other great apes. We do not know what this species was, nor do we have any fossils or evidence to study. What scientists can do is compare existing species and look for commonalities; these would most likely have been present in the common ancestor. If this is true, we can be confident that our evolutionary lineage has been a highly social one for millions of years. All

7. For a window into the internal debates and potential paradigm shift in evolutionary theory and esp. in human evolution, see Agustín Fuentes, "Towards Integrated Anthropology Again and Again: Disorderly Becomings of a (Biological) Anthropologist," *Interdisciplinary Science Reviews* 43, nos. 3–4 (2018): 333–47. For an overview of this approach to human evolution, see Fuentes, *The Creative Spark: How Imagination Made Humans Exceptional* (New York: Dutton, 2017).

8. Kenneth M. Weiss and Anne V. Buchanan, *The Mermaid's Tale: Four Billion Years of Cooperation in the Making of Living Things* (Cambridge, MA: Harvard University Press, 2009).

9. Spikins, *How Compassion Made Us Human*, 24–32.

our closest species relatives live in complex social groups and have cognitive and emotional capacities that facilitate living with others. Chimpanzees, for instance, have the cognitive capacity to recognize that others are intentional agents, and they can offer help to another agent in accomplishing a goal.[10] Chimps, and to a lesser degree other primates, can also sympathize with and offer comfort to others.[11] Humans, however, take sociality to another level.[12] Primatologist Sarah Hrdy makes this point by observing that everyday human occurrences, like three hundred people boarding an airplane and traveling together peacefully (nearly always!), would be disastrous with chimpanzees.[13] Humans do not just live together. We work together with unparalleled complexity to accomplish common goals, and we do so with pleasure and joy in the company of others. We are the consummate cooperators. How did we get this way? The question is particularly important because many evolutionary anthropologists now think that the story of how we came to cooperate is crucial to understanding much of what is distinctive about our species. Our capacity for symbolic thought, for creativity, for language, for technology—all of it has its origins in human cooperation.

Ironically, given the prominence of the human species today, the story begins not in strength and dominance but in weakness and vulnerability.[14] If we could place ourselves in Africa about three million years ago, before the emergence of the genus *Homo*, we would find bipedal hairy apes who are small brained and relatively small in stature—3.5 to 5 feet tall—and apelike in their facial features. Though walking upright, these apes, of the genus *Australopithecus* like the famous "Lucy," still had the ability to climb trees, a combination that

10. For a summary of the literature, see Michael Tomasello, *A Natural History of Human Morality* (Cambridge, MA: Harvard University Press, 2016), 20–31.

11. Frans B. M. De Waal, *Good Natured: The Origins of Right and Wrong in Humans and Other Animals* (Cambridge, MA: Harvard University Press, 1997), 40–88.

12. Considerable ink has been spilled in an effort to locate the precise capacities that divide humans from other great apes. For our purposes it is not important to identify a firm dividing line between the species. It is, rather, sufficient to observe that the degree to which humans can exercise certain capacities leads to vastly different forms of life.

13. Sarah Blaffer Hrdy, *Mothers and Others: The Evolutionary Origins of Mutual Understanding* (Cambridge, MA: Belknap, 2009), 1–3.

14. Here I follow researchers who locate the beginnings of cooperation and the associated traits needed to support it, such as tolerance, deep in hominid history. There is also considerable empirical evidence of a later shift of "self-domestication" that is visible in changes in human anatomy beginning about 300,000 years ago. See Richard Wrangham, *The Goodness Paradox: The Strange Relationship between Virtue and Violence in Human Evolution* (New York: Vintage Books, 2019). These approaches are not mutually exclusive. Penny Spikins argues that the roots of cooperation within groups go back a few million years, but that increasing tolerance across social groups was concurrent with the process of self-domestication. See Penny Spikins, *Hidden Depths: The Origin of Human Connection* (York, UK: White Rose University Press, 2022).

enabled them to branch out into the grasslands while still benefiting from the protection of the forest. One of the most striking aspects of these early hominins was their vulnerability. Consistent with their small stature, they were likely not ferocious predators. Instead, the fossil evidence overwhelmingly suggests that they were desirable prey of a variety of predator species, including now-extinct saber-toothed cats, large hyenas, wolves, and raptors.[15] In one particularly striking find from the same region in Ethiopia that Lucy comes from, anthropologist Donald Johanson and his team discovered a group of at least seventeen *Australopithecus afarensis* hominins whose remains are suggestive of carnivore damage.[16] The fact that so many died together has led some scientists to speculate that group members chose to stay and help one another rather than flee.[17]

If this speculation is correct, this Australopithecine group provides evidence that our ancestors responded to the threat of predation with strategies not of the individual level but of the group level. Many mammals compensate for a high likelihood of predation by producing multiple offspring at a time. Primates, however, ordinarily produce only one offspring at a time, and these offspring need maternal care for longer periods. Consequently, primates have lower reproductive rates.[18] In order to survive, therefore, our ancestors needed to reduce their likelihood of being eaten. We have not developed advantages like camouflage or speed, so something else must help explain the reason for primates' survival over the long term. One suggestion as to how hominins sought to escape predation is that they worked together. Living in a group is, in itself, an anti-predation strategy employed across primate species, but evolutionary theorists suggest that our ancestors began to improve on this strategy. Perhaps some members of a group scanned the landscape for predators while others foraged and then signaled with vocalizations when they spotted a threat.[19] Young males, who were slightly larger than young females and also more expendable from the perspective of reproductive success, might have tried to distract or scare away predators.[20]

15. In *Man the Hunted*, Donna Hart and Robert W. Sussman make the case that predation was an important factor in human evolution by surveying fossil evidence of ancient predation, the types of ancient predators that existed in hominin environments, and evidence of high levels of predation among contemporary primates.

16. Donald C. Johanson, "Lucy, Thirty Years Later: An Expanded View of Australopithecus Afarensis," *Journal of Anthropological Research* 60, no. 4 (Winter 2004): 471–72.

17. Fuentes, *The Creative Spark*, 30–31.

18. Hart and Sussman, *Man the Hunted*, 52–54.

19. Hart and Sussman, *Man the Hunted*, 248–50.

20. Studies of contemporary primate counterattacks on carnivores provide some confirmation that our ancestors would also have been capable of these strategies. See Erik P. Willems and

Once our hominid ancestors began these modest forms of cooperation, the success of their actions would have changed the environment in which they lived and thus also changed their evolutionary pressures. Evolutionary theorists call this process "niche construction." If our hominin ancestors began to use very basic ape capacities for cooperation—like those seen in contemporary chimpanzees—and if these strategies made them slightly more successful at evading predators, they would have created an evolutionary environment that selected for capacities that better facilitated cooperation. These slightly improved capacities would have then resulted in better cooperation, which, if beneficial for the survival and reproduction of group members, would in turn have increased evolutionary pressure for better cooperative capacities. This sort of feedback loop would lead to increasingly more sophisticated forms of cooperation.[21]

Predation is just one example of a selection pressure that would have driven cooperation among early hominins. Another possibility is a fluctuating climate. A variety of geological markers indicate that the global climate began to fluctuate approximately six million years ago, with more dramatic fluctuations occurring in the past million years.[22] Species have multiple strategies for surviving a dramatic change in their habitat, one of which is to develop increased flexibility to environmental change. Humans have several traits that suggest such flexibility—from a dental structure that can process different food types to complex cognition.[23] Our suite of advanced social capacities, and in particular our ability to learn from others, is perhaps our most powerful tool for adapting to diverse environments. As standard food sources became unavailable due to climate change, our ancestors might have begun working together to exploit food sources that they would be unable to access on their own. Over time, cooperation would have developed into capacities for learning and robust cultural transmission, which, as we shall see momentarily, would have enabled the human lineage to inhabit virtually any climate on the planet.

Carel P. van Schaik, "The Social Organization of *Homo Ergaster*: Inferences from Anti-predator Responses in Extant Primates," *Journal of Human Evolution* 109 (2017): 11–21.

21. For a discussion of niche construction and more sophisticated anti-predator strategies in the genus *Homo*, see Agustín Fuentes, Matthew A. Wyczalkowski, and Katherine C. MacKinnon, "Niche Construction through Cooperation: A Nonlinear Dynamics Contribution to Modeling Facets of the Evolutionary History in the Genus *Homo*," *Current Anthropology* 51, no. 3 (June 2010): 435–44.

22. Richard Potts, "Variability Selection in Hominid Evolution," *Evolutionary Anthropology* 7, no. 3 (1998): 81–96.

23. Potts, "Variability Selection," 84–85.

Evidence of Cooperation in Hominids

Regardless of the initial causes or triggers of increased cooperation, paleoan-thropologists do indeed find *evidence* of increasing cooperation across a range of behaviors in the hominin lineage. One of the most important is diversity in food consumption. Dental evidence indicates that the earliest hominins consumed a largely plant-based diet, with the occasional lizard or small mammal added in.[24] But this diet would not have been sufficient to support the brain sizes that appear at the beginning of the genus *Homo*. How would hominins have begun to get access to denser nutritional resources like meat? One obvious answer would be that our ancestors began to hunt larger mammals more frequently. Due to the difficulty of capturing and killing large mammals without weapons, for which the fossil record contains no evidence, most evolutionary anthropologists do not think that increased meat consumption started with hunting.[25] Instead, they argue that our ancestors began scavenging the carcasses of mammals that had been killed by other predators. One of the most fascinating recent archeological finds, discovered in 2010 in Dikika, Ethiopia, consists of two animal bones, one from a cow-sized animal and another from a goat-sized animal. These remains, which are more than 3.4 million years old, bear marks of stone-tool butchery.[26] The interpretation of these marks is still debated, but the subsequent discovery of a stone tool at this site is further suggestive of hominin carnivory of larger mammals.[27] Hominins possibly as far back as australopithecines—those small, ape-like but upright creatures—had the capacity to process the flesh of large animals. Scavenging likely started as a passive endeavor: taking a carcass left by a predator. But eventually, hominins likely experimented with taking carcasses away from other predators.[28] It is clear they could not have done this individually. To get access to a carcass, they

24. See the Smithsonian Institution's Human Origins Program for a basic overview of known ancient hominin species, including artistic renderings and the most current information regarding habitat and behavior. What Does It Mean to Be Human?, Smithsonian National Museum of Natural History (website), https://humanorigins.si.edu/.

25. Briana L. Pobiner, "The Zooarchaeology and Paleoecology of Early Hominin Scavenging," *Evolutionary Anthropology* 29 (2020): 74. Pobiner provides an overview and analysis of the current state of the "hunting versus scavenging" debate. For our purposes, it should be noted that even if the hunting of larger animals occurred earlier than currently suspected, it would have also been a cooperative endeavor.

26. Shannon P. McPherron et al., "Evidence for Stone-Tool-Assisted Consumption of Animal Tissues before 3.39 Million Years Ago at Dikika, Ethiopia," *Nature* 466 (August 2010): 857–60.

27. Pobiner, "Zooarchaeology and Paleoecology," 73. Pobiner also notes that the stone tool could have been used to process plants. On the original discovery, see Sonia Harmand et al., "3.3-Million-Year-Old Stone Tools from Lomekwi 3, West Turkana, Kenya," *Nature* 521 (2015): 310–15.

28. This kind of power scavenging is also occasionally practiced by contemporary foragers. See Pobiner, "Zooarchaeology and Paleoecology," 74.

would have needed to scare away a large predator, one that would have been just as happy to put a small hominin on the menu. Then they would have had to process a carcass, which would have been too large and heavy for one individual to move, and bring the meat to a location where they could safely consume it. And all while these hominins would have been fending off other predators and scavengers who might have wanted access to the kill.[29] Scavenging for food killed by other predators would likely have been a well-coordinated group activity, as would hunting large animals.

But what about those stone tools that were used to process carcasses? While it is possible that early hominins would have used sharp stones they found in their environment, we now also have physical evidence of hominin-made stone tools dating back over three million years. This physical evidence is important because it has enabled scientists to study the processes by which our ancestors would have made these tools. They may look unimpressive to the untrained eye, but virtually everything about the production of stone tools, from acquiring and transporting the best material, to determining where to hit one stone with another to produce the right angle of flake, to avoiding injury or the attraction of predators through noise, would have called for impressive cognitive and physical skills. Contemporary anthropologists who have learned to make these tools, especially the Acheulean tools that begin appearing roughly 1.6 million years ago, argue that it is a complex process that could not be reinvented with each generation.[30] Early hominins must have had some kind of pedagogy for passing on the skills of stone-tool making from one generation to the next. Such pedagogy, before the development of language, likely would have involved tolerance of the presence of others, careful observation, demonstration, trial and error, and correction of technique.[31] In other words, it is imaginable only in a community where individuals cooperated.

Human pedagogy, as we modern humans know it, is entangled with the unique human pattern of extended childhood. Existing fossil evidence of the genus *Homo* suggests that during the past few million years of evolution, as *Homo* brain sizes increased, so too did the length of time needed for human growth. While both apes and humans have an extended childhood, the human

29. This description of active scavenging comes from Fuentes, *Creative Spark*, 69. Pobiner notes that studies of carcasses left by contemporary lions and leopards are indicative that "passive scavenging"—taking what is leftover from a predator's kill when they have abandoned it—could have yielded more nutritional value than previously thought and would also have likely involved coordination of group members. Pobiner, "Zooarchaeology and Paleoecology," 71–73, 78.

30. Dietrich Stout, "Stone Tool-Making and the Evolution of Human Culture and Cognition," *Philosophical Transactions: Biological Sciences* 366, no. 1567 (April 2011): 1050–59.

31. Kim Sterelny theorizes this "apprentice" model of stone-tool production in *The Evolved Apprentice: How Evolution Made Humans Unique* (Cambridge, MA: MIT Press, 2012), 29–43.

pattern is longer, and studies of brain growth and metabolism suggest that human children experience much slower body growth during times of heightened brain metabolism, thereby lengthening the overall period of body growth.[32] This extended growth period also creates a longer period of learning prior to the assumption of adult behavioral patterns. Long childhoods, however, are costly, especially for mothers, who must meet not only their own caloric needs but also those of their immature offspring, all the while waiting to reproduce again until existing offspring are self-provisioning. How could early *Homo* mothers have accomplished this without their reproductive rates falling to dangerously low levels? The best theory advanced by evolutionary anthropologists—and by now we should fully expect this answer!—is cooperation.

Early human mothers had help not only from fathers but also likely from older siblings, aunts, and grandparents. Anthropologist Sarah Hrdy has persuasively argued that this is, in fact, the modern human norm for childrearing, though the structure of Western industrial societies disguises (and in some cases tragically reduces) the help that mothers receive. Unlike other great-ape mothers, who protectively guard infants and rarely allow other adults to touch or hold them, human mothers across cultures welcome and require assistance. According to Hrdy, an increasingly cooperative form of childrearing would create a niche especially suited to selecting cooperative emotional as well as cognitive capacities. Infants would develop in close contact with many other individuals, and their survival would depend on their ability to attract the attention of these other adults or adolescents and on the motivation of these individuals to carry or feed them.[33] Is it any wonder that we find young children cute or endearing or that we are able to form emotional bonds with children who are not our biological relatives?

This extended childhood is crucial for one additional unique facet of human nature. Unlike many other mammals, whose forms of life are largely biologically set (think here of the foal that begins to run almost immediately after birth), humans are capable of immense variety—in how we secure food, in where we live and how we survive in different climates, and in how we organize our social lives. We humans have a profound openness in our *becoming*, and this fact has allowed us to be creative and adapt rapidly to challenges that might mean extinction for other species.[34] We are able to do this because we rely on learning, not necessarily formal education as we know it today, but rather

32. Christopher W. Kuzawa et al., "Metabolic Costs and Evolutionary Implications of Human Brain Development," *Proceedings of the National Academy of Sciences of the United States of America* 111, no. 36 (September 2014): 13010–15.

33. Hrdy develops this argument throughout *Mothers and Others*.

34. Fuentes, *Creative Spark*, 52–54.

imitation, informal instruction, and apprentice strategies that function more organically. As we grow in childhood, we pick up specific ways of being from our cultural context that then enable us to survive and thrive in the particular context—geographic and cultural—in which we find ourselves. This openness has been particularly advantageous for the genus. Around two million years ago, early *Homo* was able to migrate out of Africa and inhabit large portions of Asia and, later, Europe.[35] *Homo sapiens* has expanded to every corner of the globe, thriving in some of the harshest climates imaginable. Humans achieve this feat by adapting and improving forms of life and passing them along from one generation to the next. Such a strategy requires humans not only to work together but also to trust others in their social group. As evolutionary anthropologist Joseph Henrich has demonstrated, we do this to a profound degree, passing on life strategies in great detail and precision, even when we do not understand why they are successful. For example, the Tukanoan people of the Colombian Amazon use a complex multistep process to prepare the root tuber of the manioc plant for consumption. Without this process, high consumption of manioc can cause cyanide poisoning, but the Tukanoan people do not necessarily know the reasoning or science behind each of the steps. They simply follow and pass on; they trust a practice they have inherited from their ancestors.[36]

What about Competition?

Given what we know about human beings—that we are not always such delightful little cooperators—the narrative of human evolution I have presented so far raises some obvious questions. What about our selfish impulses? Our desire to cheat or dominate? Our laziness? Evolution seems to account for these behaviors rather well, and they would seem to undermine the stability of cooperation. Will selfish individuals not take advantage of those trying to work together? In theorizing about the evolutionary origins of cooperation, the challenge of human selfishness has seemed so insurmountable that it has been given a special name, the problem of "free riders," and it occupies a very complex and lengthy literature dating back to the middle of the twentieth

35. For many years the earliest *Homo* remains outside Africa were of *Homo erectus*. See Susan C. Antón, "Natural History of *Homo Erectus*," *Yearbook of Physical Anthropology* 46 (2003): 126–70. Recent discoveries of stone tools that predate *Homo erectus* have now complicated this picture. See Zhaoyu Zhu et al., "Hominin Occupation of the Chinese Loess Plateau since about 2.1 Million Years Ago," *Nature* 559 (2018): 608–12.

36. Joseph Henrich, *The Secret of Our Success: How Culture Is Driving Human Evolution, Domesticating Our Species, and Making Us Smarter* (Princeton: Princeton University Press, 2016), 97–99.

century. Theorists have speculated that altruism (cooperation where one person pays a price to help someone else) emerged out of kin selection, where helping impulses prove to be evolutionarily stable because they benefit persons who share one's genetic material. Another possibility is reciprocity, in which people help because they expect that help to be reciprocated. But these sorts of explanations have not proven to be persuasive as an explanation for the kinds of cooperation and altruism we find in human communities.[37] Others have speculated that cooperation emerged as a form of group selection (natural selection operative at the group level rather than on the individual level), and rather intense debates have ensued. Outside readers of this material, however, might find that the arguments display a kind of tunnel vision. At times theorists seem to conflate human psychological motivation with Darwinian fitness incentives. They also seem to focus excessively on altruism, a specific form of human cooperation, rather than try to understand the evolution of cooperation more broadly, from which vantage specifically altruistic behaviors might make more sense.[38]

The account of human cooperation that more recent evolutionary anthropology has emphasized comes at the issue from the other direction, by looking at the evidence for cooperation in the human lineage and reflecting on the kinds of cooperation that seem to be suggested. Seen from this angle, a few differences from the earlier literature immediately come to light. First, the patterns of cooperative behavior that make sense in the particular environment of ancient hominins are ones that would involve many and not just two individuals. By contrast, older theories of the evolution of cooperation tend to start with relationships between two individuals. Second, the newer narrative proposes that ancient humans were constructing an increasingly cooperative niche in which many kinds of cooperative behaviors overlapped in complex ways. Both of these distinctions suggest that groups of ancient humans were becoming thoroughly *interdependent*. In this newer model, one individual "benefits" from helping a group mate not because someone else will return the favor down the road but because the way of life of each individual depends

37. Joseph Henrich and Michael Muthukrishna, "The Origins and Psychology of Human Cooperation," *Annual Review of Psychology* 72 (2021): 219.

38. The extensive game-theory literature fits within this perspective. I have avoided game theory in this chapter for a variety of reasons: Its games of cooperation are abstracted from ordinary life and from the environments of ancient hominins. Its assumptions are usually based on Western individualistic intuitions and then confirmed through the testing of Westerners (with the exception of the recent work of Joseph Henrich; see Henrich, *The WEIRDest People in the World: How the West Became Psychologically Peculiar and Particularly Prosperous* [New York: Farrar, Straus & Giroux, 2020]). It tends toward a very rational psychology in explaining human cooperation, avoiding more subtle cognitive and emotional mechanisms.

on the welfare of the others.[39] The idea of increasing interdependence through niche construction provides an explanation for how it might have made sense, from a Darwinian perspective, for an ancient hominin to care for someone else in the group, even if the recipient was not a biological relative and even when it brought no specific identifiable benefit to the giver.

Of course, one can readily imagine that ancient hominids would also self-ishly take advantage of the group's cooperative endeavors. Maybe one large, strong male would try to consume more of a scavenged kill. Or another might benefit from group vigilance against predators without exerting any personal effort, like spending valuable foraging time scanning the horizon or participating in a risky attack on a hyena. Some theorists suppose that group selection, where a group inclined to cooperate might, on the whole, be more successful than a group less inclined to cooperate, would both increase the overall number of cooperators and be able to absorb some free-riding behavior. Another possibility is that early humans even cooperated in their efforts to deal with selfish or cheating behavior. Perhaps they worked together to punish violators or to actively teach cooperative behaviors to the young. Unfortunately, the fossil record cannot tell us whether or when our ancestors might have attempted these sorts of strategies. We do, however, get some clues by looking at other great apes and existing human cooperative societies. Chimpanzees, bonobos, and, to a much lesser extent, gorillas do show some ability to form coalitions for social control.[40] If our common ancestor possessed this latent ability, then early humans would have had some existing capacity for working together to curb undesirable behavior from certain individuals.

Ethnographic studies of modern foragers, who are highly cooperative and egalitarian, also show a strong propensity for individuals and groups to sanction those who violate cooperative norms. Such sanctions range from mild criticism or ridicule of a behavior, to reduced sharing of resources, to social ostracism, exile, or even, on occasion, death. Polly Wiessner's ethnographic work among the Ju/'hoansi of southern Africa depicts an egalitarian society where such sanctioning was a regular part of life for individuals and groups across the society.[41] Interestingly, the Ju/'hoansi were less concerned with what we might typically think of as free riding—individuals working less and contributing less—and were much more interested in big shots or bullies who tried to dominate others or to gain power or status. Wiessner speculates that those who worked less

39. Tomasello, *Natural History of Human Morality*, 14–18.

40. Christopher Boehm, *Moral Origins: The Evolution of Virtue, Altruism, and Shame* (New York: Basic Books, 2012), 109–13.

41. Polly Wiessner, "Norm Enforcement among the Ju/'hoansi Bushmen: A Case of Strong Reciprocity?," *Human Nature* 16, no. 2 (Summer 2005): 115–45.

still contributed to the community—through knowledge, kin ties, childcare, and so forth, even if they were less productive. Big shots and bullies, however, were a greater threat to the social fabric. Even here the goal of sanctioning was to change behavior and keep offenders within the community. Basic subsistence for the Ju/'hoansi could, at times, be very fragile, and they needed all group members, even those who contributed less or whose behavior could be problematic. While groups like Ju/'hoansi are not models for early humans, studying their social interactions can help us imagine cooperative strategies outside of our large-scale industrial, market-based systems in the West. It can help us imagine how small groups of early humans might have constructed a niche to better facilitate cooperation, though they would have initially used only nonverbal strategies. Such a niche could have elicited cooperation even from those who were more inclined to take advantage of the group and could also have ensured that regularly violating communal norms was ultimately not profitable for the individual.[42]

The Human Creature Shaped by Cooperation

By this point it is quite clear that various research trajectories covering multiple aspects of human evolution from multiple disciplines, including paleoanthropology, primatology, and cultural anthropology, are converging to paint a picture of humanity emerging from a highly cooperative niche. Ancient humans did not simply live in groups. They intentionally worked together across many aspects of life to accomplish common goals. They depended on one another, and as they evolved in a cooperative niche, they came to depend on one another more and more. As we have discussed, this would likely have led to complex feedback loops that would have furthered the evolution of social and cooperative capacities and thereby strengthened the cooperative niche. It is worth taking a step back at this point and examining a little more closely what sorts of traits or capacities might have emerged in such an environment. Certainly a highly cooperative environment would select for cognitive social capacities, like the ability to recognize the intentions of others, to attend carefully to actions, and to imitate.[43] But equally important would be the emotional and

42. Christopher Boehm develops an account of evolutionarily stable cooperation using ethnographic data from multiple foraging groups and argues that it could account for the origin of moral capacities like feeling shame or having a self-evaluating conscience. See Boehm, "Purposive Social Selection and the Evolution of Human Altruism," *Cross-Cultural Research* 42, no. 4 (November 2008): 319–52.

43. See Michael Tomasello, *The Evolution of Human Thinking* (Cambridge, MA: Harvard University Press), 32–79.

moral capacities that might motivate hominins to cooperate. Here I would like to focus on two different aspects of this motivation. The first relates to how we feel about others in our social group, and the second considers how we understand ourselves as part of that group.

How would our ancestors in this highly cooperative niche have come to understand and feel about others, including those to whom they had no close biological relationship? Mammals in general have evolved neurological and hormonal capacities for care of others—such as attachment, empathy, and love—as a way of facilitating the demanding and sacrificial care that mothers provide their offspring. We humans are unique, however, in that we regularly develop deep attachments to individuals who are not relatives, and we even routinely exhibit concern for strangers. As we have just seen, this sort of care, especially robust altruism toward nonrelatives and strangers, has puzzled evolutionary biologists since Darwin, but the idea of a cooperative niche provides the most plausible explanation to date for how these capacities might have evolved. In this kind of environment, where having healthy and capable collaborators is important, it would make sense that a general tendency to be concerned for or care about others in one's social group would be an adaptive trait. It is crucial to note that this is a *genuine* concern for others. The individuals benefit, in terms of fitness and reproduction, from capacities for care, but they do not need to be motivated by or even aware of a personal benefit. In this scenario compassion is crucial to the species' survival, and its biological origin is in mutual dependence and vulnerability. We have become compassionate creatures because we continually need one another and because we are susceptible to pain, injury, and death. We begin to glimpse here a convergence with a theological anthropology of grace. When we receive life from others, the social relationships that emerge are not based on autonomous individuals who carefully repay every gift and thus maintain their independence. How could we possibly repay our very existence? Instead, these relationships are grounded in emotions like gratitude and love and a complex mutual interplay of giving and receiving, such that it does not make sense to imagine an individual separate from the community.

Evidence for this intangible human propensity for compassion shows up in the fossil record. Anthropologist Penny Spikins has written extensively on disability in ancient hominins and the likelihood that our ancestors cared for injured or even permanently disabled individuals over long periods of time, even when the injuries were severe and there was no hope for recovery. Consider just a few examples. The earliest evidence of care for the disabled is a *Homo erectus* female from 1.6 million years ago whose fossil was discovered in Kenya. This woman's skeletal remains show evidence of hypervitaminosis A, a condition identifiable in the skeleton only in the later stages of disease. To reach this point she would have survived weeks or months with an array of incapacitating symptoms and almost certainly received care from others.[44] An early *Homo erectus* skull, one from the Dmanisi site in the nation of Georgia, indicates that the individual survived for several years after losing all but one tooth. The individual's need for special soft foods has led researchers to conclude that this ancient human also could have survived only with special assistance from others.[45] As the archeological record approaches the present, such examples multiply.[46]

In considering the dynamics of early cooperative communities, some theorize that having a choice of cooperative partners would be another evolutionary pressure in a cooperative niche.[47] Individuals would be preferred and valued for their skill level and for their cooperative traits—the concern they exhibit for others, their fairness, their honesty. This might well have been important in human evolution, and I will return to it in a moment, but it does assume that there are enough members in the community to allow for a choice between cooperators. Further, it assumes that the benefits of particular cooperative endeavors were reaped by the participants and not shared equally among the broader community, as is the case with nearly all modern forager cultures. Whether either assumption was consistently true throughout hominin evolution is doubtful; some evolutionary anthropologists argue that hominins were often relatively few in number.[48] The pressures of predation and rapidly fluctuating climates would, they argue, have made these populations fragile.

For Neanderthals in particular, maintaining sufficient numbers to hunt large mammals seems to have been a constant concern, a pressure that would perhaps account for the high levels of medical care apparent in the Neanderthal fossil record.[49] If there were times when population levels were low, this

44. Spikins, *How Compassion Made Us Human*, 67–78. Some researchers argue that the fossil evidence showing care of the disabled is not necessarily an indication of compassion, since early humans might have consciously chosen to show selective care to those who were likely to contribute to their welfare. Spikins, however, persuasively argues that care in Neanderthal communities would have been uncalculating, given the severity of some illnesses and injury, from which there could have been little hope of recovery. Furthermore, the gradual emergence of emotional motivations like compassion is consistent with other aspects of early hominin life, such as shared care of children. See Penny Spikins, "Calculated or Caring? Neanderthal Healthcare in a Social Context," *World Archaeology* 50, no. 3 (2018): 384–403.
45. Spikins, "Calculated or Caring?," 68. For a list of at least twenty additional early- and middle-Pleistocene cases of pathologies that provide evidence for some level of care, see Hong Shang and Eric Trinkaus, "An Ectocranial Lesion on the Middle Pleistocene Human Cranium from Hulu Cave Nanjing, China," *American Journal of Physical Anthropology* 135 (2008): 435.
46. For more examples and debates about interpretation, see Spikins, *Hidden Depths*, 71–127.
47. Tomasello, *Natural History of Human Morality*, 57–60.
48. Hrdy, *Mothers and Others*, 18.
49. Sterelny, *Evolved Apprentice*, 62–63.

lack of community members would have exerted its own kind of evolutionary pressure. Such conditions would favor the assigning of high value to human life. Human beings, or at least those in one's own community, might come to be seen as precious or even sacred, perhaps despite failures or obvious vulnerabilities. Individuals might come to experience joy, wonder, or deep satisfaction in the presence of others, since these types of emotions would strengthen one's commitment to the community and to the care of those within it. Of course, many evolutionary theorists have also speculated that such emotional motivations would have been directed primarily or even exclusively toward those in one's own group, especially if group selection played a significant role in human evolution. Attitudes toward outsiders might have ranged from avoidance to suspicion or hostility.

A cooperative niche that shaped how human beings thought and felt about others in their community, and consequently how they acted toward them, would also likely influence how individuals saw *themselves* in relationship to that community. In the first place, it would be of utmost importance to belong. As Hart and Sussman indicate with their imaginative retelling of australopithecine life, it makes sense to think that early hominins would have had strong motivation for simply being in the physical presence of others. After all, when they might suddenly be overtaken and eaten by predators, to be alone was to be immensely vulnerable. In the next chapter, when we look at social psychology, we will find that this is certainly the case for contemporary human beings. Just being around other people is so crucial to our mental health that some argue that practices like solitary confinement are a form of torture. It also makes sense to think that as cognitive capacities for self-awareness grew, humans would be concerned with what others thought and felt about them. They would seek out, maybe even crave, signs that they were included and valued. To the extent that social sanctioning or partner choice was operative in human evolution, it would tend to increase the human propensity to be concerned with how individuals were perceived by others. A bad reputation might translate into decreased fitness, and thus an ability to monitor other's opinions and a desire to receive positive assurance would be advantageous. Similarly, earning a positive opinion from others, whether because of certain skills or character traits, might lead to benefits, such as greater influence in group decisions or more options in the choice of a mate or mates.[50] It makes sense that early humans would become increasingly aware of and motivated by how others perceived them.

50. Christopher Boehm, "Purposive Selection and the Evolution of Human Altruism," *Cross-Cultural Research: The Journal of Comparative Social Science* 43, no. 4 (2008): 319–52.

The late anthropologist Walter Goldschmidt theorized about this basic human need for affirmation and divided it into two categories: belonging and performance. The cooperative human niche, according to Goldschmidt, has taken the foundational mammalian neurological and emotional capacities for nurture, both giving and receiving, and adapted them into a broader "affect" system. According to Goldschmidt, all human beings have what he terms "affect hunger," a desire to receive expressions of worth and value from one's community. Individuals seek and receive this affirmation through the two channels of belonging and performance. By "belonging" Goldschmidt means the fundamental, and often physical, acceptance in a community that is simply a facet of birth and is not bestowed as a result of particular actions (though we would not want to say that belonging is completely noncontingent; as we have already seen, even highly egalitarian societies expel or kill members whose actions harm the community). In contrast to belonging, performance acquires the affirmation of others as a result of actions or traits specific to the individual. Goldschmidt argues that this system of affect hunger has been of tremendous import for the development of complex human societies. It provides a mechanism for groups of human beings to live together with a common purpose and to keep individuals invested in the way of life of the group.[51] Goldschmidt's theory is particularly suggestive for our purposes because his categories of belonging and performance seem analogous to theological concepts of grace and works. It will be helpful to keep his distinction between belonging and performance in mind as we consider human psychology in chapter 3 and as we think through questions of human agency and status throughout the book.

In this section we have focused on how a cooperative niche might have shaped human motivation in terms of how we see or understand others and how we want others to see us. The picture that emerges is of a humanity that is highly sensitive and responsive to a variety of social cues. It makes sense that hominins in this context would evolve the emotional capacities to care genuinely for the welfare of others, even nonrelatives. They might derive pleasure, joy, or perhaps a sense of wholeness from social relationships, and they would seek out human companionship without necessarily having any instrumental purpose. Given simultaneous motivations to seek one's own advantage and to compete with others for resources, it also makes sense that these creatures would monitor one another, develop a concern for fairness in cooperative endeavors, and take various actions to contain cheating and bullying. The same evolutionary pressures could also lead hominins to care about how others

51. Walter Goldschmidt, *The Bridge to Humanity: How Affect Hunger Trumps the Selfish Gene* (New York: Oxford University Press, 2006), 47–59, 110–19.

perceived them. They might crave indications that they were welcome and belonged, that they would themselves be cared for. Or they might seek to excel in one or more culturally valuable skills to earn the recognition and respect of others. As we continue to reflect theologically on questions related to the giving, receiving, or earning of value, we will do well to keep these embodied capacities and inclinations in mind.

Evolution and Human Social Structures

Before we leave the topic of human evolution, one final question to consider in a project on social ethics is whether human evolution points toward any particular social structure as somehow "natural" for the species. In short, and at the most basic level, the answer is no. As with so much of human life, the way we organize ourselves into social groups is not determined at the species level by our genetics but is, instead, open to human creativity and experimentation. Even the most cursory study of human history or political science confirms this variety. Usually when people pose this question, however, they are after something a little more nuanced. Is there, perhaps, a default setting for human social organization, one that emerged from the deep recesses of evolutionary time as perhaps especially suited to the creatures we are?

The question touches on the debate between anthropologists about the evolutionary significance of contemporary foraging groups. Many theorists have noted that among the groups that are mobile (i.e., without permanent dwellings, cities, etc.), some common patterns emerge, and some have speculated that these patterns were also true of ancient foragers.[52] These groups, like the Ju'/hoansi we encountered earlier in Wiessner's ethnographic work, tend to be egalitarian in both material resources and political leadership. They are highly cooperative in everyday subsistence strategies, including those used for food acquisition and childrearing, and have robust social norms regarding sharing, especially of meat. Given the type of cooperation, one might expect these groups to be highly controlling, privileging the group over the individual. In actuality, the picture is much more complex. Foraging groups practice various forms of social control to maintain social norms, but they also often have a robust commitment to personal autonomy. Outside the aforementioned norms, they resist the idea that one person can coerce the behavior of another. In the Americas, autonomy in egalitarian societies took the form of a high respect

52. Christopher Boehm, *Hierarchy in the Forest: The Evolution of Egalitarian Behavior* (Cambridge, MA: Harvard University Press, 1999), 13.

for individual differences and self-realization.[53] At times this resistance to coercion extends even to children. For instance, one study found that among
the Bayaka of the Republic of the Congo, children were frequently assigned
tasks, but compliance was not enforced. Indeed, other adults might intervene
if parents were too coercive.[54]

This combination of closely knit community and commitment to personal
autonomy might strike Westerners as an outright contradiction.[55] So much of
our political theory revolves around negotiating tensions between the individual
and the group. Could these relatively egalitarian social structures where personal
autonomy is also highly valued perhaps be the default for human society and a
path beyond our many impasses? Again, the answer must be no. It is possible
that the patterns I have described, or something resembling them, emerged with
near universality in humans prior to the development of agriculture. However, a
number of scholars point out that not all contemporary foragers are egalitarian,
that contemporary egalitarians still have some kinds of inequality, and that we
can identify some signs of stratification among upper Paleolithic foragers in the
archeological record.[56] And even without these complicating factors, forager
social organization would not be a default for the species. In the first place,
forager egalitarianism is not natural in the sense of being spontaneous or inevitable. Instead, this social structure must be actively maintained through social
norms, even to the point of capital punishment for individuals who repeatedly
violate norms.[57] Second, material egalitarianism among foragers seems to be
facilitated by the overall means of subsistence. Without permanent homes or

53. David Wengrow and David Graeber, "Farewell to the 'Childhood of Man': Ritual, Seasonal-
ity, and the Origins of Inequality," *Journal of the Royal Anthropological Institute* 21 (2015): 597–619.

54. Adam Boyette and Sheina Lew-Levy, "Socialization, Autonomy, and Cooperation: Insights
from Task Assignment among the Egalitarian BaYaka," *Ethos* 48, no. 3 (2021): 400–418. The
researchers observed a noncompliance rate of 25 to 30 percent. See also Adam Boyette and Barry
Hewlett, "Autonomy, Equality and Teaching among the Aka Foragers and Ngandu Farmers of the
Congo Basin," *Human Nature* 28 (2017): 289–322; Karen L. Endicott and Kirk M. Endicott,
"Batek Childrearing and Morality," in *Ancestral Landscapes in Human Evolution: Culture, Childrearing, and Social Wellbeing*, ed. Darcia Narvaez et al. (New York: Oxford University Press, 2014),
108–25.

55. Kirk Endicott and Karen Endicott, in their ethnographic work with the Batek of Malaysia,
call this combination "cooperative autonomy." Endicott, "Cooperative Autonomy: Social Solidarity
among the Batek of Malaysia," in *Anarchic Solidarity: Autonomy, Equality, and Fellowship in Southeast
Asia*, ed. Thomas Gibson and Kenneth Sillander (New Haven: Yale University Press, 2011), 62–87.

56. Monique Borgerhoff Muldder et al., "Intergenerational Wealth Transmission and the Dynamics of Inequality in Small-Scale Societies," *Science* 326 (October 2009): 682–88; Eric Alden Smith et
al., "Wealth Transmission and Inequality among Hunter-Gatherers," *Current Anthropology* 51, no. 1
(February 2010): 19–34; Wengrow and Graeber, "Farewell to the 'Childhood of Man.'"

57. Polly Wiessner, "The Vines of Complexity: Egalitarian Structures and the Institutionaliza-
tion of Inequality among the Enga," *Current Anthropology* 43, no. 2 (April 2002): 233–69; Boehm,
Hierarchy in the Forest, 12.

even communal dwellings in which to store goods, there is little opportunity for robust material inequality to develop.

Although contemporary foragers cannot provide an ideal model of social organization—nor could ancient foragers, even if we had better access to their institutional structures—that does not mean our study of these societies is irrelevant for the question at hand. Our imaginations benefit from seeing options beyond our restricted experience, including the juxtaposition of ideals that we find inherently contradictory. Also intriguing is what the insight into the active maintenance of equality suggests for the project at hand. What we are doing here—reflecting on how our theological tradition bestows status and worth on individuals and what this might mean for how we live together—is a thoroughly human project.

Theology, Evolution, and Human Nature

At the conclusion of the previous chapter, I argued that the history of Christian reflection on grace points to a particular understanding of creaturely humanity. The human person is created to be deeply aware and deeply trusting of the goodness of God, especially that goodness as manifest in Jesus of Nazareth. And I suggested that such an awareness of and reliance on God's gift in Christ would, in turn, imply a social ethic, a way of being in the world with others and a way of thinking about how human community might be structured. In chapter 4, I will make a stronger case for the claim that grace should be determinative of human community, and I will examine the extent to which this theology has suggested a social ethic at a few moments in Christian history. Our task in this chapter and the next, however, is to consider whether such a vision of the human coheres with empirical study of ourselves and of human nature.

Before answering this question directly, however, we must first consider which human nature, from a theological perspective, we are studying in this evolutionary history. As we saw in chapter 1, Christian accounts of human nature are multilayered, positing a created nature that is judged by God as "good," a fallen nature experiencing the corruption of sin, and a nature that receives God's grace and is rescued from sin to live in communion with God. If evolution studies human origins, do we have in our evolutionary history some kind of access to human nature as it is created to be?

Any kind of affirmative answer to this question seems highly problematic. While I have emphasized cooperation in this account, that emphasis should not be taken as a denial that the human behaviors we typically find morally wrong, such as violence or selfishness, are present within and indeed part of

our evolutionary trajectory. Quite the contrary—these behaviors and tendencies predate the genus *Homo* and persist throughout the evolutionary lineage,
at least to the extent that contemporary science is able to reconstruct it. There
seems to be very little space for an Edenic idealized "good" humanity. If we
understand a fall of humanity to entail an observable human goodness followed
by the presence of sin and perhaps accompanied by some sort of biological
alteration of the species *Homo sapiens*, we would seem to be in a bind.

Seen from another perspective, however, current theoretical accounts of
human evolution can be consistent with theological claims about human nature. The key idea is that in both evolutionary theory and in Christian theology,
human nature is not a static "thing." One prominent thread in the evolutionary
account sketched here is that of human becoming—and of human openness
to becoming *differently*. As we have seen, human life assumes many different
forms, both across time and across cultures, and these different forms are
shaped by the particular context, especially the social context. How might this
flexibility of human nature be consistent with a theological vision of humanity
as good, fallen, and redeemed? In this view we can say that human nature is
expressed differently based not just on the human context but also in relationship to God. Created goodness is thus the potential for having a relationship
with God, and it is the expression of that human nature as it would develop
in and through the divine-human intimacy evoked by Genesis 2–3. Humanity
was created to share in and reflect divine goodness through existing in relationship to God. Fallen humanity, in this construal, is any expression of human
nature as it is lived in alienation from God.[58] A humanity that "becomes" in
alienation from divine relationship will inevitably be a sinful humanity. To
the extent that human beings are in Christ, we can also speak of a humanity
that is being redeemed, precisely through relationship to God in the person of
Christ. What is shared in both the evolutionary and theological perspectives is
the notion that human nature assumes different forms according to its social
context. What is distinctive in the theological account is that this context could
be infused with or saturated by the divine presence.

Evolutionary theory, and particularly niche construction, thus offers one
way of thinking about the complexity of human nature in theological accounts.
It also affords glimpses of how our specific embodied capacities, even in the
condition of sin and alienation from God, are suitable for the relationship
of trust in and dependence on God that we observed in chapter 1. The most

---

58. In this perspective, a fall of humanity could relate to evolutionary history either historically
or ahistorically. For a survey of the theological literature on evolution and the fall, see van den Brink,
Reformed Theology and Evolutionary Theory.

striking aspect of the evolutionary history presented here is that human beings evolved to be interdependent. Put simply, self-sufficiency is not human. This is not to say that there is no personal agency or responsibility or that being able to exercise these things is not desirable. There is, rather, within the span of a human life an emergence from the profound, all-encompassing dependence of childhood into more complex forms of interdependent agency. Every human action is enabled and conditioned by other human action, although this enabling does not always follow the patterns we imagine. We might recall here the anthropological studies of nonindustrial cultures that found in them far more communal interdependence than is found in Western industrial societies but also a higher degree of respect for children's agency and freedom. In the West it would behoove us to use greater care in how we articulate these ideas in popular discourse and to consider the assumptions and expectations that accompany an uncritical valorizing of "self-sufficiency." Contemporary reflection on disability and the way this growing field of study challenges what is considered normative for human agency is also helpful in this respect. By recognizing variation in human agency, both between different persons and across the human lifespan, we are able to see more clearly that what we often take to be a human ideal—as much capacity for independent action as possible—should perhaps not be an ideal after all. It creates a division among people such that even when the person who succeeds to some degree at being self-sufficient is willing to help others, that help can be given only as from a superior to an inferior. Such a false ideal should instead be exposed as a distorted vision of human flourishing, one in which a person wishes to be isolated from human community as much as possible.

By contrast, trust in and genuine concern for others in one's community appear to be evolved capacities that are rooted in hundreds of thousands, if not millions, of years of cooperative survival. They are as much a part of human "nature" as competition, aggression, and concern for personal advantage. If we are asking about that which is *distinctively* human, we might even want to say that these capacities are more human than those that feature so prominently in our closest evolutionary relatives.[59] It is important to note that the forms of interdependent and cooperative life we glimpse in evolutionary history do not seem to take shape on a contractual basis between two equal individuals with explicit rights and duties. Rather, they take shape in complex communities

59. The claim here is not, however, that human cooperation is absolutely unique among primates. Some non-great-ape species show more cooperative features than do primates with whom humans share a more recent ancestor. See Judith Burkart et al., "Other-Regarding Preferences in a Non-human Primate: Common Marmosets Provision Food Altruistically," *Proceedings of the National Academy of Sciences* 104, no. 50 (December 2007): 19762–66.

with individuals of varying abilities and varying contributions. In the absolute dependency of infancy, all is gift. And crucially, infants receive this care not just from parents but from a community of biological and nonbiological kin. As children grow and learn, they are gradually able to contribute more, to care for others. While these capacities for trust and care are evocative of a theological perspective, the evolutionary story also presents challenges to any effort to interpret them uncritically as confirming a theological account of created human goodness.

Although interdependence is suggestive of something much like "gift" being foundational to human experience, it is not a precise human analogue for the theological concepts of grace that we have been tracing, especially to the extent that grace is not contingent on human action. It is quite clear that in the evolutionary model as we currently understand it, reciprocity and some capacity to monitor the actions of others would have been crucial to the sustainability of cooperation. And within observable human societies today, even the most egalitarian and communal are not unconditional in their acceptance of others. It would thus not be accurate to say that intrahuman community functions on the basis of grace, full stop.

Similarly, it would not be appropriate to idealize the trust and care evident in evolutionary history and conclude that humans evolved to be good or virtuous. While the evolutionary lineage suggests that these capacities would make sense in a highly cooperative niche, it also indicates that such trust and care might be highly localized. Since early humans lived in small, highly communal groups, the capacities for trust and care might more easily be directed toward those close to us, toward those we identify as our primary community or "tribe." If we have a biological predisposition to care for those close to us, we might be inclined to ignore or fear or even have animosity toward others.[60] Similarly, our interdependence and physical vulnerability shed light on our propensity to care what others think *about us*. It helps us understand why we are so desperate to belong, to matter, to be highly regarded by others, and even to have power over others. These are complex and intertwined psychological dynamics, and in the next chapter we will turn to the discipline of social psychology to try to distinguish them and to understand them better. For the moment, however, I want to note how crucial they are and also how susceptible they are to going awry. Our awareness of and concern for how others see us functions as social glue. It joins us together in common goals without the use of physical coercion.

60. Processes of human self-domestication, which many researchers believe occurred in *Homo sapiens* beginning about 300,000 years ago, may have increased tolerance between different groups of humans. See Spikins, *Hidden Depths*.

At the same time, these psychological motives can be directed to horrific and destructive ends. It does not take much observation of human behavior and human history to discover that we will do all sorts of morally objectionable things (and fail to do many good things) simply because we want our community to accept us and think well of us. These possible results of interdependence are, from an evolutionary perspective, "natural" possibilities within human communities that make sense in an evolutionary context.

Does the humanity that emerges in this evolutionary account exhibit a suitability for loving relationship with God, for a life of trusting dependence on a gracious creator? On this point the evolutionary account provides important insight. It is significant that the evolutionary history of *Homo sapiens* is one of vulnerability and mutual dependence, that members of the genus *Homo*, and perhaps even earlier hominids, survived by means of an inclination to trust and rely on one another. If such traits are indeed presuppositions of a human relationship to God—and I propose that they are—then it is worth underscoring that they have taken shape in and through our embodied human existence. Simply put, we have become creatures who can recognize and receive God's love in Christ precisely because we have evolved in interdependence with one another. A theology that subsequently abandoned or had no place for human interdependence with one another would then seem to reject one of its fundamental presuppositions.

Conclusion

In this chapter, we have sought to understand human nature by considering the deep history of human evolution. The assumption is not that science provides a more reliable or more authoritative account of human nature than theology, but that theology should help us make sense of empirical observations of humanity and that a theological anthropology attentive to the human sciences might be better equipped to speak to questions of communal flourishing in a religiously plural context. The current emphases on cooperation, interdependence, and plasticity in the study of human evolution are each suggestive of the potential for fruitful dialogue with theological anthropology. Assuming the scientific research continues to support this trajectory, it could assist theological reflection on how human community can express, rather than contradict, a fundamental rootedness in divine grace.

CHAPTER 3

BELONGING AND SELF-WORTH IN CONTEMPORARY PSYCHOLOGY

During the Summer Olympics of 2021, events in US gymnastics vividly illustrated the dynamics of performance and human worth that so frequently repeat themselves in American culture. Women's gymnastics in the United States has long been characterized by a high potential for glory and acclaim and an equally high risk of abuse and exploitation.[1] Elite women gymnasts typically undergo intense scrutiny and bear the weight of a nation's expectations, and their long-term health and well-being are treated as disposable. When Simone Biles, widely regarded as the greatest gymnast of all time, withdrew from the 2021 Olympics over health concerns, the backlash was fierce. Biles was accused by some of failure, weakness, and betrayal of team and country. Others, however, perhaps newly appreciative of the pressures and abuses gymnasts face, praised her for making a difficult decision that was necessary for her health and safety in a dangerous sport. Biles herself later commented on social media, "The outpouring of love and support I've received has made me realize I'm more than my accomplishments and gymnastics, which I never truly believed before."[2] One can imagine that most elite

---

1. Rachael Denhollander, *What Is a Girl Worth? My Story of Breaking the Silence and Exposing the Truth about Larry Nassar and USA Gymnastics* (Carol Stream, IL: Tyndale Momentum, 2019); Joan Ryan, *Little Girls in Pretty Boxes: The Making and Breaking of Elite Gymnasts and Figure Skaters* (New York: Grand Central, 2018).
2. Sophie Lewis, "Simone Biles Says She Now Realizes She Is More Than Her Gymnastics Career in Emotional Tweet," CBS News, July 29, 2021, https://www.cbsnews.com/news/simone-biles-tweet-gymnastics-olympic-games-withdrawal.

athletes who receive constant accolades for their performance have difficulty separating their worth as a human being from their success in competition. Biles's realization is even more noteworthy when one considers the pressure faced by women of color to prove themselves. Remarkably, in the midst of the ugliness of social media, Biles heard and internalized a message of noncontingent worth. She mattered more than a gold medal; she mattered regardless of the medal.

In chapter 2, I speculated that an evolutionary history where human cooperation played a major role would also facilitate the evolution of such psychological mechanisms as sensitivity to the judgments of others. In this chapter I will investigate some of these mechanisms as they are studied in social psychology. What are some of the traits that enable or motivate the individual to function cooperatively in the group? Just how strong is the hold that others, through their judgments and valuations, hold over behavior? We will find that here too, in the arena of the psyche and mental health, the human person flourishes through the gifts of others. This psychological gift comes in the form of belonging, as the person is welcomed into interpersonal community, and in the form of affirmation of value, when one's basic human dignity and worth are recognized and communicated by others. This is the kind of affirmation that Biles experienced after her abrupt exit from Olympic competition—the affirmation that one matters quite apart from one's actions and accomplishments.

In order to explore the psychological gifts that human beings receive in community with others, this chapter will first consider the discipline of psychology and some recent methodological questions and challenges concerning its reliability. Next, I will turn to two key motivations or psychological needs that facilitate human cooperation—the need to belong and the need to feel worthy. As we shall see, the psychological literature is consistent with the conclusions from evolutionary anthropology that say humans are highly cooperative and interdependent. These drives and capacities, however, can be exercised and expressed in many different ways. I will conclude the chapter with theological reflection on some of these expressions and the way they can be consistent or inconsistent with our theological purpose as creatures made for fellowship with God.

Method

Whereas the study of human evolution may be unfamiliar to many readers, each of us necessarily has some familiarity with human thought and behavior, the subject matter of psychology. Drawing on our experience of ourselves and the observations of others, we bring our own assumptions to questions about how and why human beings think and act the way they do. But how does one study human behavior from a *scientific* perspective? The question is immensely important. Understanding our behavior and motivations accurately can be helpful in addressing personal and social problems. But rigorous scientific study of human persons is also complicated and messy. There are many factors that might influence a behavior or mental process, and humans are not necessarily consistent with their choices or even aware of, and honest with themselves about, the reasons for particular actions.

The discipline of psychology uses a variety of empirical methodologies to understand human behavior and motivation. As such, it is indispensable. Without some kind of scientific approach, we are each left to generalize from our own experience or limited observations of others. At the same time, psychology, like any science, has its weaknesses and limitations. For instance, a disproportionate number of psychology studies use college students in Western countries as their primary subjects. This subject bias might lead to a distorted picture of human thought and behavior more broadly. Psychologists must also develop ways of defining and measuring the specific human characteristic they wish to study. What actually *is* gratitude or humility? The value of the results will be only as good as these initial definitions and measurement tools. One should always be aware of what specifically is being measured as well as the limitations of the conclusions one might wish to draw from the data.

In addition to requiring these kinds of disclaimers, in the last decade psychology has faced criticism of its research practices that has cast doubt on the reliability of its findings. These concerns entered the public consciousness in 2015, when a group of researchers with the Center for Open Science, carrying out what they called the Reproducibility Project, attempted to reproduce one hundred psychology experiments and were able to replicate only 36 percent of the findings. What, exactly, does this mean? A typical psychology experiment might involve several dozen subjects in a laboratory with researchers collecting data to try to discover relationships between different variables. For example, does recalling a happy memory make one more likely to give to charity? There is always the possibility that any observed relationship is due to chance rather than a genuine connection between the two variables. Psychologists seek to avoid such meaningless correlations by making sure they have a large enough sample size and by conducting statistical analysis to determine the likelihood that the findings are due to chance. Ideally, psychologists also test these results by running the same experiment repeatedly, or running very similar experiments, to see if the findings can be replicated.

What the researchers of the Reproducibility Project suspected was that common research practices were leading to a high occurrence of false positives—correlations between variables that were actually just chance results rather than indicative of a genuine relationship. In the first place, most journals in the field preferred to publish positive findings of a relationship rather than studies where no relationship was detected. Journals were also not inclined to publish replications of previous studies. These publishing decisions pressured researchers to collect information on many variables and try to find some kind of novel positive relationship, even if it was not one they initially wished to study. With enough data, researchers could usually find some correlation that was statistically significant and render their research publishable, and because there was no incentive to try to replicate findings, these relationships would be published with no follow-up experiments to confirm them. While many psychologists, especially younger researchers, are attempting to establish new best practices for the discipline, including the preregistering of experiments, these changes do not help us assess the reliability of previous research.[3] Is it possible for us, at this point, to look to psychological research for scientific insight into human behavior and thought processes?

Only time will tell as research practices are reformed and new findings are published. What this chapter will present is a snapshot of the literature as it exists now. Several criteria will guide my assessment. First, some aspects of human behavior and mental processes have been studied more thoroughly, and some findings have been replicated. This is particularly the case with belonging and self-esteem, which have been very robust areas of research. Thus, the picture of human persons and human sociality that I will present here will take a broad view and not rely on the findings of individual studies. Second, since attention to the specifics of research practices will be important even within this bigger picture, preference will be given to newer research in which the recent changes have been implemented.[4] Finally, I will seek out cross-cultural studies and experiments that do not rely only on college students or Western cultures for subjects.

3. Some changes include preregistering experiments, reporting all measured variables, and making data openly accessible. See Marcus R. Mufanò et al., "A Manifesto for Reproducible Science," *Nature Human Behaviour* 11, article 21 (January 10, 2017).

4. For example, were influential studies designed well, and were important concepts, like self-worth, carefully defined? With respect to questions of the replicability of findings, I look at sample sizes, the sizes of observed effects, and the likelihood of findings occurring by chance. Where possible I rely on more recent research that has been undertaken with newer practices, like the preregistration of experiments that clearly states the specific relationships that are being investigated. I also look for longitudinal research and laboratory experiments that study the effects of changed variables.

Motivational Structure of the Cooperative Self

Before we can speak to the motivational drives of the self, a few words are in order about the terminology and constructs that psychologists use to study the self.[5] Most prominent among these is the notion of the "self-concept." I speculated at the end of chapter 2 that the importance of interdependence to the human niche would have facilitated psychological tendencies like attending to one's location and security within the broader social group and to what other people think of them. Psychologists think of this capacity for knowing and monitoring the self as the self-concept. It is the person's ability to track their individual traits—skills, personality, emotional dispositions, and so forth—and their relationships to various social groups as well as the ability to negotiate the interplay between the two. The self-concept provides the foundation for reflection on the security of the social spaces one occupies. Am I loved? Respected? Idolized? Envied? Feared? According to most psychologists these ideas take shape gradually in childhood and adolescence, based on experience of oneself and the observations (both explicit and implicit) of others within the broader cultural context. In adulthood they assume a relatively stable form that enables the person to coordinate and direct behavior. While stable, self-concepts are not rigid or incapable of change, nor are they always internally consistent. Individuals can draw on, or "activate," different aspects of the self-concept as appropriate to a particular context. For example, while a person might prefer small groups to large crowds, they might also cultivate a networking persona that they can activate in professional contexts. In what follows I will consider two aspects of the self, belonging and self-worth, that are related to the motivational structure for cooperative agency.

Belonging

I have elsewhere examined scientific study of children's development and the need that children in particular have for belonging and affection.[6] On the whole, this literature suggests that children thrive and experience optimal development in the context of caregiving relationships that are generous with affection, unconditionally accepting of the child (though not of some behaviors!), and responsive to children's needs and agency. In short, belonging—especially if by this we mean the acceptance one experiences in close, interpersonal, affective

---

5. The following description is drawn from Daphne Oyserma, Kristen Elmore, and George Smith, "Self, Self-Concept, and Identity," in *The Handbook of Self and Identity*, ed. Mark Leary and June Tangney (New York: Guilford, 2012), 69–104.

6. Angela Carpenter, *Responsive Becoming: Moral Formation in Theological, Evolutionary, and Developmental Perspective* (London: T&T Clark, 2019): 115–47.

relationships—is critical for children's health and flourishing. While I won't revisit this literature here, an important further question is the extent to which belonging remains crucial during adulthood.

The notion that belonging or the experience of personal connections with others is a psychological need that motivates action appears in multiple theories of motivation in psychology. In a landmark 1995 essay, Roy Baumeister and Mark Leary, drawing on the prior work of Abraham Maslow, theorized a "need to belong" that consisted of "frequent, affectively pleasant interactions" occurring in the context of stable relationships in which the involved persons manifested "affective concern for each other's welfare."[7] Baumeister and Leary's article marshaled evidence from a variety of disciplines and set the stage for the next generation of research in social psychology. Shortly after the publication of this essay, the self-determination theory of Edward Deci and Richard Ryan posited that people are motivated to fulfill three basic psychological needs, one of which is what they termed "relatedness," defined as "the desire to feel connected to others—to love and care, and to be loved and cared for."[8] Both of these theories have been highly influential in psychology, and twenty-five years after its initial publication, the essay by Baumeister and Leary had been cited over twenty-two thousand times. As one commentator noted in a retrospective essay, they "identified the invisible hand that guides so much of the research in our field."[9]

Despite an initial description of close personal relationships providing a sense of belonging, the essay also mentioned the possibility that belonging could be experienced in other contexts through affiliation with a particular group or movement.[10] And indeed, much of the experimental evidence they marshal in the essay consists in less intimate group affiliations.[11] The ambiguity of this initial definition has continued in the research; the need to belong relates sometimes to interpersonal relationships, sometimes to group affiliations, and sometimes to both together. Many scholars have noted the limitations

7. Roy Baumeister and Mark Leary, "The Need to Belong: Desire for Interpersonal Attachments as a Fundamental Human Motivation," *Psychological Bulletin* 117, no. 3 (1995): 497.

8. Edward Deci and Richard Ryan, "The 'What' and 'Why' of Goal Pursuits: Human Needs and the Self-Determination of Behavior," *Psychological Inquiry* 11, no. 4 (2000): 231. A recent meta-analysis surveys the empirical findings of Deci and Ryan's program of research and concludes that the results were generally supportive, though the authors note some methodological concerns and gaps in the research. See Anja Van den Broeck et al., "A Review of Self-Determination Theory's Basic Psychological Needs at Work," *Journal of Management* 42, no. 5 (July 2016): 1195–229.

9. Shira Gabriel, "Reflections on the 25th Anniversary of Baumeister & Leary's Seminal Paper on the Need to Belong," *Self and Identity* 20, no. 1 (2021): 2.

10. Baumeister and Leary, "Need to Belong," 500.

11. Baumeister and Leary, "Need to Belong," 501–8.

this ambiguity creates for truly understanding human social needs and have recently begun to develop theoretical and experimental tools for studying these different kinds of belonging as distinct human experiences and for better understanding their interactions.[12]

As it stands, the existing literature does provide empirical evidence that humans, even in the highly individualistic American context, need regular, affective interactions with others and are motivated to associate themselves with broader groups. Some of the most robust evidence for the interpersonal need comes from decades of study on the health effects of loneliness and social isolation. Two separate meta-analyses of the research associated with loneliness concluded that it represents a significant mortality risk—an increase of approximately 25 percent, comparable to a long list of other risk factors, including obesity, substance abuse, or lack of physical activity.[13] Similar results were found for factors like social isolation or living alone, and loneliness has been associated not just with mortality but also with increased risk of specific health concerns.[14] These ill effects are observed throughout the human lifespan, not just in the elderly.[15] While more work needs to be done in understanding the causal mechanisms of the relationships, researchers suspect a variety of interacting factors. It might be the case, for instance, that partners or other family members in the house provide material support that improves health or that close others provide care in the midst of chronic illness. But there is also reason to believe that emotionally satisfying social interaction has a direct impact on the body and particularly on mental health.[16]

One body of literature that addresses the question of causality with respect to belonging is the study of ostracism. Unsurprisingly, research on "real world"

12. See Jennifer L. Hirsch and Margaret S. Clark, "Multiple Paths to Belonging That We Should Study Together," *Perspectives on Psychological Science* 14, no. 2 (2019): 238–55; Elaine Paravati, Esha Naidu, and Shira Gabriel, "From 'Love Actually' to Love, Actually: The Sociometer Takes Every Kind of Fuel," *Self and Identity* 20, no. 1 (2021): 6–24.

13. Julianne Holt-Lunstad et al., "Loneliness and Social Isolation as Risk Factors for Mortality: A Meta-Analytic Review," *Perspectives on Psychological Science* 10, no. 2 (2015): 227–37; Laura Alejandra Rico-Uribe et al., "Association of Loneliness with All-Cause Mortality: A Meta-Analysis," *PLoS ONE* 13, no. 1 (January 2018), https://doi.org/10.1371/journal.pone.0190033. Holt-Lunstad and colleagues found the increased risk factor for loneliness was 26 percent, whereas for Rico-Uribe and colleagues it was 22 percent.

14. Holt-Lunstad et al., "Loneliness and Social Isolation"; Louise Hawkley and John P. Capitanio, "Perceived Social Isolation, Evolutionary Fitness and Health Outcomes: A Lifespan Approach," *Philosophical Transactions: Biological Sciences* 370, no. 1669 (2015): 1–12.

15. Hawkley and Capitanio, "Perceived Social Isolation."

16. For a discussion of interacting causes and their empirical support, see John T. Cacioppo and William Patrick, *Loneliness: Human Nature and the Need for Social Connection* (New York: W.W. Norton, 2008), 99–109; Paula R. Pietromonaco and Nancy L. Collins, "Interpersonal Mechanisms Linking Close Relationships to Health," *American Psychologist* 72 (2017): 531–42.

experiences of ostracism, such as being ghosted, has indicated strong correlations with various negative outcomes.[17] Ostracism manipulations in the laboratory setting have helped clarify the causality. Early research on the subject using the computer game *Cyberball* indicated that experiences of social exclusion caused negative emotional responses. Across hundreds of studies, these effect sizes (the magnitude of the effect one variable had on another) were found to be strong, and research using other forms of ostracism, like "phubbing" (looking at one's phone while another person is speaking), have confirmed this immediate reaction.[18] Studies asking participants to record real-life experiences of ostracism have further supported the conclusion that it causes negative emotional responses and threatens basic psychological needs like belonging.[19]

While the evidence is strong that loneliness, social isolation, and ostracism have negative outcomes for people, scholars conducting this research do not operate with a single theoretical framework that explores why belonging is so crucial. One area of belonging research that provides a cohesive theoretical account of how belonging functions is attachment theory. Having originally been a theory about the optimal conditions for children's development, attachment theory claims that secure, affective, supportive relationships provide a context for the human person to flourish psychologically throughout life. Attachment theorists suppose that these relationships provide a sense of well-being and security that are foundational for exploration, risk taking, personal achievement, honest self-assessment, resilience in hardship, and so forth. In contrast to those with secure attachment relationship patterns, others have learned, through a history of inconsistent care or neglect, to be very anxious about their relationships (anxious attachment style) or to avoid closeness and intimacy through self-reliance (avoidant attachment style).

Both correlational and experimental evidence for the importance of secure attachment in adulthood has been growing in recent decades. Among the strongest connections is a much-replicated one between a secure pattern of close relationships and self-esteem.[20] While much of this data is correlational,

17. Gili Freedman et al., "Emotional Experiences of Ghosting," *Journal of Social Psychology* (May 2022): 367–86.

18. Chris H. J. Hartgerink et al., "The Ordinal Effects of Ostracism: A Meta-Analysis of 120 Cyberball Studies," *PLoS ONE* 10, no. 5 (May 2015), doi:10.1371/journal.pone.0127002; Judith Knausenberger, Anna Giesen-Leuchter, and Gerald Echterhoff, "Feeling Ostracized by Others' Smartphone Use: The Effect of Phubbing on Fundamental Needs, Mood, and Trust," *Frontiers in Psychology* 13, article 883901 (July 2022).

19. John B. Nezlek et al., "Ostracism in Everyday Life," *Group Dynamics: Theory, Research, and Practice* 16 (2012): 91–104.

20. For a review, see Mario Mikulincer and Phillip Shaver, *Attachment in Adulthood: Structure, Dynamics, and Change* (New York: Guilford, 2010), 155–60.

it is consistent with the idea that close, supportive relationships help establish a sense of self-efficacy that is crucial to human agency. People are able to take initiative and act because others close to them have convinced them through care and affirmation that they are capable of success. Another possibility is that the supportive presence of others makes one's personal environment feel less threatening and thus facilitates agency. Indeed, experimental manipulations that activate people's awareness of such relationships have been shown to increase self-esteem.[21] Other studies of adult attachment patterns have considered the relationship of attachment security or insecurity to various traits and behaviors such as self-concept clarity, exploration, transformational leadership, resilience in adversity, lack of prejudice, compassion, prosocial helping, authenticity, honesty, and more.[22] One set of studies found that insecure attachment styles correlated with both lower authenticity and lower honesty. However, when participants were primed both consciously and subconsciously to boost their sense of relationship security, they responded with greater authenticity and honesty.[23] Such studies are consistent with intuitive notions about acceptance and vulnerability: we are more willing to be fully ourselves, "warts and all," when we sense that even our imperfect selves are loved by others. Some of this work has been partially replicated in cross-cultural studies, which have

21. Mario Mikulincer and Phillip Shaver, "Boosting Attachment Security to Promote Mental Health, Prosocial Values, and Inter-group Tolerance," *Psychological Inquiry* 18, no. 3 (2007): 129–56.

22. For just a few relevant studies and literature reviews, see Elle M. Boag and Katherine B. Carnelly, "Attachment and Prejudice: The Mediating Role of Empathy," *British Journal of Social Psychology* 55 (2016): 337–56; Christine Goedert et al., "'Welcome or Not?—Natives' Security Feelings, Attachment and Attitudes toward Acculturation of Immigrants," *International Journal of Intercultural Relations* 69 (2019): 24–31; Mikulincer and Shaver, "Boosting Attachment Security"; Shawn T. McClean et al., "Transformed by the Family: An Episodic, Attachment Theory Perspective on Family-Work Enrichment and Transformational Leadership," *Journal of Applied Psychology* 106, no. 12 (2021): 1848–66; Michelle Anne Luke, Constantine Sedikides, and Kathy Carnelley, "Your Love Lifts Me Higher! The Energizing Quality of Secure Relationships," *Personality and Social Psychology Bulletin* 38, no. 6 (2012): 721–33; Sarah Woodhouse, Susan Ayers, and Andy P. Field, "The Relationship between Adult Attachment Style and Post-traumatic Stress Symptoms: A Meta-Analysis," *Journal of Anxiety Disorders* 35 (2015): 103–17; Lydia F. Emery et al., "You Can't See the Real Me: Attachment Avoidance, Self-Verification, and Self-Concept Clarity," *Personality and Social Psychology Bulletin* 44, no. 8 (2018): 1133–46.

23. Omri Gillath et al., "Attachment, Authenticity, and Honesty: Dispositional and Experimentally Induced Security Can Reduce Self- and Other-Deception," *Journal of Personality and Social Psychology* 98, no. 5 (2010): 841–55. Priming studies have come under scrutiny in the replication crisis in psychology. See Omri Gillath et al., "Attachment Security Priming: A Meta-Analysis," *Personality and Social Psychology Review* 26, no. 3 (2022): 183–241. If any psychological priming is likely to affect human emotion, thought, or behavior, the recalling of a significant relationship would seem to be a likely candidate. This sort of priming seems conceptually similar to reciting Psalm 23 in a moment of anxiety or encouraging someone to "remember your baptism."

also revealed some cultural differences.[24] On the whole, however, these studies support the theory that the quality of close relationships can shape a person's sense of self and can provide important psychological and material resources for agency.

Attachment theory suggests that humans experience a number of advantages when they belong in secure and supportive interpersonal relationships that are mostly unconditional. By "mostly" I simply mean to acknowledge that all human relationships have their boundaries. Some violations of trust and care are so damaging that the relationship cannot continue. But these supportive relationships are secure enough to withstand ordinary frailty and failure, and they are not contingent on things like personal success or social status. Within them there is no suggestion that belonging must be earned, and, in fact, the language of earning would seem inadequate to capture the kind of relationship that exists. Regardless of what other forms of belonging a person might experience, these relationships occupy a special role.

The literature on attachment also posits an interesting connection between human interdependence on the one hand and independence and freedom on the other. Many of the attributes that are highly valued in what we consider to be individualistic culture—autonomy, cultivation of individual ability, goal-directed activity, willingness to try new things or innovate—seem to function optimally when they are supported by a web of secure interpersonal relationships. People are able to accomplish new and extraordinary things because their basic needs—psychological but likely also material—are not a concern. There may well be other paths to recognition of individual value and agency; the person who has learned the protective strategy of avoiding close relationships out of fear of rejection is an individualist of another sort. Nevertheless, we have here at least one account of human personhood in which an understanding of interdependence is not a threat to notions like autonomy or personal accomplishment but, rather, facilitates them. At the same time, these individual traits do not necessarily imply self-sufficiency or individualism in the sense of isolation or distance from others. The secure relationships that support autonomy, authenticity, exploration, and resilience would, by definition, involve positive emotion and affective bonds between people, which

24. Wei-Wen Chen et al., "Unhappy Us, Unhappy Me, Unhappy Life: The Role of Self-Esteem in the Relation between Adult Attachment Styles and Mental Health," *Current Psychology* 41 (2022): 837–46; Chia-hue Wu and Cheng-Ta Yang, "Attachment and Exploration in Adulthood: The Mediating Effect of Social Support," *International Journal of Psychology* 47, no. 5 (2012): 346–54; Chiachih D. C. Wang et al., "Cross-Cultural Differences in Adult Attachment and Depression: A Culturally Congruent Approach," *Journal of Counseling Psychology* 69, no. 3 (2022): 298–310. Cultural differences in these studies primarily occurred with respect to avoidant attachment style, and findings regarding avoidant attachment tend to be less consistent in research in Western culture as well.

would then encourage responsive mutual support and intrinsically rewarding, rather than instrumental, social interaction.

One further area of research on attachment that is relevant for our purposes is research on attachment to God. Does secure attachment to God function similarly to attachment to humans? Many studies have found correlations between attachment to God and various positive outcomes, and one set of recent studies found these correlations held when researchers controlled for adult attachment.[25] While there is some evidence that attachment to God can fulfill a "compensatory function" for individuals with insecure human-attachment patterns, the big picture seems to be one of correlation between one's attachment to other people and one's attachment to God.[26] In other words, it seems to be the case more frequently that a person experiences the same attachment patterns in both domains, and some theorists suspect that secure human relationships, especially in childhood, establish patterns for healthy spiritual attachment.[27] If these findings are accurate, this is quite significant. It suggests that one cannot neatly separate human relationships from the relationship between a person and God. We will return to this idea in chapter 4, when I will argue that human beings mediate God's gifts to one another through human relationships of interdependence.

Thus far I have focused on interpersonal belonging. What attachment theory does not ask is whether there are also forms of collective belonging that might function in similar ways, that might be largely unconditional and thus provide a stable context for autonomy, exploration, resilience in hardship, and so forth.[28] For example, what are the implications for human agency when belonging in a community of citizens is something that is given to all by birth and is largely secure as opposed to something that is withheld from certain groups? Collective identity can be complex and multifaceted: individuals often have a national identity, a religious identity, a professional identity, and so forth. The formation of these symbolic collective identities is so ingrained in the species that even very superficial similarities between persons, such as a shared birthday,

25. David M. Njus and Alexandra Scharmer, "Evidence That God Attachment Makes a Unique Contribution to Psychological Well-Being," *International Journal for the Psychology of Religion* 30, no. 3 (2020): 178–201.

26. For a review, see Pehr Granqvist, Mario Mikulincer, and Phillip R. Shaver, "Religion as Attachment: Normative Processes and Individual Differences," *Personality and Social Psychology Review* 14, no. 1 (2010): 49–59.

27. Todd W. Hall and Elizabeth Lewis Hall, *Relational Spirituality: A Psychological-Theological Paradigm for Transformation* (Downers Grove, IL: IVP Academic, 2021).

28. For a description of the collective as opposed to the interpersonal, see Marilynn Brewer and Wendi Gardner, "Who Is This 'We'? Levels of Collective Identity and Self Representations," *Journal of Personality and Social Psychology* 71, no. 1 (1996): 83–93.

can trigger them.[29] The interpersonal and collective levels of belonging are related, but the interactions between them are not fully understood. While all people incorporate both aspects of social identity into their self-concepts, there is also some evidence that individuals may compensate for a deficiency in one area by pursuing higher belonging in another.[30] For instance, someone who is socially isolated might be more likely to find meaning and identity in conspiracy theories.[31] A member of an oppressed minority might devote more energy to and draw more value from in-group interpersonal relationships. Exploring group influence on behavior has been a robust area of research in social psychology for decades, and a vast amount of empirical evidence suggests humans act to maintain their group identities through various forms of compliance.[32] Researchers have long noted that this group influence can be both positive and negative and that the strength of the motivation to comply can be further shaped by the cultural value placed on conformity. Furthermore, identification with a group can affect a person's perceptions of and behaviors toward those outside the group. While collective identities can be the foundation for positive bias and favoritism toward in-group members as well as hatred for out-group people, the former does not necessarily lead to the latter. In fact, empirical evidence suggests that out-group hatred and conflict is primarily triggered by a threat to the in-group.[33] At minimum, current research supports the notion that both interpersonal and collective forms of belonging are important to psychological health and motivate behavior, though the relationships between them are not yet well understood.

If this literature is correct, at least in its broad strokes, and humans have a psychological need to belong, it is crucial to make the obvious observation: such a need can be fulfilled only by others. It must be bestowed and received. But under what conditions is it bestowed? Here we find natural variation even within the same cultural context. For the human infant, for example, belong-

29. For a review of this literature, see Gregory Walton et al., "Mere Belonging: The Power of Social Connections," *Journal of Personality and Social Psychology* 102, no. 3 (2012): 513–32.

30. The "quest for significance" theory is one theoretical framework that explores how the interpersonal and the collective level of belonging and approval can each function to satisfy basic psychological needs. See Arie W. Kruglanski et al., "Significance-Quest Theory," *Perspectives on Psychological Science* 17, no. 4 (2022): 1050–71. See also Katarzyna Jasko et al., "Social Context Moderates the Effects of Quest for Significance on Violent Extremism," *Journal of Personality and Social Psychology* 118, no. 6 (2020): 1165–87.

31. Kai-Tak Poon, Zhansheng Chen, and Wing-Yan Wong, "Beliefs in Conspiracy Theories Following Ostracism," *Personality and Social Psychology Bulletin* 46, no. 8 (2020): 1234–46.

32. For an overview, see David G. Myers and Jean M. Twenge, *Social Psychology* (New York: McGraw Hill, 2022), 134–265.

33. Marilynn B. Brewer, "The Importance of Being We: Human Nature and Intergroup Relations," *American Psychologist* 62, no. 8 (November 2007): 728–38.

ing can be given only unconditionally. The infant can do nothing to earn it and, at least at the beginning, can do very little by way of response. Either infants are accepted, welcomed with joy, and cared for, or tragically, they are not. Similarly, one typically does not do anything to earn one's ethnic identity or (initial) nationality. However, these forms of belonging might be affected somewhat by one's personal traits or behavior. For example, one might experience "masculinity" as given—because it is included in biological sex—but also as contingent on certain traits and behaviors.[34]

Other forms of belonging are more thoroughly bestowed on the basis of specific achievements or actions. In Western culture, for example, many people have professional identities to which they can truly belong only if they have cultivated certain skills and attained specific accomplishments: for example, a lawyer has graduated from law school and passed the bar exam. This kind of belonging is bestowed and received, but it is not a gift. Nor would one want to argue that bar associations should welcome any and all, regardless of qualifications. Friendship would seem to fall in an intermediate category. Friendship is voluntary and people generally have some sort of criteria for selecting friends, but we do not typically think of people "earning" friendship. There is an aspect of friendship that is a gift, but there are also behaviors and traits that increase the likelihood that particular people will develop and sustain a friendship with each other.

These complexities of human belonging raise questions about how we should understand this need to belong as a motivation for human behavior. Are all these forms of belonging equal? Or are some forms of belonging more important to the human psyche? As discussed in chapter 1, in Christian theology belonging to God is something that is given, and it is this givenness that makes human action possible. There is, as well, a psychological component to belonging to God that is particularly visible in Reformation thought. Knowing that one belongs to God functions very similarly to attachment theory: because every possible need has been met by God, one is set free from anxious attention to the self and is liberated to act for others. As we move forward, I will suggest that in human relationships not all belonging must be unconditional, but everyone needs some form or forms of unconditional belonging with human community and will suffer in its absence. Furthermore, because we have good theological and empirical reasons for valuing secure, largely unconditional belonging, a Christian social ethic should involve actively promoting contexts where deep interpersonal belonging can take root. By contrast, exclusionary forms of belonging may, at times, be needed, but any exclusions should always be necessary for accomplishing a good end.

34. I am indebted to Benjamin Meagher for this observation and example.

In broad perspective, the notion that belonging is a fundamental motivation is foundational and well established. Moreover, a motivation to belong
is widely understood to be adaptive, a feature of our species' highly social and
cooperative niche. When we lack belonging, we suffer in multiple ways, and
when our belonging, particularly in close relationships, is fragile, we adapt our
behavior to compensate as best we can.

Self-Esteem

In addition to the need to belong, many psychologists talk about feelings
of self-worth or self-esteem as a psychological need that functions to facilitate
interdependence. It certainly seems as though we humans like feeling good
about ourselves and want to see ourselves as persons of worth or value. Is this
a psychological need? Not all psychologists would respond in the affirmative,
but given that we have various strategies for bolstering or protecting our sense
of worth (a point to which I will return momentarily), it seems reasonable
to say that feeling positively about the self is at least a motivation and desire
for many. Throughout much of the last quarter of the twentieth century,
self-esteem was seen, both in academic and popular psychology, as a panacea
for human well-being. If measures could be taken to raise the self-esteem of
children in particular, the logic went, we would reap tremendous rewards in
mental health, academic performance, the reduction of substance abuse, and
many more areas. Subsequent empirical research prompted a reassessment
of the standard narrative. While self-esteem correlated with some positive
outcomes, most notably low rates of depression, causality was more difficult
to establish, and links between self-esteem and other desirable outcomes, like
reduced substance abuse, were found to be weak or nonexistent.[35] More recently, the pendulum has seemed to be swinging yet again, with researchers
suggesting that longitudinal and intervention studies provide good support
for a causal relationship with desired outcomes that is comparable to those of
several other suggested variables, such as self-efficacy and attachment security.
In other words, self-esteem may not be a simple cure for all that ails society,
but it may well have modest positive effects in a number of areas.[36]

Given that most self-esteem research, like most social psychology research
in general, is conducted on American college students, one might wonder if

35. Roy F. Baumeister et al., "Does High Self-Esteem Cause Better Performance, Interpersonal
Success, Happiness, or Healthier Lifestyles?," *Psychological Science in the Public Interest* 4, no. 1 (May
2003): 1–44.

36. For a more recent contribution to this debate, see Ulrich Orth and Richard Robins, "Is High
Self-Esteem Beneficial? Revisiting a Classic Question," *American Psychology* 77, no. 1 (2022): 5–17.

feeling good about oneself is a universal human motive or one that is culturally influenced and particular to certain stages of life. One frequently referenced comparison of Japanese and Western cultural understandings of the self, for instance, argues that the desire to pursue self-esteem is a phenomenon only in Western, individualistic cultures and that more collectivist Eastern cultures neither rated self-esteem as highly nor experienced negative emotional associations with low self-esteem. Rather, among the Japanese, self-criticism rather than self-esteem was the cultural norm.[37] The question has been highly contested in the past few decades, and subsequent research has created a more nuanced picture that seems to be gaining a consensus. According to this newer consensus, human beings have a universal need to view themselves positively, but the content of this positive self, the available strategies for establishing it, and the expression of positive self-evaluations are all culturally shaped.[38] Much of this research compares Eastern (East and Southeast Asian), collectivist cultures with Western (European and North American), individualist cultures. Contrary to earlier research suggesting that persons in Eastern culture did not exhibit a need for self-esteem, more recent research indicates this need simply focuses more on traits that reflect the norms and values of the culture. Thus, Easterners exhibit positivity bias (thinking more positively about themselves than objective measures would warrant) more with respect to communal qualities than with agential ones. When it comes to expressing positive self-views, Easterners, in keeping with prevailing cultural norms of modesty, are less likely to exaggerate their positive traits, as Westerners tend to do. However, when guaranteed anonymity—or, in one experiment, when paid according to the accuracy of their self-assessment—Easterners enhance their positive traits to the same degree. In both cultural contexts a positive sense of self correlates with various measures of psychological health.[39]

While this research begins the case for a universal need for self-worth, it still has a few gaps, some of which an interdisciplinary perspective could

37. Steven J. Heine et al., "Is There a Universal Need for Positive Self-Regard?," *Psychological Review* 106, no. 4 (1999): 766–94.

38. See Chi-Yue Chiu and Young-Hoon Kim, "Rethinking Culture and the Self: Some Basic Principles and Their Implications," in *Fundamental Questions in Cross-Cultural Psychology*, ed. Fons J. R. van de Vijver, Athanasios Chasiotis, and Seger Bruegelmans (Cambridge: Cambridge University Press, 2011), 518–41. See also Erica Hepper, Constantine Sedikides, and Huajian Cai, "Self-Enhancement and Self-Protection Strategies in China: Cultural Expressions of a Fundamental Human Motive," *Journal of Cross-Cultural Psychology* 44, no. 1 (2013): 5–23; Erin M. O'Mara et al., "A Longitudinal-Experimental Test of the Panculturality of Self-Enhancement: Self-Enhancement Promotes Psychological Well-Being Both in the West and in the East," *Journal of Research in Personality* 46 (2012): 157–63.

39. Chiu and Kim, "Rethinking Culture," 519. See also Huajian Cai, Qiuping Wu, and Jonathan Brown, "Is Self-Esteem a Universal Need? Evidence from the People's Republic of China," *Asian Journal of Social Psychology*, no. 12 (2009): 104–20.

help address. The literature on the East-West dichotomy is robust, but there has been surprisingly little work on Africa or Latin America. Most of the psychology research also does not attend to disciplines like history and philosophy, scholars of which have argued that Western individualism is itself a relatively recent cultural phenomenon.[40] Nor does it address the global reach of Western culture through entertainment media or the potential influence of global capitalism as the dominant economic system in both East and West. And while it is cross-cultural, most of the self-esteem research has been carried out in large-scale industrial societies, without attention to small-scale societies. One wonders how members of some of the small-scale or forager societies referenced in chapter 2, cultures that combine communal economic practices with a high respect for individual freedom from coercion, would respond to these self-assessment questionnaires. At the very least, however, this literature indicates that a desire to feel that one has value is not limited to an American or European context. Indeed, one might argue that a historical and anthropological approach would likely strengthen this case and deepen our understanding by attending to related categories of honor, shame, and pride.

Evidence that self-worth is assessed and expressed differently according to one's cultural context would seem to support the notion that this psychological motivation is oriented toward the security of the individual's place within the social group. In other words, it suggests that one evolutionary benefit of our deep desire to feel worthy, of our anxious insecurities, and of our pursuit of status or success, is that these behaviors enable us to cleave to and entrench ourselves within our social groups and thereby reap the benefits of cooperation. Within social psychology, sociometer theory has most thoroughly explored this explanation of the self-esteem motive. For Leary and Baumeister, the authors of the initial essay on the need to belong, self-esteem functions as a barometer of a person's social value and thus of their security within various networks of belonging.[41] Of course, our desire to think well of ourselves does not function this way in a vacuum. It does so in and through the reactions of others in our social context, in accordance with the broader social values and norms and the forms of approval or disapproval that are salient in our context. Self-esteem is thus not simply a way for us to track our social value; it is also a tool with which social groups can exert influence over the behaviors of individuals. Empirical evidence supporting this interpretation of self-esteem includes the literature surveyed above exploring connections between low self-esteem

40. Charles Taylor, *Sources of the Self: The Making of Modern Identity* (Cambridge, MA: Harvard University Press, 1992).

41. Mark R. Leary and Roy F. Baumeister, "The Nature and Function of Self-Esteem: Sociometer Theory," *Advances in Experimental Social Psychology* 32 (2000): 1–61.

and a personal history of rejection and abuse as well as the high correlation between self-esteem and one's sense of social acceptance and support. Some empirical evidence also suggests that humans feel less good about themselves on the basis of random areas of skill or competence than they do on the basis of those that are socially valued.[42]

Given the power for social control that such a psychological need gives to the community, it is important to recognize that social evaluation of the person is not the only factor in self-esteem. One of the most substantiated findings of social psychology is that individuals have a tendency to exaggerate their self-image—to see themselves as more capable or skilled than objective measures would indicate and as better at most things than the average person. Not only are people likely to exaggerate their own positive traits, but they have psychological mechanisms to protect this self-image, such as practicing selective memory and attention, diminishing the abilities of others, dismissing negative feedback, engaging in self-sabotage, deflecting responsibility for failure, and distancing the self from more successful people.[43] Just how common are these behaviors? The literature suggests they are fairly common, as the honest and introspective reader could, in all likelihood, anecdotally attest. For example, studies of the "better than average effect" indicate that anywhere from 60 percent to 94 percent (the latter in one survey of university professors regarding their teaching!) of respondents claim to be above average on the trait surveyed.[44] Critics of these surveys, however, have pointed out that many of these respondents would, in fact, be above average and that "above average" as a metric is problematic.[45] Perhaps not everyone self-enhances, but it does seem relatively common for people to have positive and often exaggerated self-views and for them to protect these self-images through a variety of strategies.

From a theological perspective, these behaviors seem problematic for human behavior and agency. Exaggerating one's abilities or thinking one is better than others is suggestive of pride, and the various mechanisms of self-deception

42. Geoff MacDonald and Mark R. Leary, "Individual Differences in Self-Esteem," in *Handbook of Self and Identity*, ed. Mark Leary and J. P. Tangney (New York: Guilford, 2012), 355–57.

43. For a comprehensive list and discussion of each protective mechanism, see Constantine Sedikides, "Self-Protection," in *Handbook of Self and Identity*, ed. Mark Leary and J. P. Tangney (New York: Guilford, 2012), 327–53.

44. K. Patricia Cross, "Not Can, But Will College Teaching Be Improved," *New Directions for Higher Education* 17 (1977): 1–15. Studies of the better than average effect have asked research subjects to rank a wide variety of traits including intelligence, appearance, moral character, athletic ability, and so forth.

45. Young-Hoon Kim, Heewon Kwon, and Chi-Yue Chiu, "The Better-Than-Average Effect Is Observed Because 'Average' Is Often Construed as Below-Median Ability," *Frontiers in Psychology* 8, article 898 (June 2017), https://doi.org/10.3389/fpsyg.2017.00898.

used to sustain wrong self-images seem, to put it mildly, detrimental to the cultivation of good action, both morally good action as well as excellence in other domains. How can we act rightly or well when we cannot be honest about our failures? How can we cultivate genuine concern for others and honor their value as fellow creatures of God when their successes threaten our sense of self? When initially encountering this psychology literature, one might be surprised to discover that these behaviors are considered by many psychologists, perhaps even the majority, to be "adaptive." By this the researchers do not mean just that the behaviors have evolved and, therefore, must be advantageous for survival and reproduction for the individuals who use them. They also understand these behaviors to contribute to the health and flourishing of the person according to widely accepted standards, like being motivated to act in pursuit of personal goals or not being depressed, and they understand this framing to be important for the clinical or therapeutic setting.

The literature on this question is mixed, and it remains a contentious issue. There does seem to be substantial evidence correlating self-enhancement—as well as other "positive self-illusions," such as a sense of control or a presumption that negative life events will not happen to oneself—with mental health, especially subjective well-being.[46] Indeed, there is even a theory, depressive realism, that depression itself is linked with a realistic understanding of the self and of personal agency. Empirical evidence consistently shows that depressed persons are less optimistic about their ability to control a situation, that they recall a smaller quantity of positive feedback and a larger quantity of negative feedback, and that they evaluate themselves more negatively than nondepressed persons. The evidence varies, however, regarding whether the assessments of depressed persons are more accurate than nondepressed persons or whether they exhibit inaccurate negative bias.[47] Regarding self-enhancement and self-protection in particular, Constantine Sedikides has recently theorized that they function much like the biological immune system, detecting threats to psychological stability and working to eradicate them so that the organism can maintain a stable and healthy self-concept that is foundational to agency.[48]

Given the theological concerns mentioned above, what are we to make of this research and the normative claims regarding human flourishing that at

46. Michael Dufner et al., "Self-Enhancement and Psychological Adjustment: A Meta-Analytic Review," *Personality and Social Psychology Review* 23, no. 1 (2019): 48–72.

47. For a review, see Lauren B. Alloy et al., "The Breakdown of Self-Enhancing and Self-Protecting Cognitive Biases in Depression," in *Handbook of Self-Enhancement and Self-Protection* (New York: Guilford, 2010), 358–79.

48. Constantine Sedikides, "Self-Construction, Self-Protection, and Self-Enhancement: A Homeostatic Model of Identity Protection," *Psychological Inquiry* 32, no. 4 (2021): 197–221.

least some researchers are inclined to make? Should we endeavor to truly know ourselves? Or are self-illusions crucial to our psychological well-being? First, it is worth noting that not all illusions are the same. One can see how a false sense of control in a situation or an exaggerated likelihood of positive outcomes might be important in motivating action. Similarly, a belief that one has the particular capacities needed to succeed at an endeavor might encourage effort and lead to eventual success. We could even point to theological versions of this sort of optimism. The apostle Paul, for instance, claims that the secret to not being anxious is trusting that "I can do all things through [Christ] who strengthens me" (Phil. 4:13). Of course, built into this version of optimistic agency is the recognition that God in Christ is also acting and is the source of Paul's ability. Implied as well is that "all things," expansive as the language may sound, would not include action that would contradict the character or person of Christ.

On the other hand, some forms of self-enhancement might be particularly problematic from a Christian perspective. If one's sense of self-worth includes a notion that one is superior to others, not just with respect to certain skills but as a human being, then reference to the sin of pride is appropriate. Research on entitlement, social class, and reduced prosociality suggests that this comparative form of self-enhancement could impact how a person treats other people.[49] Another danger of self-enhancement is that success in a particular area may become crucial to a person's self-worth as a whole. Such individuals might be susceptible to a future loss of worth if their illusion is shattered, or they may maintain their sense of self by taking steps that harm others. There is some research to suggest, for instance, that when self-worth is threatened, one defensive strategy is denigrating others, particularly those of minority groups, though this research is relatively old and has not been replicated.[50] Biased self-views also seem to be related to the capacity to repair and sustain relationships after wrongdoing. Persons scoring high in defensiveness are less likely to apologize, whereas persons who see themselves as capable of transgressions are more willing to forgive others.[51] One type of self-enhancement that is worth

49. For a review, see Paul K. Piff and Angela R. Robinson, "Social Class and Prosocial Behavior: Current Evidence, Caveats, and Questions," *Current Opinion in Psychology* 18 (2017): 6–10.

50. Steven Fein and Steven J. Spencer, "Prejudice as Self-Image Maintenance: Affirming the Self through Derogating Others," *Journal of Personality and Social Psychology* 73, no. 1 (1997): 31–44; Lisa Sinclair and Ziva Kunda, "Reactions to a Black Professional: Motivated Inhibition and Activation of Conflicting Stereotypes," *Journal of Personality and Social Psychology* 77, no. 5 (1999): 885–904; Lisa Sinclair and Ziva Kunda, "Motivated Stereotyping of Women: She's Fine If She Praised Me but Incompetent If She Criticized Me," *Personality and Social Psychology Bulletin* 26, no. 11 (2000): 1329–42.

51. Joost Leunissen, Karina Schumann, and Constantine Sedikides, "Self-Protection Predicts Lower Willingness to Apologize," *Journal of Social Psychology* 162, no. 6 (July 2021): 691–700; Julie

giving special consideration to is enhancement in the moral domain. Whereas self-enhancement regarding my ability to run long distances might make me more likely to train to run a marathon, enhancing my moral self might have the opposite effect: enabling me to think that I am basically a good person while actually violating moral principles that I claim are important. Even if persons who engage in these behaviors tend to be more satisfied with life or less likely to be depressed, it does not follow that this sort of enhancement should be encouraged in a clinical setting.

Why is it that illusions of self might correlate with psychological health? Some very recent research supports the theory that the psychological benefits of self-enhancement are not actually due to enhancement per se but are actually basic effects of feeling positively about oneself, regardless of whether that positive sense is inflated or illusory.[52] In other words, people who feel good about themselves also tend to feel good about life in general, and conversely, it is generally bad for people to feel that they are not of value. This sort of connection is hardly surprising. Indeed, there is a theological point here as well: apart from the question of sin, to see oneself in a predominantly negative way is to reject the goodness of creation. We human beings are creatures of remarkable dignity and beauty, and we should value both ourselves and others. Even if the enhancement of the self does relate to positive psychological outcomes, there is some uncertainty among researchers as to how one should interpret this connection. Most studies have looked for predictive relationships in a single moment of time between self-enhancement and various measures of mental health. But as noted, it is hardly surprising if feeling good about oneself now, for whatever reason, correlates to a subjective sense of well-being. The empirical data that is needed is longitudinal. How does inflating one's traits and capabilities now relate to future well-being? Here the data is mostly older, so the conclusions must be tentative, but the available evidence suggests a much murkier picture, with modest evidence that certain kinds of positive illusions are predictive of maladaptive outcomes.[53]

Juola Exline et al., "Not So Innocent: Does Seeing One's Own Capability for Wrongdoing Predict Forgiveness?," *Journal of Personality and Social Psychology* 94, no. 3 (2008): 495–515.

52. Sarah Humberg et al., "Enhanced versus Simply Positive: A New Condition-Based Regression Analysis to Disentangle Effects of Self-Enhancement from Effects of Positivity of Self-View," *Journal of Personality and Social Psychology* 114, no. 2 (2018): 303–22; Sarah Humberg et al., "Is Accurate, Positive, or Inflated Self-Perception Most Advantageous for Psychological Adjustment? A Comparative Test of Key Hypotheses," *Journal of Personality and Social Psychology* 116, no. 5 (2019): 835–59.

53. Annmarie Callahan Churchill and Christopher G. Davis, "Realistic Orientation and the Transition to Motherhood," *Journal of Social and Clinical Psychology* 29, no. 1 (2010): 39–67; C. Randall Colvin, Jack Block, and David C. Funder, "Overly Positive Self-Evaluations and Personality," *Journal of Personality and Social Psychology* 68, no. 6 (1995): 1152–62; Richard W. Robins and Jennifer S. Beer,

If this is the case, it seems that what is most desirable is a form of self-worth that befits the finite nature of human beings, one that takes into account frailty and failure. A few theoretical approaches seek to use this nuanced understanding of self-worth. Attachment theorists have suggested, with some initial empirical support, that individuals who experience secure attachment patterns will have less need to self-enhance or to employ protective strategies like ignoring negative feedback or diminishing the abilities of others. Researchers suspect this might be because their worth is regularly affirmed in close interpersonal relationships.[54] Researchers who distinguish stable from contingent self-worth similarly argue that some people do not need to self-protect because their sense of self is firmly rooted in noncontingent sources and is therefore not subject to dramatic fluctuations in everyday life.[55] Finally, research in self-compassion tracks the ability of some individuals to treat themselves with kindness, recognizing that no one is or can be perfect.[56] What each of these approaches share is a commitment to the idea that it is possible to see the self as valuable while also recognizing weakness, failure, and frailty—even recognizing that these are ordinary aspects of all human experience.

These nuanced approaches to self-assessment resemble the complexity we have already observed in theological accounts of the human person. Theological anthropology, with its distinctions between created, sinful, and redeemed humanity, also calls for complexity in a person's self-assessment. Human limitation and finitude, for example, are part of creaturely goodness and should be recognized and affirmed, whereas sin should be confessed and repented. A blanket affirmation of all positive illusions of the self as "adaptive" does not allow this nuance. It suggests that healthy people must avoid seeing themselves as limited or vulnerable to hardship and leads to ambiguity about the need to recognize and take responsibility for wrong actions. At the same time, demonizing these optimistic biases does not make sense either. Believing that we are capable of accomplishing a goal, even if impartial observers would disagree, would seem to be crucial to human agency. Having a natural tendency to see ourselves as

"Positive Illusions about the Self: Short-Term Benefits and Long-Term Costs," *Journal of Personality and Social Psychology* 60, no. 2 (2001): 340–52; Gabriele Oettingen, Doris Mayer, and Sam Portnow, "Pleasure Now, Pain Later: Positive Fantasies about the Future Predict Symptoms of Depression," *Psychological Science* 27, no. 3 (2016): 345–53.

54. Phillip R. Shaver and Mario Mikulincer, "An Attachment Perspective on Self-Protection and Self-Enhancement," in *Handbook of Self-Enhancement and Self-Protection* (New York: Guilford, 2010), 279–97.

55. Michael H. Kernis, "Toward a Conceptualization of Optimal Self-Esteem," *Psychological Inquiry* 14, no. 1 (2003): 1–26.

56. Kristin Neff, "Self-Compassion: An Alternative Conceptualization of a Healthy Attitude toward Oneself," *Self and Identity* 2 (2003): 85–101.

valuable and competent can protect us against those who would shame and demean us for their own purposes, as Simone Biles's detractors attempted to do. Such a tendency, one might argue, could itself be seen as a gift of God. It is perhaps not the complete protection of seeing ourselves as God sees us or the more secure sense of self we might receive from the love of those closest to us, but it affords some resistance against abuses of social influence.

Belonging, Self-Worth, and a Psychology of Grace

What are we to make of the psychological mechanisms of belonging and self-esteem for an interdependent humanity? At the very least, we should note that they are consistent with the conclusions in chapter 2. The need to belong is clearly connected to the human history of survival in community with others, and if sociometer theory is correct, self-esteem functions as a barometer for one's value to the broader community. Here again, interdependence is foundational for human existence, and absolute self-reliance is not. The intense psychological need to belong and to feel worthy enables humans to sustain and navigate this interdependence throughout life. As they operate at the individual and societal levels, people meet these psychological needs in various ways, and it is well worth attending to the implications of these differences.

Specifically, it seems that whether these needs are met has implications for human freedom and agency. It matters whether our belonging and value are contingent, and thus in some way "up to us," or whether, to at least some degree, they are freely offered and received, a gift rather than something we must earn. As with so much of the Christian narrative of sin and salvation detailed in chapter 1, the freedom afforded through gifts is one of capacity, of what is actually possible for human agency, rather than the simple absence of restrictions on choice. Receiving love and support and affirmation of worth enables humans to be more confident in their power to act. On the other hand, if we must anxiously devote our energy and attention to fulfilling these psychological needs, we are less free to pursue those courses of action we deem to be genuinely good for their own sake. Receiving or not receiving this support, therefore, affects whether we devote energy to helping or forgiving others and whether we can acknowledge our limitations, failures, and wrongdoing instead of refusing to entertain the notion that we could be wrong.

The discerning reader will note that this research echoes much of the Reformation psychology of grace. Martin Luther and John Calvin thought that genuinely trusting in God's love and grace also enabled a different kind of agency, one capable of serving the neighbor precisely because self-anxiety had been quieted. This need for grace is a facet of theological anthropology, of being a human creature of God, and is not simply an arbitrary truth about how God chooses to save. The literature on attachment to God, however, might press the theologian to consider carefully the relationship between receiving God's love and grace and receiving human love. It might be the ordinary course of events that we come to perceive the former in and through our experience of the latter. If these findings regarding attachment to God are sound, then we have all the more reason to consider, from a theological perspective, the choices we make as communities regarding human belonging and human worth.

If this literature, along with the study of evolutionary anthropology, tells us anything about our individual and social responses to interdependence, it is that we are adaptable. There is no single or universal form of belonging, though some forms might be preferable. And this fact only serves to underscore the importance of the task before us. It is possible for us to ask which forms of belonging and value we want to cultivate as a society and which we should discourage. We can recognize that these psychological needs are powerful tools for social cohesion, likely ones that no society could dispense with. But we can also recognize and try to minimize their liabilities. What difference would it make, for example, for people to ground their basic sense of worth in the recognition that they are children of God and are loved by God? I will have much more to say on this score in future chapters, so I will limit myself here to the basic observation that our own culture seems very conflicted on this point. We recognize the importance of children enjoying unconditional belonging and a stable sense of self-worth, but we also place a high premium on self-sufficiency and certain markers of status and achievement as contributors to our self-concepts. The result is a fundamental cultural incoherence in which we affirm an individual's inherent worth and dignity with common cultural platitudes but then undermine these claims in very concrete ways—for example, using a dehumanizing criminal-justice system or enabling children to engage in excessive social comparison on social media. If the human person is constituted by grace, we cannot avoid asking how such a dependence on gifts might be recognized and embodied in our institutions, our social norms, and our personal choices.

Conclusion

The scientist may or may not find the conceptual overlap between these scientific and theological anthropologies to be interesting, but for the theologian, the convergence is illuminating. It suggests, as I speculated from the start, that when we think of human capacities for social relationship, we are considering a consistent aspect of human nature, one that is expressed differently, depending on the relationship partner or partners, but is recognizably the same human nature. It is not the case that human beings are thoroughly *dependent* in relation to God (receivers of good gifts who then act joyfully in response) but then subsequently *independent* and *self-sufficient* in their relationships with others (capable of acting and of achieving their own objectives without initial and ongoing contributions from others). Furthermore, as we have seen in both of these scientific disciplines, the form that human interdependence assumes can vary widely between and within human communities. This openness of human life allows for the possibility that human sociality might be shaped by the human relationship to God. In chapter 4, I will argue that this is precisely what Christian theology claims. In the early church, as we encounter it in the New Testament, the assumption is that God's action in Christ is foundational for human community. Even more specifically, it is God's grace, in Christ and the Spirit, that is explicitly intended to structure relationships within the community of those who follow Christ and have received the Spirit. Modern pluralist societies are not, of course, coterminous with the church nor did Luther and Calvin think that the temporal social and political entities of the sixteenth century were to be equated with the church. At the same time, none would deny that the church is always also afflicted by sin and subject to the formative influences of the surrounding culture. These realities make it very difficult to claim that the implications of a doctrine of grace for human community apply to the church but not to other aspects of society. It is to these crucial questions of how an anthropology of grace might apply to human community—whether a fellowship of those claiming to be Christian or a broader pluralist society—that we now turn.

CHAPTER 4

GRACE AND INTERDEPENDENCE IN HUMAN SOCIETY

The primary argument of this book is that grace, far from undermining ethics, actually calls for a social ethic. Theological claims about God's grace are not simply claims about how God happens to relate to and save human beings. Grace in Christian thought is deeper than that. Grace involves claims about the kind of creature we are. It involves the kind of realization that Olympic gymnast Simone Biles expressed—that however impressive human achievements may be, they are not the source of human worth, that human action and achievement are always based on prior gifts and thus are never independently ours (see chap. 3). If this is true for the human person before God, then I argue it has important implications for human relationships with one another. But why should this be the case? Why could we not be dependent before a God of grace and empowered through this grace to exercise independent action and agency among other humans, establishing human relationships and communities governed by the categories of working, earning, and deserving rather than by gift? Why should God's gifts to us matter for how we live in human community?

In this chapter I will respond to questions such as these. The argument here employs both a bottom-up and a top-down approach. The bottom-up approach involves reflecting on the scientific perspectives from chapters 2 and 3. Empirical study of the human person is not definitive for a theological anthropology, but it does afford a picture of human nature that is, at the very least, suitable for the kind of existence with God that I have described.[1] In taking this bottom-up approach, I hope that the points of overlap or convergence between scientific and theological depictions of the human person not only strengthen the case that grace grounds and calls for a social ethic but also provide some reasoning that makes such an ethic salient to those who do not profess the Christian faith. With the top-down approach, I intend to make a stronger theological claim. As Christians, we cannot be the persons we are called to be, in fellowship with a God who is gracious to us, if we are not also this same creature, with this same nature, in relationship to our fellow humanity. Put more starkly yet, it cannot be the ethos of our lives in human society that we must each establish our worth through our own actions and abilities—at least this cannot be the ethos if we are to be faithful to the fundamental theological insight that who we are, in our entirety and at every level, is nothing other than the gift of God.[2]

I will develop this argument, first, by drawing on the theological and scientific discussions of the first three chapters to observe some common features of human existence that have emerged. Again, these anthropological similarities should not be understood as proof of a particular theology. They can, however, increase our confidence that the creaturely relationship we have to God is consistent with who we are in relationship to our fellow human beings. Next, I will discuss why theological anthropology, quite apart from any consideration of science, itself demands a correspondence between our vertical (who we are with God) and horizontal (who we are with one another) dimensions. In the second part of the chapter, I will look at two historical expressions of Christian theologies of grace—first, that of the apostle Paul and, second, his reinterpretation by Martin Luther and John Calvin in the early Reformation—to demonstrate that this move from the vertical to the horizontal, from thinking about God's grace to thinking about human community, has been a regular feature of theologies of grace.

Grace, Identity, and Human Agency

To begin, a brief review of grace and its implications for human agency is in order. Grace, as I have now repeatedly observed, is everywhere in Christian

1. In the words of Karl Barth, human "creaturely essence cannot be alien or opposed to this grace of God but must confront it with a certain familiarity." Barth, *Church Dogmatics* III/2, *The Doctrine of Creation*, ed. Thomas F. Torrance, trans. Geoffrey William Bromiley (Edinburgh: T&T Clark, 1956), 224.

2. We must examine more closely how sin fits into this equation—a task for chap. 6.

theology. God creates *ex nihilo*, meaning that our very existence is a gift. God's providential care constantly sustains creation, and when confronted with human sin, God freely remains with humanity, first in his relationship with Israel and then in the incarnation, life, death, and resurrection of Jesus. The incarnation cannot be overstated in its radical character as gift. Here divine nature irrevocably joins with human nature. As Karl Barth puts it, "Basically and comprehensively, therefore, to be a man is to be with God."[3] In Christ, God also responds to human sin by forgiving and transforming humanity. Crucially, this gift of salvation is not based on any prior human characteristics or accomplishments. None of this, at any point, is earned or deserved. In fact, if one is tempted to locate differential human worth in the differences of created humanity, the grace of salvation is a decisive rebuttal. The incarnation occurs in weakness, oppression, and poverty, thereby affirming those forms of humanity that human societies so often diminish. And as we shall see, a crucial emphasis of Pauline salvation in the New Testament is that this gift is for every human person, regardless of status or any other human characteristics.

One implication of this theology is that it is part and parcel of being human to be radically dependent on God. To say we are dependent, however, is not to deny that we are agents—conscious selves who desire and reflect and eventually make choices for which we are, to varying degrees, responsible. Rather, it is to define and understand human agency in a specific way. Human agency is *enabled*. It is always agency carried out in response to other action, ultimately God's action. Dependency, however, can be a somewhat ambivalent status for human beings. At times it seems that there is very little distinction between dependence, on the one hand, and subjection to domination, on the other. If one is utterly dependent on someone or something, that other has tremendous power to compel and control. This is why it is absolutely crucial that Christian dependence on God is dependence on God's grace. Because God gives without regard for human status and achievement, grace makes possible a relationship with God that is not one of domination and subservience but is, instead, one of free and loving response. Grace means that we are dependent, but it also means that we are free. According to liberation theologian Gustavo Gutiérrez, grace means that our faith in God can be "disinterested," not based on the instrumental desire to receive certain things from God, because in Christ, God has already given everything.[4] Instead, our faith can function for the sake of the relationship itself.

3. Barth, *Church Dogmatics* III/2, 135.
4. Gustavo Gutiérrez, *On Job: God-Talk and the Suffering of the Innocent*, trans. Matthew O'Connell (Maryknoll, NY: Orbis Books, 1987).

This connection between grace and loving relationship introduces a second implication of the theology of grace for human nature. This aspect is psychological, and while it is not exclusive to the Reformation, it was developed there most explicitly and forcefully. From a Christian standpoint, human beings are meant to *understand* that God is gracious to them. This understanding shapes human identity and, by extension, human agency. Those who understand God's grace see themselves as established by it; they do not merely assent intellectually. As we saw in chapter 1, this distinct psychology makes possible and then characterizes one's relationship to God. By displacing the preoccupation with the self, who is vulnerable and in need of protection, grace makes it possible to truly see and know God. God is not the object of fear and thus can be seen as the God of love and gift. Human beings can then genuinely return love to God rather than seek to control God through their actions.

By now it should be fairly evident that I find a significant convergence or analogy between this theological picture of human agency and identity and what we have observed in the scientific studies. Whereas humans are entirely dependent on God, we are thoroughly *interdependent* with one another. The evolutionary picture is one of creatures who became the distinctive hominids they are by way of increasingly cooperative forms of life. Just as there is no human action that is not dependent on God at every moment, there is also no human action that is not founded on, enabled by, and responsive to other human action. One might even go so far as to say this is what makes it human action. As Michael Tomasello has observed, humans inherit culture like a fish inherits water.[5] We become who we are in and through culture. Whenever we speak of human independence or self-sufficiency, both of which, when carefully defined, do have their place, we are always talking about action that is predicated on this more foundational interdependence. And interdependence, in the empirical picture, is rooted in gift. We are born into a community as vulnerable infants. We receive our sustenance long before we contribute, and even more, we receive our very being and identity through our specific culture, with its practices, institutions, language, and accumulated knowledge.

If the evolutionary theory is correct, it makes sense to think that humans would be especially attuned to their status within their social group and the opinions others held of them. Our study of the psychological literature on belonging and self-worth certainly bears this out. As we saw in the previous chapter, humans flourish in supportive personal relationships that, while perhaps not unconditional in a strict sense, are stable and not based on categories

5. Michael Tomasello, *Becoming Human: A Theory of Ontogeny* (Cambridge, MA: Harvard University Press, 2019), 7.

of earning or deserving. In this context, one in which an individual senses secure belonging and value, that person is actually empowered to act, to take risks, to be creative, to think about those other than the self. We also saw that humans are sensitive to broader judgments on their worth as persons and suffer psychologically when that worth is diminished because of their failure to meet some personal or social standard of deservingness. In fact, humans will apparently go to great lengths to hide such failures, even from themselves. We also see glimpses—and it remains to be seen whether empirical study will bear these out—of a different option for humans, of a sense of worth that is not rooted in contingent aspects of the self and is cognizant of human frailty. This is a sense of self that is capable of admitting mistakes, that does not need to receive special treatment or to demean others to feel better, that is not constantly in pursuit of greater achievement just for the sake of feeling valuable.

While these points of analogy are striking, it is also crucial to note some differences in how human sociality is portrayed. Perhaps most obviously, human dependence on God is of a different order altogether than interdependence in human community. The former is asymmetrical and involves a God who is wholly other. It is this radical difference that makes it possible for God to be the source of all existence, including humanity. Human interdependence, by contrast, presupposes a likeness in kind and thus some form of equality and mutuality. We should, therefore, not expect or wish the divine-human relationship to be replicated in human communities. There is also a normative distinction between the theological and scientific claims, which is to say that these disciplines are making different kinds of claims about human nature. Theology, speaking of God as creator, makes claims about God's intentions for humanity and about what humans should and should not be. Scientific study typically sees itself as making purely descriptive claims: this is what humanity looks like as we observe it. And as we have seen, one important feature of this descriptive approach is that it displays the diverse ways of being human. For example, it seems as though humans in general have psychological mechanisms that facilitate group life and cooperation, but these psychological needs can be pursued and satisfied in different ways. Our evolutionary history tells us that humans survive together, with a kind of togetherness unparalleled among other species, but our ways of life and social organization vary tremendously. The empirical literature can describe these differences and explore their effects, but these disciplines face challenges when trying to translate the empirical findings into normative claims.

Even granting these differences, the points of convergence suggest that the insights of the Reformers might provide resources for thinking about questions of belonging, worth, and merit for human communities, even in secular spaces. Those who are concerned about the failures of meritocracy, especially the relentless pressure on individuals to establish their own worth and the tendency to establish hierarchies, might find unlikely conversation partners in Luther and Calvin and might discover secular analogues to theological notions of grace and freedom. The alignment between Christian dependence on God's grace and human interdependence might suggest that human societies should give adequate attention to what their members must *receive* in order to be capable of acting well. If acting as completely independent agents is not a part of our religious heritage and is contrary to our embodied existence, why do we valorize more extreme forms of self-sufficiency? If human agency has different needs and capacities as we grow from the pronounced asymmetrical dependence of childhood into diverse interdependencies throughout the lifespan, should we then find other ways of thinking and talking about ideals of human agency?

However useful this analogy may or may not be from a secular perspective, for Christians the reasons for turning to a theology of grace for guidance in social ethics go deeper than simply observing analogues between human relationships and the relationship between God and humanity. I contend that in order to truly live into the identity of one who receives God's gift in Christ, we *must* reenact this pattern in our human relationships, even, to the extent that we can, influencing the broader, less personal structures that establish the range of possibilities for how we will relate to one another. It is essential to Christian identity that we do so.

The theological reasons for this claim are ontological, pedagogical, and sacramental. By "ontological" I mean having to do with our fundamental being as creatures of God. A theology of grace tells us that we are created to be persons who receive all good things from God and respond in loving relationship. If this is truly who humans *are*, in the deepest sense, we must ask how this being is expressed in our embodied existence with other humans. If, as Luther claimed, God provides all that a person could possibly need, one might be tempted to think that human fulfillment is restricted to the vertical dimension of dependence on God and does not have any corollary in human interdependence. Indeed, Luther himself says that the Christian, the one who is liberated by God's grace, becomes a servant of all precisely because such a person has no unmet need. Is this not, after all, *independence* from others rather than interdependence? A little more reflection, however, shows that this conclusion cannot possibly hold.

Within Christian theology, human beatitude (or perfection or salvation) is to know and love God, to have fellowship with God, to experience union with God, or to participate in God. We need not concern ourselves here with debates regarding these different formulations. They all involve a claim that the human person is to image God or to reflect God. In short, the human person is to love because God is love and one, therefore, cannot participate in God without loving. To whom should this love be directed? The human person is to love God, certainly, but as we explored in chapter 1, God has no need that human self-offering can fill. We can marvel at and adore divine beauty, and indeed, we are meant to enjoy God in this way, but there is no way for the human person to benefit God. We can offer the very lives and gifts we have received from God back in service, but to what end? What need does God have of these gifts?

The repeated response of the New Testament to this question is that human beings love God by loving their neighbor. It is only because we are finite creatures who exist in interdependent communities that human self-offering of love becomes a possibility. Crucially, this must entail all persons being in positions of giving and receiving. If we each received all provision directly from God, how could we have any opportunity to love through offering our gifts beyond ourselves? We would essentially be isolated monads, ever receiving but never able to reflect divine being through the giving of ourselves. The only possible alternative to this scenario is that in our finitude and genuinely human interdependence, we mediate God's gifts to one another. All comes from God and is rooted in the eternal divine act of self-offering, and we receive these gifts in and through God's creation, including through the self-offering of others.

It is instructive here that even Jesus, in his earthly ministry, received care from other humans. He entered human existence, as all of us do, as an infant in a position of absolute dependence and need. He was supported financially by women (Luke 8:2–3), he desperately asked his disciples to remain with him in his sorrow and keep watch as he prayed in Gethsemane (Matt. 26:36–38), and he was even anointed by a woman who bathed his feet with her hair (Luke 7:37–38). The apostle Paul also exemplified this human interdependence. To take one particularly instructive example, at the end of the letter to the Philippians, Paul radically claims, in a manner consistent with Luther, that whether in a situation of plenty or want, he ultimately has no "need" (4:11). God is his provider. And yet Paul has been in "distress" (v. 14), and the relief of this distress illustrates the way that humans mediate God's gifts. Whereas previously the Philippians "were concerned for [Paul] but had no opportunity to show it" (v. 10), in his time of distress they have been able to help him by sending gifts, which have also been "a sacrifice acceptable and pleasing to God" (v. 18). Likewise, Paul confidently asserts, God will also meet their needs (v. 19). Paul is not anxious regarding his lack, but he gratefully receives gifts from the Philippians, knowing that through these gifts they express both their love for

Paul and their love for God. The human reality of living by the gifts of God and in loving relationship to God is mediated by human interdependence.

If we are to express and not contradict this nature in our embodied existence, we must attend to pedagogy, to questions of formation and transformation. We thus come now to my second reason for insisting that human community ought to reflect the patterns of gift and dependency between God and humanity: the pedagogical argument. Human beings do not automatically emerge from their processes of growth and maturation to be persons who wholeheartedly trust God and are therefore able to trust and love others. Quite the opposite is true, in fact: we are often fearful of our finitude and our dependence on others, and we act to protect ourselves as much as possible. This fear and protection are, no doubt, related to the tragic exploitation of those who are in greater positions of dependency by those who have power. If my primary experience has been that other people are out to use me and get what they can, there is little mystery in my self-isolation, my determination to make my own way, and my disavowal of any assistance from or responsibility to others. Theologically, the exploitation of others and the alienation and distorted relationships that ensue fall under the category of sin, and a crucial aspect of Christian salvation is not just the forgiveness of sin but liberation from it—transformation of the person into the image of Christ. Even if we were not sinful, however, the pattern of human life indicates that such trust would need to be cultivated and coaxed into existence. As we observed in our study of human evolution, human beings are open to their environment, especially the social and cultural environment, and to a lifelong process of becoming. This openness to becoming is one of *the* distinguishing features of the species *Homo sapiens*. Christian theology also recognizes that embodied social becoming is an essential feature of humanity. From its beginning in the ministry of Jesus, Christian discipleship has been communal, and it has largely continued to be so throughout its history. The image provided in the New Testament is one in which this communal context of transformation— the church—is itself conditioned by the incarnation of Jesus, by the presence of Jesus among humanity, and by the Spirit, who joins believers, individually and communally, to Christ.[6]

All of this might lead one to assume that the path to formation in grace runs exclusively through the church, such that Christians should isolate themselves and focus on cultivating the kinds of communities within which a graced

6. I develop an account of sanctification along these lines in Angela Carpenter, *Responsive Becoming: Moral Formation in Theological, Evolutionary, and Developmental Perspective* (London: T&T Clark, 2019).

identity can flourish. The moral thought of Stanley Hauerwas develops this kind of approach, and others have advocated similar strategies.[7] The church is indeed a crucial context for the formation and expression of a graced existence, and discussion of social life within the church is itself an important and necessary form of social ethics. In this project, however, I presume that most Christians are leading and will continue to lead lives that overlap substantially with other kinds of communities and thus are formed by and exist within multiple social spaces. Regardless of which approach one takes, however, the important point here is that participation in the Spirit's work of redemption calls us to attend not simply to our personal lives and personal virtues but also to the broader social context.

This claim is not a statement about the relative import of social concerns compared to that of personal morality but is instead a claim that the two cannot be separated. Contemporary evolutionary theory and Christian theology both suggest a complex interplay between the personal and the social in human becoming, and we must hold both of them in view as we think about human redemption. To take just one example, in many Christian megachurches the established culture affords tremendous power and status to men who have dynamic personalities and who are gifted public speakers. Often, these men are seen as so integral to the health and success of the community that their authority and behavior goes unquestioned. In such settings, how are these leaders supposed to cultivate personal virtues like humility, kindness, or self-control? How can Christians in these contexts truly internalize and believe the message that their worth or value is given in Christ when concrete evidence of what the community actually values in human beings is so readily available? Is it any wonder that these leaders so often fail spectacularly and with devastating impact? To the extent that our overlapping social worlds encourage ways of being that are contrary to one founded on grace, we are drawn into a denial of our identity in Christ, which is a denial of our true being.

At this point it is important to sound a note of caution. What I have said thus far could be interpreted as a renewal of nineteenth-century liberal Protestant optimism regarding the capacity of Christians, through dedication to social change, to usher in the kingdom of God. If only we can construct the perfect society, we will become good people. It could simultaneously be read as a new and expanded legalism whereby we must accomplish not only our own sanctification but the perfection of society as well. But part of the lesson

7. Stanley Hauerwas, *The Peaceable Kingdom: A Primer in Christian Ethics* (Notre Dame, IN: University of Notre Dame Press, 1983). See also Rod Dreher, *The Benedict Option: A Strategy for Christians in a Post-Christian Nation* (New York: Sentinel, 2017).

of accepting human finitude and turning to God's grace is recognizing that we do not have this sort of control. While we invariably participate in God's redemption—it is, after all, God's redemption *of humanity*—its ultimate reality is not our accomplishment. How, then, should we speak theologically about our efforts, particularly as they relate to the transformation of our social contexts?

Here we come to the third and final kind of argument, the sacramental argument, for the expectation that grace will be enacted and visible in human communities. As I have noted before, Christians have long held that the natural world signifies God's grace and is a means for us to know, understand, and receive grace—not in the abstract but in real and tangible ways. For instance, God "sends rain on the righteous and on the unrighteous" (Matt. 5:45). Our need for food reminds us we are not the source of our existence, and we receive life from that which is outside of us. Mysteriously, in the book of Job we find that even human suffering, precisely because it is *not* God's punishment on the unrighteous, shows us that the world, and God as its creator, does not operate on the basis of what we deserve because of our actions. And for many Christians, certainly Catholics and Orthodox but also the Protestants who follow Luther's and Calvin's theology on this point, it is in or through the material elements of communion that we receive Jesus.

Building on this sacramental understanding, one way to think about the expression of grace in human relationships is to conceive of it as a sign and witness to God's fellowship with humanity.[8] To the extent that our interpersonal relationships and the structures of our various institutions—political, civic, economic, religious—are consistent with our nature as creatures who find their origin, sustenance, and agency in God's gift, they signify or testify to that grace. Barth articulates this point in his reflection on the church's political responsibility: "Among the political possibilities open at any particular moment [the church] will choose those which most suggest a correspondence to, an analogy and a reflection of, the content of its own faith and gospel."[9] The language of signification, as opposed to actualization, recognizes the ongoing presence of sin in human life and also the role of eschatological hope in Christian theology. But at the same time, it also conveys the reality of redemption and the genuine presence of the Spirit within the world and particularly in the lives of those who have faith in Christ.

8. I am indebted here to Gerald McKenny's analysis of Barth's theology of grace and particularly of Barth's account of ordinary life in its "natural, political, and social dimensions" as signs of grace. See McKenny, *The Analogy of Grace: Karl Barth's Moral Theology* (Oxford: Oxford University Press, 2010), 289–90.

9. Karl Barth, "Christian Community and Civil Community," in *Community, State, and Church: Three Essays* (Garden City, NY: Anchor, 1960), 170.

In review, the grace of Christ must be expressed not only in our personal fellowship with God but also in our social existence. Because we are creatures who find our origin and worth in Christ, we must discover how to be this kind of creature with one another. The expression of our being is always found in interdependent life with others, so we anticipate that God's grace will operate at a personal level as well as in and through human community, including our social structures, in ways we will not be able to disentangle. The points at which we discern coherence in our being, rather than an internal conflict, signify the goodness and gift of God and anticipate their eschatological fullness.

At this point, the description of God's grace in Christ might sound somewhat strange and distant from descriptions found in popular religious discourse. Contemporary discourse frequently emphasizes grace as forgiveness of sins and personal salvation without making any connection to what salvation *as a gift* means for how we understand human relationships, human communities, and particularly the structural features that shape these communities. While novelty is often prized among scholars, it is typically a cause for skepticism in theology. After all, the appearance of new ideas in a religious tradition might be taken as a sign that the tradition has gotten things wrong in the past, and this notion would raise questions about the legitimacy of the tradition. But is this idea, that grace tells us something fundamental about humanity not just in its relationship to God but also in its social existence, actually novel? In the next section I will draw on the work of biblical scholars and historians to examine the two most significant sources for Protestant theologies of grace: Pauline theology and the theology of the early Reformation. Here we see that in both of these instances the insistence on grace has explicit and significant implications for human social life. As Pauline scholar John Barclay puts it, "Social practice is for Paul the necessary expression of the Christian gift."[10] At the same time, in each of these historical examples we also see inconsistencies, particularly regarding the relevance of grace for social and political structures. We therefore encounter questions about the ultimate significance of grace for social ethics.

The Social Expression of Grace in the Christian Past

Pauline Theology

Readers who have even a passing familiarity with the previous generation of Pauline scholarship will likely be well aware that the interpretation of his

10. John Barclay, *Paul and the Gift* (Grand Rapids: Eerdmans, 2015), 425.

theology of grace has been much contested. Scholars like E. P. Sanders and
James Dunn, building on the earlier insights of Krister Stendahl, have argued
that the Reformers, and particularly Martin Luther, fundamentally misunder-
stood Paul.[11] The apostle's primary concern, these scholars contend, was not
the tortured conscience of the believer facing divine judgment but, rather, the
ethnic divisions between Jews and gentiles that threatened the unity of the
church. While these interpretations have become widely accepted among biblical scholars, they have left something of a theological vacuum. Did Paul then
not want to make any claims about salvation as a gift of God that is not earned?

In his recent study of Paul's theology of grace, John Barclay accommodates
many of the insights of these recent interpretations while also giving renewed
attention to the multiple dimensions of Paul's language of gift, particularly
as they exist in Paul's Jewish context. Barclay agrees that much of Protestant
theology has, in its interpretation of Paul, unfairly portrayed Judaism as a
"works righteousness" religion. At the same time, however, he outlines a nuanced typology of the different "perfections" of grace, thereby enabling himself
to better specify where Paul disagreed with the Jewish theology of his day.[12]
Barclay believes that what is crucial and distinctive about Paul's theology is the
incongruity of grace—grace, for Paul, is given without regard for any standard of
the recipient's worth. Because of this, the Christ event fundamentally disrupts
and subverts all previous systems of worth.

Barclay develops this account by tracing Paul's theology in Galatians and
Romans, where Paul retells the story of Israel to emphasize the prominent role
of God's power and grace in Israel's election. God chose Abraham without
regard for worth or status by giving the promise first, prior to the command
to circumcise all males and prior to the giving of the law. In Romans this point
is underscored when Paul distinguishes Jacob from Esau and Pharaoh from
Israel based solely on God's choice and God's mercy (Rom. 9:12–16).[13] For
Barclay, it is clear that Paul's interpretation of Scripture and his theological
commitments grow out of what he has seen and experienced of the Christ
event. In his ministry Paul has observed that Christ comes to gentiles as well
as Jews without regard for factors like circumcision, gender, or status as a free
person. Shockingly, at least from the perspective of the ancient notion that

11. Krister Stendahl, "The Apostle Paul and the Introspective Conscience of the West," *Harvard Theological Review* 56, no. 3 (1963): 199–215.
12. Barclay, *Paul and the Gift*, 66–75.
13. Barclay provides an insightful interpretation of a notoriously difficult passage. At every stage Paul employs a strategy of "not . . . but . . ." to illustrate that the formation of Israel is not based on ethnicity, or biological descent, or good versus bad actions, or human effort. It is, therefore, God's power and grace that provides the foundation of hope for the ultimate salvation of Israel. See Barclay, *Paul and the Gift*, 524–36.

gifts are given to those who are worthy of them, God does not give based on the moral goodness of the recipient: "For while we were still weak, at the right time Christ died for the ungodly"[14] (Rom. 5:6). Because grace does not depend on any form of prior worth, Barclay notes that it can also be without limit. There is not a particular subset of human beings who are candidates for receiving grace. All of this, he argues, relativizes or subverts cultural systems of worth. This subversion then takes concrete shape in the communities established by faith in Christ.

Critics of this Pauline tradition have sometimes suggested that Paul cannot completely dispense with markers of worth that are grounded in human action, because faith itself becomes a kind of "work." Barclay rejects this notion, at least as far as Pauline theology is concerned. Faith, for Paul, is not a kind of human accomplishment but instead is a disavowal of all accomplishment. It is a "declaration of bankruptcy" and a recognition that Christ is the only source of worth.[15] This declaration of bankruptcy does not, however, entail that God (or Paul) has a disregard for righteousness, a critique that some of Paul's own hearers have apparently leveled at his theology. Instead, what begins as an unfitting gift actually creates the fit that was expected.[16] In Romans 5–8 Paul describes how the gift of Christ creates new life in the Spirit, a life in which believers die to sin or the "flesh" and live a new existence that consists in growth in holiness. For Barclay, however, this gift remains "incongruous" because the new life is not the possession or accomplishment of the person but is the creation of the resurrected Christ, powered by Jesus's life through the presence of the Spirit.[17]

Before we see how this theology of grace is expressed in the believing community, I want to pause and note that the theology Barclay draws out of Paul's

14. Barclay, *Paul and the Gift*, 478.
15. Barclay, *Paul and the Gift*, 383.
16. Barclay, *Paul and the Gift*, 473.
17. Barclay, *Paul and the Gift*, 500–503. Barclay is concerned here to distinguish his interpretation of Paul from Luther's. Where Luther goes wrong, he maintains, is in thinking that an *unconditioned* gift would necessarily imply that it was *unconditional*—that it did not carry subsequent expectations or demands (500). Barclay wants to preclude what he sees as a tendency toward antinomianism in Lutheran theology. He is also, like the proponents of the New Perspective on Paul, concerned that Luther's reading is overly focused on efforts to merit salvation (works righteousness) rather than a broader understanding of grace as opposed to all cultural systems of worth, which function "objectively" through social systems of value rather than through subjective motivation (444). On this point, however, Barclay distances himself too much from the Reformers. After all, notions of merit or human accomplishment can certainly be instantiations of socially constructed systems of value. Furthermore, while these systems may not be limited to the human subject, they certainly operate *through* human subjectivity. It is unclear how grace could counteract these systems without the agent being, on some level, subjectively aware that their value is in Christ and received as a gift.

letters is simultaneously a theology of grace and a theological anthropology. Paul's claims about grace are claims about human nature. The idea that God in Christ has no regard for prior status or worth is a rejection of a theory of human value that claims that people's worth comes from particular traits or characteristics or behaviors. This is the case for both moral worth and for what we might think of as morally neutral human excellence or accomplishment. But at the same time, and in contrast with popular self-help manuals and pop psychology, Paul's theology does not offer a generic affirmation of any human behavior that happens to manifest itself, especially with respect to virtue or morality. This is not the theological equivalent of showing blatant disregard for the evidence at hand and telling all children they are the next Mozart or Gandhi. Quite the opposite is true, in fact. Paul's theology of grace affirms human value solely on the basis of Christ, and precisely because of this grounding, it is able to genuinely affirm all human value while simultaneously being honest about human failures and accomplishments. In Paul's reading of the human condition, all people fail to attain moral worthiness, but human sin does not preclude the possibility that God values the person. Nonmoral abilities and accomplishments, often the source of special status within human communities, are also relativized by Pauline grace. They come from God as gifts, and as we will see, they are given for the good of the community and the glory of God, not to establish individual honor or glory.

The emphasis on the communal purpose of distinctive human gifts highlights what Barclay and others take to be a *relational* anthropology in Paul. Barclay interprets Paul's personification of sin, the "flesh" (e.g., Rom. 7:5) or the "body of sin" (Rom. 6:6) that opposes the Spirit, as indicative of the way the human person is "commandeered" by external forces, "such that its dispositions, emotions, speech-patterns, and habitual gestures are bound to systems of honor, self-aggrandizement, and license that are fundamentally at odds with the will of God."[18] This portrayal of the person formed in human culture is consistent with Paul's use of the body-of-Christ metaphor to depict the church. Believers in Christ are so interdependent that each is essential to the other, and while each is "individuated" in the sense of having a unique personhood and gift, no one operates or even makes sense independent of the community (Rom. 12:4–7).

Barclay is not alone in this emphasis. New Testament scholar Susan Eastman also detects a relational anthropology in Paul, one she finds consistent with depictions of the human in developmental psychology and neuroscience. For instance, in Eastman's reading, the "flesh" of Romans 7 does not just communi-

18. Barclay, *Paul and the Gift*, 508.

cate vulnerability to sin or temptation but conceives of the person as "constituted inextricably in relationship to sin." It is consequently only in relationship to the Spirit that one can be reconstituted.[19] To connect this back to our scientific study of the person, according to these scholars what we find in Paul is a human agency that, because it by nature *becomes* or *emerges* in a complex, multilayered, embodied cultural context, is therefore at the mercy of that context and under the power of these forces.

If this reading of Paul is correct, it should come as no surprise that Paul expects the reconstitution of the person in Christ by grace to find expression in human community. Much of Barclay's analysis thus carefully connects the moral and communal advice Paul offers at the end of Galatians and Romans to the theology he has developed throughout each letter. Whereas many scholars have puzzled over whether the two sections in each letter have an integral connection, Barclay argues that the moral guidance is thoroughly consistent with the fact that Paul is writing to communities of people chosen by grace without regard for prior worth or status. Barclay locates these passages in the context of Roman honor society, where "self-advertisement, rivalry, and public competition were a perpetual cause of tension in everyday life."[20] At every level of society, ancient Romans were intensely concerned with honor, which was based on public reputation and was established and defended by the competitive comparison of persons on a hierarchical scale. Placed in this context, much of Paul's advice to the Christian communities in Galatia and Rome subverts and ultimately rejects such a system. His list of vices in Galatians 5 includes many that would be destructive of community: enmities, strife, jealousy, anger, quarrels, dissensions, and factions (Gal. 5:20–21). His virtues, the fruit of the Spirit, are, by contrast, prosocial dispositions (Gal. 5:22–23). He also cautions against pride and competition and (controversially, as we shall see) uses the metaphor of mutual slavery to upend a hierarchical relationship. With respect to cases of people acting destructively in the community, Paul agrees that the behavior must be dealt with, but it is done so with gentleness and with the broader objective of restoring the offender (Gal. 6:1).

In Romans, Paul's communal advice is even more explicitly connected to his theology of grace than it is in Galatians. As Paul develops that theology in the early parts of the letter, he repeatedly mentions the wrongheaded tendency to judge others or to boast in one's own status or accomplishments (Rom. 2:1–3, 17–23). He then claims that boasting is excluded under the "law of faith,"

19. Susan Grove Eastman, *Paul and the Person: Reframing Paul's Anthropology* (Grand Rapids: Eerdmans, 2017), 90–91.

20. Barclay, *Paul and the Gift*, 433.

because believers have been justified apart from their status under the torah (Rom. 3:27–29). In a later section of moral instruction, prefaced by a reminder about "God's mercy" (Rom. 12:1), Paul sketches a vision of communal life that emphasizes humility, mutual love, honoring others, and provision for others (vv. 3–13). Revenge must be refused, and community members should seek to live peacefully with all, including outsiders (vv. 14–18). Passing judgment on those who are "weak" (Rom. 14:1) is discouraged because "God has welcomed them" and God is the one who will make them stand (Rom. 14:3–4). As Barclay puts it, "To judge or despise a fellow believer is to impose a valuation of worth wholly contrary to that person's evaluation by God."[21]

It is at this point—the question of status and its subversion in early Christian communities—that the astute reader might well question Barclay's insistence that, for Paul, the incongruity of grace, the fact that it is given without any regard for prior status, must necessarily find social expression. After all, Paul has not exactly been seen as unambiguously egalitarian when it comes to social hierarchies. What about the relations of power between husbands and wives? What about the institution of slavery? At times Paul even seems to argue that these inequalities in human social relationships do not really matter because believers in Christ are equal before God. In other words, a spiritual reversal of status means that inequalities in human social relationships can continue with no real problems. One's identity in Christ means that no other identity matters, and thus there is no reason to attempt to change other differences in status. A crucial text here is 1 Corinthians 7:21, where Paul tells slaves not to worry about their status. An ambiguity in the Greek has made this passage rather difficult to interpret. Either Paul is telling slaves *not* to take advantage of any opportunities to gain their freedom, or he is saying that, yes, they should take advantage of such an opportunity.[22] The fact that the context here provides little help in resolving the issue underscores how ambiguous Paul is on this point. It is difficult to argue that Paul opposes the institution of slavery on the grounds of the gospel.

All of this is often quite surprising to my undergraduate students when we read the New Testament household codes regarding the relationship between slave and master. Contemporary Christians are virtually unanimous in the belief that slavery is immoral and that it contradicts the message of Jesus.[23]

21. Barclay, *Paul and the Gift*, 512.

22. See J. Albert Harrill, "Paul and Slavery: The Problem of 1 Corinthians 7:21," *Biblical Research* 39 (1994): 5–28.

23. For an exception, see J. Stephen Wilkins and Douglas Wilson, *Southern Slavery: As It Was* (Moscow, ID: Canon, 1995). The few exceptions are controversial precisely because the point is so readily taken as obvious.

It seems there is widespread agreement that in this instance the gospel must be expressed in our social structures and to fail to do so is to fail catastrophically in our Christian calling. As a result, Christians like William Wilberforce who in the past condemned or fought slavery are lifted up as exemplars of the faith,[24] while the many who supported slavery are conveniently forgotten and the biblical passages that accept it are read with embarrassment or, more commonly, avoided altogether.

Among Christian biblical scholars and historians who take up the issue, a common argument is that Paul undermines the ideology on which slavery depends, even though he leaves the institution itself intact.[25] At the popular level some apologists gesture to the entrenched nature of slavery or offer some qualification of its horrors—for example, "Many Roman slaves had a high standard of living"—despite the fact that these horrors are recognized in Scripture itself (e.g., 1 Pet. 2:18–21).[26] Eventually, it is argued, the contradiction between the gospel and the institution of slavery could no longer be sustained, and Christian societies largely rejected slavery. While these accounts certainly have their critics, they may, in the final analysis, be correct.[27] It might be that holding together the lordship of Christ with the institution of slavery was ultimately unsustainable and led to its decline. What is important for my purposes, however, is that any claim that grace is only about personal salvation with no social implications is contradicted by the very embarrassment with which Christians now look back on centuries of slavery within Christian societies and the fervor with which many, especially within American evangelicalism, have now taken up the cause of opposing slavery globally. Regardless of whether the defenses of Paul have any merit, what matters here is that they need to be offered at all. Even if Paul is inconsistent on this point, the history of interpretation and the efforts to sanitize Paul's inconsistencies on slavery point to the necessity of the social expression of our graced identity—if we

24. See, e.g., the 2006 film *Amazing Grace*, directed by Michael Apted and released by 20th Century Studios.

25. N. T. Wright, *Colossians and Philemon: An Introduction and Commentary* (Downers Grove, IL: IVP Academic, 2008).

26. Academic discussion of Roman slavery is more nuanced. Dale Martin, e.g., discusses aspects like varied standards of living or educational attainment while readily acknowledging the horrors of the institution and opposing efforts to make it seem more palatable. See Martin, *Slavery as Salvation: The Metaphor of Slavery in Pauline Christianity* (New Haven: Yale University Press, 1990), 1–49.

27. Chris de Wet, e.g., challenges the ideas that Christianity ameliorated the institution or that various features of Greco-Roman slavery made it less oppressive. De Wet, *Preaching Bondage: John Chrysostom and the Discourse of Slavery in Early Christianity* (Berkeley: University of California Press, 2015). See also Jennifer A. Glancy, "To Serve Them All the More: Christian Slaveholders and Christian Slaves in Antiquity," in *Slaving Zones: Cultural Identities, Ideologies, and Institutions in the Evolution of Global Slavery*, ed. Jeff Fynn-Paul and Damian Alan Pargas (Boston: Brill, 2018), 28–49.

are to be the people we were created to be and if we are to witness to the God of Jesus Christ. Christians may not succeed in efforts to effect social change, but to pretend the contradiction between the gospel of grace and our social structures does not exist is the worst kind of failure.

Luther's and Calvin's Economic Thought

After the writings of Paul, the next most significant moment for Protestant doctrines of grace is the creative reinterpretation of Paul by Luther that is then sustained and developed in Calvin and others. When it comes to questions of grace and freedom in society, however, most Christians who have any awareness of the early Reformers' stance on these issues think primarily of Luther's two-kingdoms theology and his advocacy of harsh and brutal suppression of the Peasants' Revolt in Germany. For Luther, Christ's kingdom does not entail any legal restriction on a person's freedom because those who act in faith will naturally act rightly without the assistance of law. But since the kingdom of the world must deal with human sin, and because there are so few true believers who live a Christian life, Luther argues that law and civil government are needed in order to restrain immoral behavior and guarantee a provisional, external peace. True Christians, while not in need of this law, still abide by it and do everything they can to aid temporal authorities.[28] Many have taken the two-kingdoms theology as evidence that Luther's revolutionary thought regarding grace and freedom could have little impact on a human society that was still largely under the influence of sin, and indeed, Luther's actions in the context of the Peasants' Revolt would seem to support such an interpretation. More recent scholarship on Luther, however, has turned to his many writings on economics, as well as comments within other treatises, sermons, and commentaries, to paint a more complicated picture. It is a side of Luther that, until recently, has received very little attention and relies on portions of his extensive theological output that have been largely neglected.[29]

Given the late medieval entanglement between wealth and salvation, Luther's primary theological conviction had economic implications from the very beginning. Not only did Luther draw on salvation by grace through faith to oppose the sale of indulgences, but he also critiqued the wealthy usurer who could oppress the poor and then use the profit to gain salvation.[30] Even here,

28. Martin Luther, "Temporal Authority: To What Extent It Should Be Obeyed," *Martin Luther's Basic Theological Writings*, ed. Timothy Lull (Minneapolis: Fortress, 1989), 662–68.
29. Carter Lindberg, "Luther on a Market Economy," *Lutheran Quarterly* 30, no. 4 (Winter 2016): 379.
30. Lindberg, "Luther on a Market Economy," 375.

in one of his most infamous teachings, Luther hardly appears to be an anti-nomian whose view of grace allows societal injustice to continue unchecked. Instead, grace entails a totally different relationship to God, one in which exploitation of one's neighbor is inconsistent with a foundational trust in God for one's entire being and security. We saw this dynamic in chapter 1 when we considered Luther's critique of excessive wealth as being fundamentally contrary to faith in God because the pursuit of wealth entails a competing trust in money to provide personal security. Luther employs a similar analysis when he advocates on behalf of the poor in his treatises on trade and usury. For example, he says that Christians can indeed fulfill the radical commands of Jesus to give to those who ask, for God will support them. He urges ruling authorities to stop monopolies, arguing that they profit by exploiting people's needs "as if God's creatures and God's goods were created and given for them alone."[31] For Luther, both care for the poor and work that contributes to the common good are expressions of worship, not "good works" performed to earn salvation. They are grounded in the theology of grace whereby God's gift of salvation in Christ liberates the person from preoccupation with the self so they can serve others.[32]

Recent scholarship on Luther has illustrated that he translated these kinds of theological commitments into very specific policy proposals in the ecclesial and civil spheres. Luther advocated for the establishment of the "common chest," an early kind of social welfare that involved both the church and local government. He also called for government regulation of business and bank-ing to prevent exploitation of the poor and frequently spoke of the evils of usury, which, for Luther, included not only charging excessive interest but also a variety of other harmful financial practices.[33] Luther's opposition to these practices came through public condemnation in sermons rather than mere private correspondence. He preached that usurers were headed for damnation if they did not repent, and he urged other pastors to unmask injustice publicly in their sermons as well. Luther even called for the excommunication of usurers and himself denied someone communion because of usury on at least one oc-casion.[34] In addition to opposing exploitation, Luther also advocated for the establishment of public institutions for the good of the poor and society more

31. Martin Luther, *Trade and Usury* in *The Christian in Society*, ed. Walther I. Brandt, trans. Charles M. Jacobs, vol. 45 of *Luther's Works* (Philadelphia: Fortress, 1962), 262.

32. Carter Lindberg, *Beyond Charity: Reformation Initiatives for the Poor* (Minneapolis: Fortress, 1993), 100–111.

33. For instance, after a widespread crop failure followed by drought, Luther urged civil authori-ties to act when economic interests were prompting people to withhold grain from markets to drive up prices. See Lindberg, "Luther on a Market Economy," 381–82.

34. See Lindberg, "Luther on a Market Economy," 381–83.

broadly, including public education and public libraries.[35] Such actions suggest
that Luther was highly committed to his theology's economic implications for
public life and especially for the poor.

Luther was not alone in this commitment. John Calvin's teachings on
wealth and poverty often sound far more radical than one might anticipate.
In Geneva he, like Luther, advocated for civil-ecclesial partnerships that would
help meet the needs of the poor, and the Reformers in Geneva established
public institutions, like compulsory education and hospitals supported by
public funds, to benefit the poor. For Calvin, these issues were particularly
urgent given the massive influx of Protestant refugees fleeing persecution in
France. But caring for the poor went beyond a practical necessity; it also made
sense in the context of his theology of grace, in which the material goods of
creation were signs of God's gracious provision. In the *Institutes*, Calvin made
explicit connections between God's grace, on the one hand, and the activity of
believers with respect to the gifts of God, on the other hand. Both a person's
particular abilities as well as his material possessions came from God as gifts
and thus could not be a source of pride or honor that created superiority over
others.[36] Instead, they were to be used for the good of the community, "and
therefore the lawful use of all benefits consists in a liberal and kindly sharing
of them with others."[37]

Calvin located this giving of gifts within the Pauline theology of the body
of Christ, and his vision of interdependence is reminiscent of our study of
human evolution. Because he understood people to be intimately joined and
dependent on one another, as parts of the same body, it did not make sense to
Calvin that a person should be solely concerned with his individual welfare.
Instead, each should "have his mind intent on the common upbuilding of
the church."[38] So, one should not insist on repayment of a debt from those in
need, for this would be like one part of a human body insisting that a sick or
injured body part owes a debt to the whole.[39] While much of this discussion
focused on the context of the church, Calvin also encouraged doing good to
all people, regardless of merit, on account of the image of God within them.[40]

This brief treatment of the subject in the *Institutes* is consistent with Calvin's
extensive consideration of these topics in his broader corpus, particularly his

35. Lindberg, "Luther on a Market Economy," 384.
36. Calvin, *Institutes of the Christian Religion* 3.7.4.
37. John Calvin, *Institutes of the Christian Religion* 3.7.5, ed. John T. McNeill, trans. Ford Lewis
Battles (Philadelphia: Westminster, 1950), 695.
38. Calvin, *Institutes of the Christian Religion* 3.7.5, p. 695.
39. Calvin, *Institutes of the Christian Religion* 3.7.7.
40. Calvin, *Institutes of the Christian Religion* 3.7.6.

biblical commentaries.[41] In his treatment of the law of Moses, the Sermon on the Mount, and the economic parables of Jesus, Calvin consistently held that material goods were gifts of God and were intended to signify God's generosity and goodness. As such, these goods were to be distributed broadly to all so that all could experience the signs of God's grace. Like John Chrysostom and many other Christians throughout the centuries, Calvin did not mince words in condemning the wealthy for failing to give of their abundance, and he equated this failure with theft or even murder, should their neighbors perish for want of their help.[42] His treatment of these themes in sermons and commentaries also went beyond the analysis in the *Institutes*, particularly in the vivid depiction of human interdependence and the role of wages in the distribution of material goods. According to Calvin, God ordained human communities, through the bestowal of various gifts, the distribution of labor, and the exchange of goods, so that there would be natural interdependence as all contributed to the common good. In his commentary on Isaiah, for instance, Calvin remarked that the covetous, who would like the whole earth to themselves, could experience nothing more detrimental than to get their wish. "Were they alone," he wrote, "they could not plough, or reap, or perform other offices necessary for life. For God has linked people together in such a way that they need each other's assistance and labour; and no one in their right mind would reject others as hurtful or useless to him."[43] For Calvin, not only were all people dependent on God and intended to live by trusting in God's goodness and care, but they were also to live interdependently with one another, receiving in community the goods that were ultimately to be had from God.

An emphasis on divine grace and generosity and a rejection of merit were not, in Calvin's thinking, contrary to the reception of this sustenance through wages, nor did they preclude strong language about what was due to the worker by right. Calvin's references to wages fit within his broader understanding that all provision for human sustenance was a result of divine gift. So, for instance, in a sermon on Deuteronomy 15, Calvin told his congregation that if they had profited off the labor of another—which is to say, if they were in a position of hiring other workers—then the people who worked for them had been the means of God's blessing. Note that in his discussion of employers and employees, Calvin kept the ultimate source of material goods—God—firmly in

41. In this section I rely on French historian André Biéler's classic study of Calvin's economic and social thought in order to locate appropriate passages in his broader corpus. See André Biéler, *Calvin's Economic and Social Thought*, ed. Edward Dommen, trans. James Greig (Geneva: World Alliance of Reformed Churches and World Council of Churches, 2005).

42. Biéler, *Calvin's Economic and Social Thought*, 299.

43. Biéler, *Calvin's Economic and Social Thought*, 298.

view. He then argued that employers were thus obligated, according to their means, to share with such persons the fruit of their labor. How much should the laborer receive? Calvin was quite clear that this should be a sharing in fruit and that it should be sufficient to sustain the worker and provide for his life. Even with wages, however, Calvin insisted that what one received was not something merited but was instead "a token of blessing when we clearly see the fruit of our labor."[44]

In a sermon on Deuteronomy 24, Calvin castigated those who tried to take advantage of a worker's need by paying less than he required to live simply because the worker had no options. Here Calvin described what Marx might call the motives of capital with astonishing clarity. "A rich man," he wrote, "will note this: 'that fellow lacks everything: I shall have him for a bite of bread, for he must offer himself to me even if it means gritting his teeth—I will give him half a wage and even so he will have to count himself satisfied.'"[45] The logic of Calvin's thought regarding wages seems to run like this: God has made gracious provision for human life through the earth and through human participation with their labor to gain their sustenance from creation. None of this is merited—it is all gift. Therefore, those with the economic power in the situation must make available to those who are without such power their proper share of the fruit. At minimum this must be enough to provide for a person's needs.[46] The notion of sharing in the fruit, however, could also suggest that all involved in an endeavor should also share in the extent of its success even after basic needs are provided.[47] We see here that Calvin's insistence that gift is foundational does not rule out concerns of justice in distribution.

Lest the listener think that I am content to portray Calvin as a proto-Marxist, it is also important to clarify what Calvin did not say, at least to the best of my knowledge. He did not reject private property, nor did he believe that social equality was a reasonable goal. It might, perhaps, have been a human reality in Eden, but this side of the fall the world was governed hierarchically. We may or may not wish to quibble with him on these points. What is important for my argument here is that his theology of grace, and particularly the disposition of trust in God as the giver of all good things, had very clear implications for how human beings were to live together in community. We are inherently

---

44. John Calvin, "Commentary on Isaiah 65:23," quoted in Biéler, *Calvin's Economic and Social Thought*, 368.

45. John Calvin, "Sermon 140 on Deuteronomy 24:14–18," quoted in Biéler, *Calvin's Economic and Social Thought*, 371.

46. Biéler, *Calvin's Economic and Social Thought*, 366–72.

47. Calvin does say that wages should be in line with the employer's resources because the employee has been the means of that blessing. See Biéler, *Calvin's Economic and Social Thought*, 368.

interdependent, according to Calvin, and we all constantly receive from others. To reduce such exchanges to categories of merit and deserts obscures their ultimate origin in God's grace and inculcates a disposition that is opposed to living by grace.

Moving Forward: Grace, the Human Person, and a Social Ethic

Part 1 of this book has been building toward an anthropology of grace that also implies a social ethic. Along the way we have considered theological and scientific sources, both because a theological anthropology should be intelligible in the context of our experience of human beings and because it is helpful if a social ethic for a pluralist society is intelligible to those outside the Christian faith. My contention has been that engaging the human sciences along with theology furthers both of these goals. In this final section I will sketch a picture of the human person viewed from these two perspectives by drawing out four key theological principles. These principles are a distillation of the conceptual work undertaken throughout part 1 and will serve as a guide in part 2 as we explore specific contemporary issues in social ethics.

The first theological principle is that human life is dependent on God and interdependent with all of creation, particularly with other human beings. We did not create ourselves. Rather, our very existence is received as a gift from the God who has brought all things into being. We begin in grace, and any earning or deserving on our part is always established in this prior and ongoing grace. Within this foundational dependence on God, the mutual dependence of human persons in the broader community signifies and reveals our deeper spiritual source and teaches us the beginnings of trust, humility, and care. This consistency between our spiritual life and our embodied existence suggests a unity of our being; we are not meant to be one sort of creature with God and a different sort in our lives together. Rather, mutuality and interdependence are the proper expression of our humanity as we live it in fellowship with one another.

When we deny or disguise our interdependence by using wealth or abilities or skills to isolate ourselves, or when we insist that others must solve their problems by themselves, we move our societies away from this potential to communicate our deep dependence on God and toward pride, resentment, and fear. Luther and Calvin saw that there is a spiritual cost here: when we think we can secure our existence through wealth or power, we trust God less or not at all. Moreover, when we live this way we harm others. Our actions may not be depriving others of what they have earned or merited—and this is one way in which the language of justice can be misleading as the primary framework for social ethics—but when we withhold the support and care that human creatures naturally need from one another, we exploit and cause harm all the same.[48]

Being dependent and interdependent does not negate human agency. We are made to be actors; in fact, we are made to be lovers. And when we learn to act well, most especially to love well using the specific gifts we are given, it is entirely appropriate to experience joy and satisfaction in human excellence and accomplishment. What we must not do, however, is forget that this action flows from gift—not a one-time "starter" gift but a continuous, moment-by-moment gifting that often comes to us by way of other people. Thus, we must resist the subtle and insidious impulses to claim these accomplishments as entirely our own, to think that receiving help from others diminishes our actions or diminishes us, or to think that we are better than others when they need our help.

The second theological principle, a corollary of creaturely dependence, is that the gifts of God in creation are intended for all humanity. In the Christian creation stories, humanity comes into the picture at the very end and is not involved in or even present for the fashioning of the rest of creation. Indeed, what human beings need for food is explicitly presented to the first couple as a gift not only to them but to animal life as well (Gen. 1:29–30). This creation account thus rules out any possibility that human beings are responsible for and have a claim on creation on the basis of their own action. All of this appears in the context of the divine celebration of the goodness of creation, so there is no room for crude assumptions that the creation is of purely instrumental value and is to be used however human beings see fit.[49] All life is dependent on God, and God has, out of eternal goodness, abundantly provided. We have already seen that this notion is important for Calvin, but the idea has been foundational to Christian thought about material goods.

The third principle is about the source of human worth or value. Human worth arises from God's love of creation, and even the tragedy of sin does not erase it. The creation of humanity out of nothing prohibits any claims that human beings must be the source of their value or must establish their value through their actions. Because people's very existence is a gift, no special

48. A social ethic of grace is not necessarily an entirely novel ethic or wholly distinct from other approaches. On this point there is some affinity with communitarian approaches. See Michael Sandel, *Liberalism and the Limits of Justice*, 2nd ed. (Cambridge: Cambridge University Press, 1998).

49. Mary Hirschfeld, "What Is the Technocratic Paradigm and Must Business Be Structured by It?," *Business Ethics and Catholic Social Thought*, ed. Daniel K. Finn (Washington, DC: Georgetown University Press, 2021), 93–113.

abilities or actions can independently attest human value. Anything human beings might point to has already been received from God. And because God was not restrained in creation by preexisting matter, humans can confidently say that they are the creatures God wanted. Furthermore, God could not have made them to be instrumentally useful to God in some way, because God has no prior need or lack. The only possible conclusion within the parameters of a Christian doctrine of creation is that God made human beings out of love and that they matter because God loves them and made them. This conclusion about human worth is supported by the doctrines of the *imago Dei* and the incarnation. Not only has God made human beings, along with the rest of creation, purely out of love, but God has seen fit to associate Godself with such vulnerable and small creatures.

Even the tragic reality of human sin, traditionally conveyed through the doctrine of the fall or original sin, does not ultimately alter the reality or source of human worth. The Christian doctrine of original sin is crucial not because it says something about how horrible or worthless human beings are (an unfortunate caricature of the doctrine) but because it insists that all humans share the need for grace. People cannot claw their own way out of sin through their actions. Grace is not the backup plan for those who cannot hack it on their own or the stopgap for the unfortunate times when people's actions fall short. The work of Christ and the Spirit is, instead, everything. Grace *enables* good action, and all human goodness springs from God's grace. As the apostle Paul tells us, no one can boast. In the midst of human sinfulness, God continues to sustain human life *ex nihilo* and is acting through Christ and the Spirit to redeem and restore humanity. At the same time, the fact that human worth is a gift and not earned does not thereby render human action irrelevant. Instead, the reason human sin matters so much is that it is destructive of the human life and community that God created and loves. The reality of sin continually confronts humanity, and our reflection on social ethics will need to reckon with it; sin will be particularly salient in our discussion of criminal justice. Yet the work of Christ makes clear that sin does not make human beings any less loved by God. On the contrary, it is the occasion for the greatest demonstration of God's love.

In one of the most profound insights of the Reformation, the psychological aspect of human worth is crucial: it matters that we understand we are not the source of our own value but instead receive it as a gift. What we have internalized about ourselves and our status or worth affects our agency. When we believe that our worth or our security within the community is contingent on our action, these actions are undertaken out of fear or anxiety. We act because we feel we must prove to God, to others, or to ourselves that we are worthy.

Understanding that our value comes from God, however, means that we can use our gifts in the service of what is truly good or excellent instead of pursuing status or power and therefore placing our gifts in the service of the values or ends that are most cherished in our cultural contexts. In this sense an ethic grounded in grace is attuned to human excellence, as counterintuitive as the claim may seem. External motives for good action are always susceptible to various kinds of corruption, and our need to see ourselves as worthy, or to be seen by others as worthy, prevents us from examining this action very closely. As we saw in chapter 3, there is considerable overlap between the Reformers' account of human psychology and contemporary studies of worth and belonging. One way of thinking about the Christian life is to conceive of it as the process whereby the truth of the gospel becomes the truth of a person's existence and is inscribed in all knowledge of the self.

When we grasp the radical sense in which God is for us and we understand that we no longer need to be for ourselves, a new kind of social existence can take shape. Space to love others without worrying about our need opens up. As Luther intuited, because God's grace is sufficient and everything a person needs is provided through it, recipients of grace have no cause to fear that their lives will be lacking in anything. They can trust God completely. This is not an easy calling. It is instead a disposition that must grow over time through the experience of God's love. But in those moments where people are able to trust God's grace, they are set free, opened up to lead lives that are not focused inwardly on manipulating all life circumstances to their own ends. Instead, their lives can be directed outward in love and service of their neighbors. Similarly, a person can receive care from others as the way appointed by God for human provision without needing to feel inferior or to maintain a rigorous accounting of gifts that must somehow be repaid. This mutual love involves sharing with at least some other persons an intimacy of life in the sharing of joy and sorrow. Such genuine presence with one another is difficult to maintain if the participants are always concerned with how they can use the others to meet their own needs.

This revolution in our personal identity should change how we see others. We should become suspicious of cultural status markers and of competitive efforts to establish worth, and we should instead acknowledge the worth that is given by God, expecting that each person possesses gifts that should be nurtured and honored. As Barclay emphasizes in his reading of Paul, such suspicions should extend to the broader ways in which societies divide people and assign differential value based on these divisions. In other words, we should become suspicious of the various tribalisms and in-group/out-group distinctions we are tempted, and perhaps evolutionarily predisposed, to rely on. In the community established by grace, even the believer/nonbeliever distinction is porous;

the nonbeliever is always invited into the community of faith, the faith of the believer can be false, and the life of the believer is always deeply compromised by sin. In the same vein a recognition of grace also invites us to see the sins and failings of others differently. While there is always the potential for sin to wreak havoc in communal life, and while we may be forced to make painful choices to protect the community (e.g., 1 Cor. 5:13), Jesus's incarnation, death, and resurrection require us to say that sin cannot erase or negate the value God bestows on the person, a fact for which we can only be grateful given our own sin.

If we are to cultivate this sort of graced identity, we must beware of the potential for wealth, privilege, and power to corrupt it. The wealthy and powerful will be tempted to think they deserve some special status, and the experience of being treated with deference by others could obscure the truth about human worth. Seen from this angle, the teachings of Jesus with respect to wealth and power are invitations to continue discovering God's grace. Thus, in the Gospels, true power is connected not with personal advantage but with service, and those in positions of power are invited to consider themselves last. The rich are asked to relinquish their wealth (Luke 6:24; 14:33; 18:18–30). These teachings are not a rigid and uncompromising moralism; they are forms of social realignment that enable people of status, power, or privilege to see and recognize their need for God's grace.

The fourth theological principle is that this entire story of the creation, sustenance, and redemption of humanity through gift has a distinct purpose: a life of friendship with God and neighbor. Humans exist for loving community. It is crucial here to observe that only a creation characterized by grace and gift could be the foundation for lives of friendship or of what theological tradition has called "charity." Concepts like merit and deservingness, and even justice, crucial as they are in their proper place, establish an entirely different dynamic when they are the foundation for life with God or for human relationships. If all exchange is based on what one has earned or merited, it becomes impossible for exchange to be an expression of love. It becomes impossible for people to know whether the actions of others toward them flow from love or from a desire to gain something in return. It is the excess, that which goes beyond earning and into the realm of generosity and gift, that creates the possibility of expressions of loving relationship and the true realization of human purpose in love.

Conclusion

In this chapter, I have sketched a vision of the human person established in gift and argued that this anthropology must also be expressed in human

community. In part 2, this vision of human personhood as dependent on the
good gifts of God, interdependent in human community, and psychologically
formed by the awareness of these foundational and unearned relationships will
guide our reflection on specific social issues. This emphasis on grace in theological anthropology does not supplant other anthropological claims; we will
still need to grapple with the ongoing presence of sin and with the "already
but not yet" tension of redemption in Christ.[50] Christian social and political
thought throughout the centuries has, however, been excessively focused on
these tensions despite the fact that the social thought of Jesus's Sermon on
the Mount and the Pauline epistles seems to be driven much more by the
implications of God's grace. In what follows I will attempt to give priority, in
reflecting on specific social issues, to the notion of the human person as a gift.

50. This term is frequently used in theology to refer to the time between the resurrection of Jesus
and the second coming. It is a time of tension when Christ has "already" defeated evil but the fullness
of Christ's victory has "not yet" been realized in creation.

PART 2

SOCIAL ETHICS AND GRACE

CHAPTER 5

WORK

In the sixteenth century Martin Luther challenged the obsessive efforts of his contemporaries to ensure that they had done enough to achieve salvation. Luther was concerned with both the anxiety and the hubris of the ordinary Christian: the anxiety that there was always just a little more to be done and the hubristic notion that mere mortals could control the grace of God by earning it. Not very many of our contemporaries obsess about their eternal destiny. We do, however, obsess over our accomplishments. We wonder if we have done enough, not to merit grace but to get into a good college, to gain a new job or promotion, to be successful and stand out among our peers, to feel worthy. Our efforts still involve plenty of anxiety and hubris. For many, these impulses are so strong that various observers have suggested that work is becoming a kind of religion. In this chapter we will discover that the basic intuition that human value derives from action and productivity permeates our culture of work. It is a system of value that is deeply antithetical to the gospel and distorts and diminishes human life. A Christian ethic of work must resist this impulse and seek to limit its destructive impact.

Before we turn to the specifics of work in the twenty-first century, we should take a moment to place the topic of work in the broader context of Christian theology, focusing on both history and the theology of grace developed in this book. The New Testament has relatively little to say about the theological significance of what we would consider paid employment. Jesus and many of his followers left ordinary occupations to preach throughout Palestine. The apostle Paul was a tentmaker and, in an oft-quoted verse, told the church at

Thessalonica that those who did not work should not eat (2 Thess. 3:10). Beyond this, work in a secular sense does not appear to be much of a pre-occupation of the New Testament writers. Paul, for instance, is far more inter-ested in people's work on behalf of the gospel than in how his readers acquired food and shelter. As the faith spread in the early centuries, work was portrayed in broadly positive terms. It was a means of contributing to Christian com-munity and acquiring resources to give to the poor, and it served the spiritual function of distracting the believer from potential temptation. This positive valuation was also significant from a class perspective against the backdrop of a Greco-Roman culture where work signified low status. To affirm work was to affirm the dignity of those whose lives were spent in manual labor on behalf of the wealthy, leisured class.

In the monastic tradition, the motto *Ora et labora* ("Pray and work") con-stituted the ideal of the Christian life. Monks and nuns devoted themselves to life with God, and part of this life was a discipline of work as an ascetic practice of self-denial.[1] Their labor also supported the community of brothers or sisters. In the sixteenth century the Reformers, wanting to resist the division of the church into vowed "religious" (monks, nuns, etc.) and laity, argued that secular work itself constituted a vocation, or "calling," from God. For Luther, this notion of vocation did not involve the sense of spiritual discernment that it often does today. He simply wanted to insist that a Christian life of devotion could be lived in and through whatever work one happened to do.[2] However, over time Luther's notion of vocation has, in some circles, taken on a sense of spiritual discernment and obedience and thus transformed into the notion that God calls people to a particular profession that a person must seek out and pursue.

The positive approach to work in Christian history remains theologically important. At the same time, the way work functions in our broader culture has changed significantly from previous eras, so we should question whether work as it exists today continues to play the same role in Christian life and discipleship. The specifics of contemporary work have also raised new questions that are not necessarily addressed by a theological approach that analyzes work primarily in terms of its relationship to personal character. How should the proceeds of work be distributed in a market economy? What does a worker

---

1. As Miroslav Volf notes, reflection on work throughout much of Christian history occurred within the context of the doctrine of sanctification. Volf, *Work in the Spirit: Toward a Theology of Work* (Eugene, OR: Wipf & Stock, 2001), 71–73.

2. While I generally agree with Luther that Christians should not adopt a two-tiered standard of discipleship, his concept of vocation has several weaknesses. For a critique, see Volf, *Work in the Spirit*, 107–9.

deserve, and how should a society make such assessments? How much should a person work? What sorts of work conditions are reasonable for workers in various occupations? How should work relate to social status? How should we think about unpaid work, like caring for children or housework? I will consider many of these questions in this chapter as I examine the contemporary world of work from the perspective of a theology of grace. Broadly speaking, what I aim to investigate in this chapter is whether work, as it is experienced in the United States in the twenty-first century, is consistent with our theological vision of the human person as having been established in grace for friendship with God. With this objective in mind, what do the theological principles with which we concluded chapter 4 have to say about work?

Grace and Work

An understanding of human dependence and interdependence is particularly relevant for any economic topic because human dependence is necessarily material. We survive only by depending on that which is not us. As human creatures, we survive in human community. Even the most self-sufficient naturalist, living in an isolated wilderness cabin, survives based on skills learned from others. Most of us rely on human community in much more obvious ways, since we do not grow our own food, build our own houses, and so forth. The complexity of these networks of interdependence, and the fact that each of us enters life having contributed nothing to them, belies any superficial assumption that we are all owed the entire fruit of our labor. This labor is premised on a prior receiving—from God but also from human community. In a very real sense it is all God's (a point of which we should regularly remind ourselves) and is to be directed to the flourishing of God's creation, especially to the ongoing work of redemption. In terms of human deserving, it is foolish to think that some kind of absolute determination or calculation of what each person is owed is possible, given the complex networks of cooperation in human community. Human communities will establish pragmatic determinations regarding how best to distribute material goods, but we must not confuse the justice that comes from following these legal conventions with an absolute deservingness that would make other possible configurations unjust.[3]

3. According to Mary Hirschfeld, even though Thomas Aquinas defended private property as a means of God's providence over creation, he did not connect labor to property in an absolute sense. Rather, Aquinas argued that the distribution of property was determined by human convention. See Hirschfeld, *Aquinas and the Market: Toward a Humane Economy* (Cambridge, MA: Harvard University Press, 2018), 164–68.

It might help here to consider a concrete example. Ryan Avent observes that tremendously successful US entrepreneurs like Bill Gates or Jeff Bezos would never have achieved anything like the success they have if they had been born and had lived in one of the poorer nations of the Global South.[4] While they have undoubtedly employed their talents and worked hard, they also owe their success, perhaps the vast majority of it, to the social and communal resources of a wealthy Western nation with a stable government, an educated and largely law-abiding citizenry, modern infrastructure, and so forth. Given this complexity, even if one agrees that material rewards should correspond to one's labor, is there any way to adjudicate how much profit they deserve in an absolute sense? The reality of dependence and interdependence complicates any simple story we might tell about earning and deserving.

The second theological principle, that the gifts of creation are given to all, has particular relevance for questions about work and the distribution of material goods. While I affirm a connection between laboring and receiving the sustenance necessary for life, such a connection does not change the fundamental truth that at a deeper level these material goods are gifts. Nor does it change the obligation to provide access to the means of sustenance to everyone, even those unable to work in the paid economy. It bears repeating that this has been a core Christian commitment in theological reflection on wealth and material goods, so much so that retaining more than one needs while others do without has been considered the moral equivalent of theft. Very few wealthy Christians—I would include here much of the American middle class—have attempted to live out such radical claims. This failure, however, should not prevent us from reflecting on and embracing the universal destination of goods—the notion that the goods of creation are intended for all people—in our economic thinking.[5]

The third principle, that human worth is grounded in the gift of God rather than in human action or achievement, will be critical for thinking about the role and structure of work in contemporary society. At present the de facto reality is the opposite of this principle. Among educated professionals in the

---

4. Ryan Avent, *The Wealth of Humans: Work, Power, and Status in the Twenty-First Century* (New York: St. Martin's Press, 2016), 18.

5. Even Christian affirmation of private property by Thomas Aquinas and other medieval theologians maintains this assumption regarding the universal destination of goods. For Aquinas, private property makes sense as a practical way to care for the various goods of creation, but it does not alter the theological truth that, in terms of use, a person should think of these goods "as common, so that, to wit, he is ready to communicate them to others in their need." It is also important to note that, for Aquinas, the particular distribution of goods is determined not by natural law but by human agreement. See Thomas Aquinas, *Summa Theologica*, trans. fathers of the English Dominican Province (New York: Benziger, 1911–1965), II-II, q. 66, a. 2, https://www.newadvent.org/summa/3066.htm.

contemporary US context, it is perfectly normal to derive one's identity and worth from a career or, in more pious language, a vocation. More insidiously, it is quite common for contemporary Americans to implicitly assess the worth of others on the same basis. However, locating human value in gift does not mean that a sense of accomplishment or a feeling of satisfaction in a job well done are illegitimate human responses. Nor does it mean that a kind of pride in one's contributions to the common life is to be discouraged or rejected. Part of the task of this chapter will be to tease out these conceptual distinctions and think through their implications for how people should live out the role of "worker." Christians in particular should be attentive to the ways we learn from our culture to evaluate people on the basis of employment, and we should consider what sorts of actions the giftedness of human value calls for, both in terms of actions performed at the individual level and in the ways we structure our lives together.

Finally, in this discussion we must remember that the truest and most comprehensive human vocation is the calling to friendship with God and neighbor. This is the end result of all God's gifts and is itself the ultimate gift. It is fully realized in the friendship of Jesus with the Father and is shared by all who are adopted into Christ. Given this centrality, it is somewhat unfortunate that Protestant theological analysis of work in the twentieth century focused prominently on the notion of vocation or calling, displacing the more basic association of vocation with discipleship. In doing so, Protestants continued the Reformation emphasis on the sacredness of ordinary Christian life and the Reformation rejection of a two-tiered system consisting of the laity and vowed religious persons. However, this discourse has, in contemporary settings, produced the idea that those on the cusp of adulthood need to discern their particular "callings"—generally meaning the specific form of work they will do in order to support themselves in life. In American culture in particular, the language of discerning one's vocation blends into secular notions of professional identity and thereby becomes a powerful force in individual lives, one that risks distorting the central human *telos* of friendship or love.

Work in American Society

As I have stated, I contend that work must be considered within the broader theological understanding of grace. This perspective is quite different from the dominant assumptions about work in the United States today. Most Americans think of work as a virtue through which individuals earn or deserve a place in society and that, when combined with skill, is appropriately rewarded through wages or salary, fringe benefits, and social status.[6] One of the most common ways to describe this system is the term "meritocracy." The term does not simply capture a pragmatic approach to the assignment of work and the distribution of goods in a society; it is also value laden. Meritocracy suggests, on the one hand, that those who have wealth or status or other social privileges have these things because they have earned them and thus deserve them, and, on the other hand, those who do not have them have not earned them.

While the general public has largely embraced meritocracy, within the past decade a number of books and essays in various fields have analyzed and critiqued it. In *The Tyranny of Merit*, philosopher Michael Sandel traces the prevalence of meritocratic ideas in American popular culture and public life and offers a rigorous critique. He contends that meritocracy is premised on a fundamental falsehood: the idea that what we achieve in life is what we deserve. For Sandel, our talents and innate abilities are not of our own creation, and it is therefore illogical to maintain that because these particular skills happen to be valued in our current context, we deserve what we receive from them. The truth is that we are simply fortunate to have these skills and "it is a mistake and a conceit to assume we deserve the benefits that flow from them."[7] Even success that results from hard work, on Sandel's reading of the situation, is more about gift than we would like to admit. He notes that success rarely results from effort alone without skill, and that emphasizing hard work without acknowledgment of gift will simply "inflate the moral significance of effort and striving."[8] Ultimately, for Sandel, those who embrace this fiction will believe that success is indicative of goodness and that failure is deserved.

Sandel has captured and critiqued a prevailing, almost commonsense American ethos, although it is possible that the beliefs of ordinary Americans are somewhat more nuanced than he allows.[9] This is an ethos that bears some affinity with the way work has been conceived of in Christian history

6. According to Gallup, 70 percent of Americans believe that "if you work hard and play by the rules, you will be able to attain the American dream in your lifetime." Mohamed Younis, "Most Americans See the American Dream as Achievable," News, Gallup, July 17, 2019, https://news.gallup.com/poll/260741/americans-american-dream-achievable.aspx. In a recent poll, 94 percent of respondents said hard work was either "very important" or "somewhat important" to them. WSJ/NORC, "WSJ/NORC Poll March 2023," https://s.wsj.net/public/resources/documents/WSJ_NORC_ToplineMarc_2023.pdf.

7. Sandel, *The Tyranny of Merit: What's Become of the Common Good?* (New York: Farrar, Straus & Giroux, 2020), 123.

8. Sandel, *Tyranny of Merit*, 125.

9. According to the Pew Research Center, since 2017 Americans have begun to attribute wealth more to received advantages than to hard work, though this survey still indicates that a sizable minority of Americans are willing to make assessments about work ethic based on financial status. "Most Americans Point to Circumstances, Not Work Ethic, for Why People Are Rich or Poor," Pew Research

(as generally good, necessary, and even virtuous), but it is also in tension with the theological commitments regarding the origin of creation in gift, the interdependence of human life, and the true source of human value in God and not in human striving. The meritocratic ethos, however, is not just about abstract values. It is woven into the structures of work and is visible in the everyday working lives of millions of Americans. Those who examine the concrete realities surrounding work in the twenty-first century will see a stark divide in the treatment of different forms of work and, by extension, different workers. In practice, it is not just that educated and highly skilled workers receive higher pay than low-skilled workers. As we will see, the situations of different workers extend to the very capacity to live a dignified life. One might well maintain that these differences are simply the result of market forces and the demand for different types of labor. People in these jobs, the argument goes, should have worked harder and trained for something better. Undoubtedly, market forces have a role in determining the conditions and compensation for different forms of labor, but by accepting all differences that emerge, we as a society are also saying something about what we think is just and what we think different people deserve, reinforcing a cultural tendency to value people on the basis of their work.

The Indignities of Low-Skilled Work

The struggles of today's workers are certainly not new in the industrial era, though the current situation has changed substantially from the period following the Second World War. According to the standard narrative, several pronounced social and cultural shifts have thoroughly transformed work in a global economy.[10] Technological advancement led to increased automation, eliminating the need for many low-skilled jobs, particularly in manufacturing. In the United States these sectors were further reduced by economic globalization and the ability of firms to move the production of goods or the delivery of services to developing economies in the Global South. Because many US workers were unable to acquire new skills or education for jobs in an increasingly information-based economy, the workforce experienced an excess of workers

---

Center, March 2, 2020, https://www.pewresearch.org/politics/2020/03/02/most-americans-point-to-circumstances-not-work-ethic-as-reasons-people-are-rich-or-poor/.

10. Versions of this can be found in Avent, *Wealth of Humans*; Arne Kalleberg, *Good Jobs, Bad Jobs: The Rise of Polarized and Precarious Employment Systems in the United States, 1970s to 2000s* (New York: Russell Sage Foundation, 2011); Guy Standing, *The Precariat: The New Dangerous Class* (London: Bloomsbury, 2011).

competing for the remaining low-skilled jobs. During this time, regulatory changes at the federal level made it easier for corporations to be bought and sold, increasing pressure on firms to maximize efficiency and shareholder value. The sale and restructuring of firms, and the pressure to avoid hostile takeovers, led to efforts to reduce labor costs, which in turn produced widespread layoffs and further changes in the ways companies structured employment. Other regulatory and legislative changes weakened the power of organized labor. Furthermore, throughout this period the nation saw an influx of immigrants from Mexico and from South and Central America.

While economists and policymakers dispute the relative weight that should be given to these various factors, it is their combined effect on the experience of work in the United States that is our primary interest at present. Particularly, though not exclusively, in low-skilled professions, these combined shifts have reduced worker power and have given employers substantial latitude to restructure work in the interest of profit and efficiency. According to some scholars, a downward pressure on the quality of jobs has left workers with a precarious existence that threatens their health, relationships, and broader quality of life.[11]

The most obvious way work can be precarious is by being subject to simple disappearance, particularly during an economic downturn such as the Great Recession. However, sociologists of work note several other producers of job instability, including temporary jobs, part-time hours, subcontracted work, and involuntary reassignment. Such strategies have been widely adopted to increase the flexibility of firms and their capacity to adjust rapidly to market fluctuations, but their impact on workers is profound.[12] Instability in such a crucial aspect of life as one's ability to support oneself and one's family is understandably a source of anxiety. The sense that one's current existence, as undesirable as it may be, is always balancing on a knife's edge leaves many workers desperate and willing to tolerate all sorts of indignities to retain their current status.

The precarious nature of employment has other psychological effects as well. Workers in these situations have little reason to hope that circumstances will change; better jobs are not just around the corner for them, nor do they have the time, money, or energy to acquire skills that might open up further

---

11. See Kalleberg, *Good Jobs, Bad Jobs*, and Standing, *The Precariat*. At present there is some evidence that these dynamics are shifting. Unemployment is low, and worker wages have risen, though many of these gains have been erased by inflation. It remains to be seen whether these shifts are temporary or whether they signal a lasting change. See Annie Lowery, "Low-Wage Jobs Are Becoming Middle-Class Jobs," *The Atlantic*, March 4, 2023, https://www.theatlantic.com/ideas/archive/2023/03/wage-growth-income-inequality-labor-market/673277/.

12. Standing, *Precariat*, 19–24.

opportunities. In these circumstances, the development of family and community is also stifled. Why get married or have children when life is so uncertain and has such little chance of improvement?[13] At the same time, the broader social and cultural context is filled with many people who do have such skills and opportunities, simply by the "accident of birth," and whose lives appear much more comfortable and satisfying. Understandably, this kind of disparity sets the stage for social division and resentment. While these phenomena have been noted by social scientists in a variety of disciplines for a few decades, they have taken on a new salience since the 2016 election and the rise of populist politics fed by social alienation and resentment.

In addition to the precarious nature of work itself, low-skilled workers experience other life vulnerabilities such as low wages and a life at or near poverty. During this era of technological advancement and globalization, wages in the United States have continued to rise, but this growth has been noticeably unequal, with workers in the lowest income brackets experiencing little to no increase and in some cases even seeing decline. Low wages are a factor in the nation's poverty levels, which are high in comparison to those of similarly wealthy nations. According to the most recent data, 11.6 percent of the population, or 37.9 million Americans, lived below the poverty level in 2021.[14] These United States Census Bureau numbers are disputed by many poverty researchers, both because they rely on an outdated method for calculating poverty, which is based on the cost of food, and because they do not take into account government assistance to alleviate poverty. When both of these problems had been adjusted for, the poverty estimate in 2020 was 8.4 percent, a number that reflects the robust financial assistance provided during the COVID-19 pandemic.[15] The final pre-COVID estimate from 2019 was 11.2 percent. What is particularly noteworthy about the adjusted poverty data is that without government transfers like the Earned Income Tax Credit and food stamps, which is to say using only market income, the poverty rate in 2020 would have been

13. Jennifer Silva, *Coming Up Short: Working Class Adulthood in an Age of Uncertainty* (Oxford: Oxford University Press, 2013), 53–80.

14. John Creamer et al., "Poverty in the United States: 2021," US Census Bureau, September 2022, https://www.census.gov/content/dam/Census/library/publications/2022/demo/p60-277.pdf. There is also some evidence that wages have, very recently, been rising. Given the unusual context of high inflation and low unemployment, it remains to be seen whether these changes reflect increasing power of low-skill workers or whether they are a brief respite from broader trends. See Lowery, "Low-Wage Jobs."

15. These adjusted estimates come from Historical Supplemental Poverty Measure Data, Center on Poverty and Public Policy at Columbia University, accessed April 6, 2024, https://www.povertycenter.columbia.edu/historical-spm-data. This data is anchored to 2012 thresholds. It is a measure of absolute poverty, meaning the changes reflect a change in material standard of living and not a relative change with respect to the income of others in society.

24.9 percent, only 1.5 percent less than the poverty rate of 1967, despite the increase in GDP throughout the past fifty years.[16] Clearly, the current system by itself is not producing increases in material well-being for the least well-off workers.

It is also worth noting that the structure of poverty-reducing programs in the United States also presents challenges for workers. Cash transfers via the Earned Income Tax Credit or the Child Tax Credit are paid in a lump sum once a year and thus do not provide the stable income that secure full-time wages do. Other programs, like food stamps and Medicaid, require a time-consuming and confusing application process that can stigmatize recipients.[17] They also often come with work requirements, which add to the administrative burden and end up pushing people out of the programs when they are laid off or see their hours drastically reduced.[18] Furthermore, virtually any assistance for poor people in the United States comes with cultural stigma of failure and of shame at not being able to support oneself or being a drain on the system. Thus, while these programs are indispensable for the well-being of many Americans, they do not communicate the sense of dignity and worth that many people associate with well-paid and well-respected work.

For middle-class and affluent Americans, the experience of low wages can seem quite abstract. After all, with the declining cost of many consumer goods, one might assume that the lives of low-income workers today are relatively comfortable compared to those of such workers in previous generations. Poverty researchers provide a profound service by putting a human face on the experience of poverty.[19] What is it like to be the working poor in the United States? In this research, poverty is juggling multiple part-time jobs until one passes out from exhaustion. It is barely making ends meet month to month until an economic shock like a canceled shift, unexpected car repair, or emergency-room visit upends the fragile balance. In that case, poverty entails incurring high-cost debt from payday loans or credit cards or pawning valuables for a fraction of their value. Then it means deciding which bill can wait a month

16. I am indebted here to Steven McMullen, "Redistribution to Expand Economic Opportunity," in Steven McMullen and James R. Otteson, *Should Wealth Be Redistributed? A Debate* (New York: Routledge, 2023), 27. McMullen makes this point using a different study with data from 2012.

17. Annie Lowery, "The Time Tax," *The Atlantic*, July 27, 2021, https://www.theatlantic.com /politics/archive/2021/07/how-government-learned-waste-your-time-tax/619568/.

18. Annie Lowery, "Work Requirements Just Won't Die," *The Atlantic*, May 31, 2023, https:// www.theatlantic.com/ideas/archive/2023/05/work-requirements-snap-debt-ceiling/674246/.

19. See Matthew Desmond, *Poverty, by America* (New York: Crown, 2023); Sarah Halpern-Meekin et al., *It's Not Like I'm Poor: How Working Families Make Ends Meet in a Post-Welfare World* (Oakland: University of California Press, 2015); Jennifer Silva, *We're Still Here: Pain and Politics in the Heart of America* (Oxford: Oxford University Press, 2019).

and making minimum payments on debt without ever touching the principal. Poverty usually means living in unsafe neighborhoods and worrying that even a small increase in income will mean that one no longer qualifies for a housing voucher. It means regularly risking one's health in physically demanding work and living with constant pain. For many, poverty in the midst of the current opioid crisis means turning to drugs to deal with physical or mental pain. It means suffering the abuse of a partner and not being able to afford to leave. Poverty is constant stress and anxiety. Many among the working class do not fall within the official poverty boundaries, but as sociologist Matthew Desmond writes, "What then is the term for trying to raise two kids on $50,000 a year in Miami or Portland? What do you call it when you don't qualify for a housing voucher but can't get a mortgage either? When the rent takes half your paycheck, and your student loan debt takes another quarter?"[20]

In addition to low wages, another dimension of work precarity is irregular scheduling. Not only do low-wage workers labor in industries that require them to work outside the standard 8-to-5 workday, but many of these workers also have a schedule that fluctuates from week to week, often with little notice. Time-saving technologies that were initially harnessed to schedule the supply of goods to assembly lines for maximum efficiency are now also used to schedule human persons. Corporations can track data on the demand for workers at various times and places, and they can use this data to schedule employees on short notice to match the current algorithmic predictions. Employees may thus be constantly "on call," being expected to remain available to their employer as the need for labor arises. Or they might show up on time for a scheduled shift only to be told they are no longer needed.

Data regarding the prevalence of nonstandard work schedules can be difficult to come by. According to some estimates, as many as two in five workers have nonstandard work times, and nearly one in five knows their schedule less than one week in advance.[21] While not all these workers are low income, nonstandard schedules and just-in-time scheduling are heavily used in service industries that have a low-wage workforce. These schedules present distinct challenges, especially for those who have caregiving responsibilities. Most childcare facilities operate only during standard working hours, and even those that maintain extended hours can hardly be expected to provide care for children

20. Desmond, *Poverty*, 17.

21. Kadri Täht and Melinda Mills, *Out of Time: The Consequences of Non-standard Employment Schedules for Family Cohesion* (New York: Springer, 2016), 32; Katherine Guyot and Richard V. Reeves, "Unpredictable Work Hours and Volatile Incomes Are Long-Term Risks for American Workers," Brookings, August 18, 2020, https://www.brookings.edu/articles/unpredictable-work-hours-and-volatile-incomes-are-long-term-risks-for-american-workers/.

on a schedule that changes constantly or to have space available for a child whose parent is called to work on short notice. Parents who work nonstandard schedules may find themselves cobbling together care from family, friends, and neighbors and making painful choices between losing a job, leaving a child with someone the parent does not trust, or even leaving young children unattended.[22]

As nonstandard schedules have risen in prominence over the past forty years, a growing literature in the social sciences has tracked the effects of such scheduling on the health of workers and children. The literature on nonstandard but predictable schedules is mixed. Here much depends on the household's other resources for coping with the unusual schedule and on the kinds of public supports available locally and nationally. With unpredictable on-call or just-in-time schedules, however, the story is different. Schedule instability is associated with psychological distress, difficulty sleeping, and lower subjective well-being than that associated with a regular day schedule.[23] Parents with unstable schedules are more likely to use multiple childcare arrangements, including informal care and sibling care, and to observe behavioral problems in their children.[24] Furthermore, workers with unpredictable schedules were more than twice as likely to experience material hardship than workers with stable schedules.[25]

While low-wage employers will often adjust workers' schedules to meet the changing needs of the company, the reverse is not the case. Employers are not obligated to adjust to worker needs by providing paid leave for illness, the birth of a child, or to care for an unwell family member. Nearly half of workers in the lowest 25 percent income bracket have no access to paid sick leave or paid vacation.[26] Low-wage workers are asked to be increasingly flexible

22. Kristen Harknett, Daniel Schneider, and Sigrid Luhr, "Who Cares If Parents Have Unpredictable Work Schedules? Just-in-Time Work Schedules and Child Care Arrangements," *Social Problems* 69 (2022): 164–83.

23. Daniel Schneider and Kristen Harknett, "Consequences of Routine Work-Schedule Instability for Worker Health and Well-Being," *American Sociological Review* 84, no. 1 (2019): 82–114. These correlations were higher than they were for a regular night shift in each category except sleep. Researchers also note the effect sizes are strong, with a high level of statistical significance. In a subsequent study, the sleep disruptions were found to be worse than those experienced by a parent of a preschool child or a worker who works night shifts. Kristen Harknett, Daniel Schneider, and Rebecca Wolfe, "Losing Sleep Over Work Scheduling? The Relationship between Work Schedules and Sleep Quality for Service Sector Workers," *Population Health* 12, article 100681 (2020).

24. Harknett, Schneider, and Luhr, "Who Cares If Parents Have Unpredictable Work Schedules?"; Anna K. Walther and Alejandra Ros Pilarz, "Associations between Parental Precarious Work Schedules and Child Behavior Problems among Low-Income Families," *Journal of Marriage and Family* 86, no. 3 (June 2024): 551–73.

25. Daniel Schneider and Kristen Harknett, "Hard Times: Routine Schedule Unpredictability and Material Hardship among Service Sector Workers," *Social Forces* 99, no. 4 (2021): 1682–709.

26. "Higher Paid Workers More Likely Than Lower Paid Workers to Have Paid Leave Benefits in 2022," US Bureau of Labor Statistics, February 15, 2023, https://www.bls.gov/opub/ted/2023

with all aspects of their lives in order to maximize the business's profits, but businesses are not obligated to recognize that employees are embodied social creatures with needs and responsibilities that cannot be neatly segregated from their lives as workers.

The last aspect of low-skill precarious work that we should consider is the work environment itself. While workplace safety has undeniably improved since the beginning of the industrial era, there is still ample evidence that these occupations are more dangerous than they need to be. As I write this chapter, a massive heat wave is gripping the American South and Southwest, and the state of Texas has passed a law that invalidates local ordinances mandating ten-minute water breaks every four hours for construction workers.[27] In the meat-processing industry, accidental amputations, usually of fingers or hands, occur on a weekly basis.[28] Eyal Press describes the physical pain and injuries that meat packers routinely experience as well as the verbal abuse dished out by supervisors who are themselves pressured to keep the lines moving as fast as possible.[29] Recounting his interviews with poultry workers, Press noted, "As they recounted their experiences, all but one of the women wept openly. As the tears suggested, the workers at the plant did not just feel mistreated. They felt degraded and demeaned."[30]

Not all the indignities of low-wage work environments are life threatening, but they still contribute to environments that produce varying degrees of misery and affronts to human dignity. Journalist Emily Guendelsberger, for instance, describes her experiences working in an Amazon warehouse, a call center, and a fast-food restaurant.[31] She documents the surveillance techniques used to squeeze the highest amount of labor possible from workers, at the expense of their health, and notes her surprise in discovering that Amazon warehouses provide vending machines offering free over-the-counter pain medication. Guendelsberger also observes that the tight scheduling of fast-food restaurants leaves them routinely understaffed, creating a frantic environment for workers as well as poor service, with long waits, for customers. This environment,

/higher-paid-workers-more-likely-than-lower-paid-workers-to-have-paid-leave-benefits-in-2022 .htm.

27. Betsy Reed, "'The Cruelty Olympics': Texas Workers Condemn Elimination of Water Breaks," *The Guardian*, August 2, 2023, https://www.theguardian.com/us-news/2023/aug/02/texas-construc tion-worker-water-break-law-heat-exhaustion-abbott.

28. Desmond, *Poverty*, 14.

29. Eyal Press, *Dirty Work: Essential Jobs and the Hidden Toll of Inequality in America* (New York: Farrar, Straus & Giroux, 2021), 168–208.

30. Press, *Dirty Work*, 169.

31. Emily Guendelsberger, *On the Clock: What Low-Wage Work Did to Me and How It Drives America Insane* (New York: Back Bay Books, 2019).

predictably, leads to hot tempers, with customers yelling and pelting workers with various items from the menu. Guendelsberger is particularly gifted at documenting how company policies gradually erode worker dignity. After she is denied the employee discount at McDonald's because the meal is already on sale, she comments, "But of course I'm still mad, because obviously it's not about the $2.50. It's because my worth may be greater than zero, but I now also have proof that it's less than three bucks."

Many of these features of wage labor are exemplified in recent changes in the railway industry, which culminated in the suppressed worker strike and the subsequent calamitous train derailment in East Palestine, Pennsylvania. In the late twentieth century, when US railways were struggling to remain profitable, companies began instituting a series of changes in operating procedures and employment to increase efficiency and decrease costs. As these changes proved financially successful, they were gradually increased through a set of policies that came to be known as Precision Railway Scheduling (PRS). These changes involved dramatically increasing the length of trains (though the same number of, or fewer, employees operated them), assembling trains as quickly as possible (often with decreased attention to planning the weight distribution of various cars), shrinking the labor force, decreasing time allotments for safety checks, and decreasing inspection points.

Most importantly for our purposes, efficiency involved substantial changes to worker scheduling. Instead of having set times for train departures and thus maintaining reliable scheduling for workers, precision scheduling involved waiting until a train had sufficient cargo and then running it, regardless of the time of day or night. Workers in the new system were thus an entirely on-call workforce, being required to work whenever the trains happened to be ready. In January 2022, one railroad instituted the most draconian scheduling system yet, requiring workers to be on call approximately 90 percent of the time and installing a harsh point system to manage workers who needed to request time off for any reason.

What this meant for a typical worker would be something like this: The worker is on call, always reachable by phone and available to work within ninety minutes. Once called in, they work a twelve-hour shift, after which they disembark the train in a town along the route. They remain there for between twelve and forty-eight hours until they are able to work on a train going back to their hometown, where the process starts again. In this system, roughly half of the worker's nonworking (unpaid) time is spent in a hotel room away from their home and family. The time they do have at home is always up in the air, always coming with the understanding that they could be called away at a moment's notice. When a call comes in the middle of the night, a worker might have slept for only a few hours before beginning a shift on which they are responsible for transporting dangerous chemicals. Major life events, like weddings or the birth of a child, have to be carefully planned, and unplanned events or emergencies often force workers into horrible choices: do they call off work to stay with a brother on his deathbed, or do they go to work so they will be able to attend the brother's eventual funeral?[32] Ordinary life is impossible. Will they be able to attend a child's soccer game? Or take a spouse to a doctor's appointment? Or be present for a family meal? It is impossible to say. In essence, the worker's entire life is claimed by work.

As one might imagine, unionized railway workers have vigorously opposed many of these changes, objecting both to the sharp decline in quality of life and to the decreased safety for workers and the general public. In the weeks leading up to the planned strike in December 2022, before Congress and the Biden administration legally prohibited workers from striking, the coverage in the mainstream press depicted the conflict as one about "sick time." In-depth reporting from several sources, however, revealed that the concerns went much deeper. One former Norfolk Southern employee remarked, "That job changed me. I didn't feel as if I was even a person anymore. I'd lost my hobbies, my friends, and my fiancée. More importantly I'd lost any reason to live."[33] Another worker spoke to the loss of time with family, saying, "We have to parent our children via FaceTime. In order to discipline my children or console them when they're upset about something or why they never see me, I have to do it via FaceTime. To go to a sporting event, I have to go via FaceTime."[34] Another commented, "I average 110 hours a week away from home. I have no scheduled days off at all. I'm on call 24/7 and work all hours of the day and night while BNSF [Railway Company] makes me watch training every two years on sleeping well and eating healthy while they do everything they can to prevent that."[35]

Conditions like these communicate important information about how the worker as a human person is understood within the system. In the first place, and as we see dramatically in the case of freight-rail workers, the worker is disposable. The living and working situations of the workers are not a reflection

32. This heartbreaking dilemma is described by Aaron Gordon in "'What Choice Do I Have?' Freight Train Conductors Are Forced to Work Tired, Sick and Stressed," Motherboard, Tech by Vice, April 18, 2022, https://www.vice.com/en/article/pkp9m8/what-choice-do-i-have-freight-train -conductors-are-forced-to-work-tired-sick-and-stressed.

33. Aaron Gordon, "28 Freight Rail Workers Tell Us What They Want You to Know about Their Lives," Motherboard, Tech by Vice, September 15, 2022, https://www.vice.com/en/article/qjkzbq/28 -freight-rail-workers-tell-us-what-they-want-you-to-know-about-their-lives.

34. Gordon, "28 Freight Rail Workers."

35. Gordon, "28 Freight Rail Workers."

of their inherent dignity as people or of the human value of the work they perform—as we saw in the early days of the COVID-19 pandemic, much low-skilled labor is essential to human society—but instead to the value of their work in the labor market. Due to an excess of low-skilled laborers, these workers are not worth much to their employers, and thus, they are not cared for. They are not treated as human beings who must sleep to function safely, who have limbs that can be sawed off, who have body temperatures that can rise to excessive and life-threatening heights, who are parents of children who need their stable presence, who might become sick or need to care for a spouse after surgery. Not only are such workers disposable, but they are also increasingly claimed for the world of work. In the extremes of nonstandard schedules, there is no time that is unclaimable by employers. Employees always exist for the sake of work. And during working hours, surveillance technologies ensure that the employees remain workers, expending the maximum amount of effort for the sake of work.

Worker disposability translates into broader social status. How could it not? If we collectively accept that some workers should be treated as less than human, can we continue to value them as human in any meaningful sense? Can they continue to value themselves? Similarly, the absolute claim of the worker's time and effort communicates certain assumptions about human personhood. The human person is *for* work. Even when they are not being paid, workers are encouraged to understand themselves as existing for the sake of work. Both the disposability of the worker and the absolute claims of work offer what is, from a Christian perspective, a false vision of the human person. As we have seen, in Christian theology human value is graciously given. It is not the sort of thing that can be earned through work.

One would imagine that the precarious state of many workers would make them eager for assistance and for stronger social support that could enable low-income and low-skill workers to live a dignified life. When sociologist Jennifer Silva interviewed working-class young adults during the Great Recession, however, she found that many of these workers distrusted government assistance and instead embraced radical self-sufficiency.[36] Silva observed that her research subjects felt betrayed not just by the difficulties of employment—many had college degrees or some college education but found themselves stuck in precarious low-wage jobs—but also by the various institutions that had failed them, especially the state. Such experiences, Silva noted, had "hardened" her subjects, convincing many of them that they were on their own and that self-reliance was a virtue. They made a virtue "out of not asking for help, out of

36. Silva, *Coming Up Short*, 88–111.

rejecting dependence and surviving completely on their own, mapping these traits onto their definitions of adulthood."[37] The flip side of this moral vision was that these young adults expected the same of others, distancing themselves emotionally from others who were struggling and rejecting values like solidarity and mutual concern.[38] The workers in Silva's ethnography embraced and strengthened a meritocratic system of value.

Professional Work

Our discussion of work has focused largely on the low-wage and/or low-skilled sector, but the economic changes of the late twentieth and early twenty-first centuries have also presented challenges for higher-skilled professional labor. Although the instability of work is less pronounced than it is for low-skilled workers, these laborers can still face precarious work circumstances like part-time or subcontract work and low wages. Many people in service professions, like teachers (especially adjunct professors) and social workers, receive salaries that are not enough to live on in the major metropolitan areas they serve. Other knowledge-sector workers are currently experiencing the threat of technological redundancy. At the time of writing, both the Writers Guild of America and the Screen Actors Guild are on strike, and the use of artificial intelligence in each of these sectors is a fundamental point of contestation. It may be the case that artificial intelligence rapidly changes the world of work in relatively short order, necessitating theological reflection on the shrinking opportunities for work across the board. These concerns, while important, go beyond the scope of this chapter. At present I want to explore the ways in which professional labor is, in its own way, subject to the absolute claims of labor on the human person in the existing economy.

Among highly educated and skilled American workers, work is tied to identity. This reality reflects a process that begins quite early—young children are regularly asked what they want to "be" when they grow up. For many, work is the defining feature of who they are, and it enables them to pursue their particular passions and put their distinctive skills to use. Work provides a sense of meaning, self-worth, and belonging. Work can, in theory, fulfill these same psychological needs for workers without a college degree, especially when the work involves other kinds of vocational training, but as we have seen, the de-meaning ways in which much low-skilled work is often structured make this relationship much more complicated. For the more highly educated, many of

37. Silva, *Coming Up Short*, 96.
38. Silva, *Coming Up Short*, 97–109.

the demeaning features that characterize low-wage work are not present. These workers generally earn more money, receive sick time and vacation time, have consistent schedules, and work in generally safe environments. There are, of course, exceptions. Some highly educated workers are financially strapped. Hospital physicians and nurses often work nonstandard schedules. Many educated workers might not feel that their work is particularly meaningful or necessary.[39] On the whole, however, working conditions for the highly educated avoid the sorts of demeaning conditions that might threaten identity and self-worth.

It is precisely because work is, for professionals, so closely tied to identity that they also allow their lives to be claimed by and for work. When work is integral to self-understanding, self-worth, and meaning in life, people are willing to invest considerable effort in their work. This investment is, in many respects, culturally encouraged or even mandated. Aspiring young people on the cusp of entering the workforce are encouraged to "do what you love."[40] Prominent business leaders brag about their extreme dedication to work, which leaves them barely enough time to eat and sleep. Corporations add perks like meals and exercise facilities, structuring the work environment in a way that reduces the amount of time employees need to spend elsewhere. Many organizations seek to enhance productivity by increasing workers' commitment to the organization and its mission or goals. Such environments often involve strong competition for advancement, salary increases, and accolades, and success can further enhance the psychological rewards of work.[41] Jonathan Malesic notes, however, that there is a catch-22 with this love of work: "If work is well-paid, comfortable, and even enjoyable, then why not do it all the time?"[42]

This is precisely what many American workers have done in the past thirty years.[43] In 2022, 12 percent of respondents to a Gallup poll reported working over sixty hours a week, and an additional 29 percent reported working forty-five to fifty-nine hours a week.[44] Newer communication technologies allow

39. David Graeber, *Bullshit Jobs: A Theory* (New York: Simon & Schuster, 2018).

40. Lindsay J. DePalma, "The Passion Paradigm: Professional Adherence to and Consequences of the Ideology of 'Do What You Love,'" *Sociological Forum* 36, no. 1 (March 2021): 134–58.

41. For discussion and examples of these trends, see Erin Griffith, "Why Are Young People Pretending to Love Work?," *New York Times*, January 26, 2019, https://www.nytimes.com/2019/01/26/business/against-hustle-culture-rise-and-grind-tgim.html.

42. Jonathan Malesic, *The End of Burnout: Why Work Drains Us and How to Build Better Lives* (Oakland: University of California Press, 2022), 158.

43. Juliet Schor initially noted this trend in *The Overworked American: The Unexpected Decline of Leisure* (New York: Basic Books, 1991).

44. Data is not broken down by type of work, so some of these workers undoubtedly are low-skilled and working overtime or working more than one job. See "Work and Workplace," Gallup, accessed April 6, 2024, https://news.gallup.com/poll/1720/work-work-place.aspx.

workers to be accessible all the time, creating the sense that all time is for work and that constant accessibility should be the norm. For salaried employees, the number of working hours is not limited legally or curbed by a requirement of overtime pay. Thus, workers are largely on their own to establish work-life balance, even as the structural incentives of advancement and professional success pressure them to give more and more to work. More time spent working means less time given to other aspects of life, like maintaining relationships, participating in civic activities, or being involved in a local church. For many workers, it is also a recipe for anxiety, depression, and burnout.[45] It is in this context that commentators begin to speak of work as a religion—it requires absolute devotion and substantial personal sacrifice, and it becomes the locus of meaning and the object of trust.

These features of professional work are especially visible in ethnographies of the world of high-powered finance.[46] Wall Street employers begin by heavily recruiting among a handful of Ivy League universities and appealing to a sense of self-worth that is rooted in intelligence.[47] In keeping with a meritocratic ethos, new graduates are encouraged to combine hard work with the raw skills of intelligence, leadership, and ambition in order to earn the rewards of material success and high status that come with the profession. In the first two years, new employees in financial services are expected to work one-hundred-hour weeks, including Saturdays and Sundays, with regular all-nighters. According to one employee, "It's akin to slavery and it will break you." Another remarks, "For a year you have no personal life. It's hard enough just to do my laundry."[48] Even if one wants to maintain some semblance of normalcy, the competitive nature of the work environment does not allow it. As one worker puts it, "It is like, 'oh, yeah, work is your life, and if it is not, you are going to get hung by somebody whose life it is.'"[49] According to these ethnographers, the world of finance creates a hefty sense of entitlement, as workers who have been told of their brilliance all their lives spend several years totally dedicated to work for which they reap substantial material and psychological rewards that seem, to them, to be entirely deserved and justified. Of course, the financial sector is only one small slice of the professional workforce, but as these scholars observe, it is outsized in its influence on the broader work culture.[50] Workers in the

45. See Malesic, *End of Burnout*.

46. Alexandra Michel, "Participation and Self-Entrapment: A 12-Year Ethnography of Wall Street Participation Practices' Diffusion and Evolving Consequences," *Sociological Quarterly* 55 (2014): 514–36; Karen Ho, *Liquidated: An Ethnography of Wall Street* (Durham, NC: Duke University Press, 2009).

47. Ho, *Liquidated*, 39–72.

48. Ho, *Liquidated*, 88.

49. Ho, *Liquidated*, 98.

50. Michel, "Participation and Self-Entrapment," 528; Ho, *Liquidated*, 214.

financial sector set the expectations for efficiency and productivity in business more generally, both through the restructuring they force on companies and through the expectations they carry with them when they leave finance and enter other sectors of the economy.

While there is nothing wrong with finding work that is meaningful and in which one finds satisfaction exercising skills with excellence, the particular confluence of identity, meaning, and productive work among the professional classes does stand in complex tension with the theological understanding of grace. Work in this context exemplifies and contributes to a culture that is all too willing to locate human worth and dignity in productivity, to see highly imbalanced rewards for different work as normal and deserved, and, ultimately, to make the human person serve the ends of work. In the final section of this chapter, I will explore these tensions in greater detail and ask what kind of response a social ethic rooted in grace might call for.

Work and Christian Social Ethics: The Question of Structural Change

We have seen in this chapter that the existing structures of work do not allow some members of society to share in the fruit of creation. The lives of too many are marked by constant anxiety about their ability to meet their basic needs. Many people endure precarious work circumstances in which employers do not recognize fundamental aspects of their embodied humanity. These circumstances do not acknowledge that humans have a deeper purpose than paid labor—the purpose of loving God and loving their neighbor. Current structures of work both depend on and perpetuate a culture where human value comes from what type of labor one does in the paid economy rather than from the reality of having been created by and for God's love. Given this reality of work, how should Christians respond? I contend that both structural and personal approaches are needed. As a broader society, we need to shape work to serve human persons, and at the personal and cultural level, we need to interrogate our values and actively seek a spiritual transformation. Each of these responses can support and enhance the other.

As one might expect, at the structural level there are myriad proposals for ways to improve the lives of low-wage workers, such as minimum basic income, minimum-wage increases, an expanded Earned Income Tax Credit, child tax credits, investment in early-childhood education, increases to the feasibility of labor organization, and so on. As a theologian, my primary role is not to weigh in on the empirical questions about the efficacy of specific proposals, though I will offer some reflections on which ones I find more appealing. Rather, as a theologian I can assess the ideological and theological objections that are used to resist structural change, especially since so many of these objections center on questions of merit, deservingness, gift, dependency, and self-sufficiency—core themes of this book. The four objections I encounter most frequently are worthy of special attention.

Objection 1. Addressing the distribution of goods so that all can share in the gifts of creation will always involve taking what another person has rightfully earned and will be unjust.

I should begin by observing that many structural changes to work need not involve what we commonly call "redistribution." Some local jurisdictions, for example, have taken steps to reduce or eliminate inhumane scheduling practices.[51] Other approaches, like support for collective bargaining or the removal of zoning restrictions on housing construction in high-demand areas, or even minimum-wage increases, do not involve redistribution. At the same time, however, I want to argue that practices that fall under the broad umbrella of redistribution do not necessarily involve taking from people what they have rightfully earned.[52]

In general, I have no theological objection to a system where, for most adults, work is directly connected to personal sustenance. This is not the only valid option for structuring human community,[53] and it may need greater theological scrutiny if work continues to disappear with technological advancement, but on the whole a system where the receipt of material goods corresponds directly to work is consistent with God's establishing and sustaining human agency. It is also consistent with a Christian tradition that has valued work as a social and even spiritual good. Valuing work in this way respects our creaturely nature and specifically the fact that we have each been given various abilities that can be exercised for the benefit of creation and human community. As Calvin affirmed, it is reasonable to think that one who works deserves a share of the fruit of their labor, even as we recognize that everything is ultimately a gift from God.

However, any economic system will have to specify how much of the fruit is due to the laborer. To simply assume that the present system represents absolute moral deservingness rather than social and legal convention is simply to beg the question. And this question begging assumes an individualistic and

---

51. Elizabeth O. Ananat, Anna Gassman-Pines, and John A. Fitz-Henley II, "The Effects of the Emeryville Fair Workweek Ordinance on the Daily Lives of Low-Wage Workers and Their Families," *Russell Sage Foundation Journal of the Social Sciences* 8, no. 5 (2022): 45–56.

52. The opposite argument, that redistribution does involve taking from one person what they have rightfully earned, is made by James Otteson in Steven McMullen and James R. Otteson, *Should Wealth Be Redistributed? A Debate* (New York: Routledge, 2023), 70–77.

53. Monastic communities, e.g., do not operate on this basis.

meritocratic framework that overlooks the many ways in which we all depend on and are indebted to one another. As I have suggested throughout this book, these various forms of human interdependence are signs of our deeper dependence on God and are woven into our being so that we can live out our vocation of love. It will never be possible to add up all that one has received from others and render financial repayment in order to even the score and assert absolute independence, nor should we wish to do so. To return to an earlier example, Jeff Bezos, in founding Amazon, undoubtedly worked hard, was extraordinarily creative, and acted as a visionary. But he was also successful because he exercised these abilities in a society with a wealthy, educated, and largely law-abiding populace. He capitalized on existing legal structures and existing infrastructure like roads—infrastructure that has been further worn down by the volume of Amazon deliveries.[54] It is no easy matter to say what is owed to Jeff Bezos, to the various employees of Amazon, and to the wider society that enabled his success. Making these kinds of determinations will always be a judgment call that must be negotiated through various social and political structures and must balance many considerations. But to establish an economic system where some of the profit of Amazon is due not to Bezos or Amazon's investors, but to the broader public, is not to take from Bezos or Amazon shareholders something they deserve in an absolute sense.

Objection 2. Government handouts encourage laziness and dependence, but rewarding hard work encourages virtue and human excellence. It is good and right for people to be proud of a job well done, and it is socially destructive to reward laziness.

There is something quite right and important about this intuition that I must begin by affirming. It is indeed crucial to our humanity and sense of agency to be able to contribute to our communities through work. And it is indeed good and right to find satisfaction in having done so. All too often we say to people, such as low-skilled workers, the elderly, or people with disabilities, "You have nothing to contribute." This sentiment is a denial of created human goodness and a denial of the wisdom of God, who has made humans with much diversity and particularity in giftedness.

We should note, however, the subtle differences in the potential emotional responses to professional accomplishment. To use an example from my own profession, when a scholar writes an essay that persuasively captures just what they want to communicate, they might feel a deep satisfaction at a job well

---

54. See, e.g., Amanda Mull, "America Is Drowning in Packages: UPS Workers Have an Impossible Job in the Amazon Age," *The Atlantic*, July 29, 2023, https://www.theatlantic.com/technology/archive/2023/07/ups-strike-union-contract-package-deliveries/674864/.

done, at having used their particular skill set to accomplish a goal with excellence. They might experience greater rejoicing and satisfaction when this work is recognized and celebrated by their peers, as this recognition confirms their own sense of having done something well and having made a contribution to the common cause. Our basic intuitions are to affirm this response, and I would agree, with the caveat that their sense of accomplishment and pride should be accompanied by gratitude—to the many neighbors who contributed to the work and ultimately to God for the writer's abilities and their drive to use them. In fact, their deepest satisfaction should be the glory reflected back to the creator through the goodness of creation. In other words, this good and healthy joy and satisfaction in excellent human action should always be a shared satisfaction and joy. And it should be enhanced by virtue of being shared. This sort of pride and satisfaction is quite different from one that is primarily comparative, where the person rejoices in being better than others or has a sense of entitlement or cannot stand to assess their actions and accomplishments honestly because any failure would be psychologically devastating. Ultimately, this latter kind of motivation and pride risks undermining worthwhile action because the true focus is the enhancement of the self, not the action and its intrinsic goodness.

In this context, where excellent human action is both one's own and shared with one's community and ultimately with God, the issue is not so much about "handouts" creating dependency. We are all necessarily and gloriously dependent in all our actions. All of us have received "handouts." As I have endeavored to show, this idea is actually a central Christian claim. Gift precedes and enables action. As the Christian philosopher Josef Pieper puts it in his classic reflections on work and leisure, "Everything gained and everything claimed follows upon something given and comes after something gratuitous and unearned."[55] Christians, of all people, should be incredibly suspicious of any blanket critique of "handouts." Instead, we should be asking what kind of gift or support is needed in the present moment, since every human being needs ongoing support of various kinds. While this support often comes through networks of family and interpersonal relationships, a point to which we will return momentarily, relying on these networks alone can lead to deep social divisions and perpetuate historical injustice. The impact of slavery and segregation on the resources of black communities is, of course, the most blatant example in the US context, though it is certainly not the only one.[56] It is also

55. Joseph Pieper, *Leisure: The Basis of Culture*, trans. Alexander Dru (San Francisco: Ignatius, 2009), 36.

56. Richard Rothstein documents how black people were systematically and legally excluded from home ownership in good neighborhoods. Rothstein, *The Color of Law: A Forgotten History of How Our Government Segregated America* (New York: Liveright, 2017).

disingenuous to pretend that the middle and upper classes have not benefited from many past and previous "handouts" that were not available to others. The Homestead Act of 1862 and the GI Bill are two of the most significant, but as Matthew Desmond argues, handouts to the middle and upper classes that support the creation of wealth continue in the present system.[57]

We should also challenge the belief that giving people necessary resources incentivizes laziness while wages or salaries incentivize virtuous work. There is plenty of empirical evidence to contradict both of these claims. As we discovered in chapter 3, people are generally enabled to take initiative, be creative, care for others, and so forth when they themselves have received social, emotional, and material support from others. The contemporary literature on poverty and cash transfers offers additional confirmation.[58] When poor people receive higher wages or a windfall payment or a housing voucher, they can make better choices for their health, be more present to their children, and think about long-term plans.[59] In one particularly striking case, when the Eastern Cherokee Tribe of North Carolina opted to distribute some of the proceeds from a new casino equally among its members, providing each person with about $6,000 annually, researchers found rather large effects in health outcomes. Poorer children receiving the stipend had fewer behavioral problems and were more likely to graduate high school. In early adulthood they had lower rates of substance abuse and better mental health compared with poor rural white children in the area.[60] Even in cases where we might be tempted to think that giving someone the resources they need supports laziness—we might think here of the stereotyped and denigrated "welfare" recipient—we should perhaps reexamine our assumptions about laziness and responsible action. Is it lazy if a parent uses a child allowance to stay home and care for a young child? Caring for children, after all, is not easy and is also a social good. Perhaps we should see a child tax credit dispersed monthly as supporting good parenting and children's health for the overall well-being of society.

57. Desmond, *Poverty*, 80–102.

58. See Joseph Hanlon, Armando Barrientos, and David Hulme, *Just Give Money to the Poor* (Sterling, VA: Kumarian, 2010).

59. Minimum-wage increases, e.g., are associated with lower rates of smoking and lower rates of child maltreatment. See J. Paul Leigh, Wesley A. Leigh, and Juan Du, "Minimum Wages and Public Health: A Literature Review," *Preventative Medicine* 118 (2019): 122–34; Kerri M. Raissian and Lindsey Rose Bullinger, "Money Matters: Does the Minimum Wage Affect Child Maltreatment Rates?," *Children and Youth Services Review* 72 (2017): 60–70.

60. Moises Velasquez-Manoff, "What Happens When the Poor Receive a Stipend," *New York Times*, January 18, 2014, https://archive.nytimes.com/opinionator.blogs.nytimes.com/2014/01 /18/what-happens-when-the-poor-receive-a-stipend/?_php=true&_type=blogs&_php=true&_type= blogs&emc=edit_tnt_20140119&tntemail0=y&_r=1&.

With respect to wages incentivizing virtuous work, it is by no means clear that market-based approaches reliably function in this manner. No doubt, employees of pharmaceutical companies worked hard and were well compensated to market the drugs at the center of the opioid crisis, and these companies clearly made lots of money as a result. But the results of their labor were tragically destructive of communities. This example raises the question of what we really mean by virtuous work and laziness. In the Christian tradition the vice of sloth is a sin against the virtue of charity. Sloth means neglecting love toward God or one's neighbor. As Christopher Jones and Conor Kelly argue, this theological conception of sloth raises the possibility that one could be devoted to working long hours in the paid economy but neglect care for one's own children or one's spiritual state, thus exhibiting sloth.[61]

Objection 3. The response to human need should be interpersonal acts of love. This is a fundamental Christian calling, and we should not look to the government to fulfill it for us.[62]

Debates about the relationship between charity and justice have been common in recent work in Christian ethics, and they are too extensive to engage fully here.[63] For our purposes, it is crucial to affirm that personal acts of love for the neighbor, the stranger, and even the enemy are integral to human purpose. As I argued in chapter 4, it is because we are interdependent creatures that we can participate in the love that is God. However, the centrality of love to human purpose and meaning does not require *all* human needs to be met interpersonally or by the church. We meet many needs through our own agency, with the important caveat that this agency is always enabled by God and other people. Other needs can be met best, or perhaps only, by other human beings and in an interpersonal way. This is the case when we comfort someone grieving a loss or when we offer companionship to the lonely or when we provide the physical touch that all human beings need in order to thrive. There are other cases, however, where it might make more sense for human needs to be met through broadly available public goods. Most industrialized societies, for example, have concluded that making at least some education a public good that is available to all contributes to the flourishing of the whole community by promoting broad opportunity, the cultivation of skills, and the development of responsible citizens. Providing for needs like this collectively can reinforce communal

61. Christopher D. Jones and Conor M. Kelly, "Sloth: America's Iconic Structural Vice," *Journal of the Society of Christian Ethics* 37, no. 2 (2017): 117–34.

62. Versions of this argument are common. For one example, see Robert Sirico, *Defending the Free Market: The Moral Case for a Free Economy* (Washington, DC: Regnery, 2012), 115–31.

63. For a good discussion, see Hirschfeld, *Aquinas and the Market*, 181–90.

awareness of the many ways we are linked together and thrive as societies and
not just as individuals. It is far too simplistic to say that any human need not
met by individuals themselves should be met through person-to-person giving
or through the church rather than through public services.

In this chapter I am especially concerned with whether the structure of
work respects human dignity and the universal destination of goods. When
the problems, like the absolute claim of employers on the human person, are
at least partly structural, then working toward structural responses rather than
just relying on interpersonal or nonprofit charity can also be a form of love
for one's neighbor, as so many advocates of the working poor have profoundly
illustrated. One can affirm this while also maintaining that many Christians
would benefit spiritually from reflecting on overconsumption and the ever-
rising standards of living that do not serve any authentic human purpose. The
church must not forget the constant reminders of Christian theologians and
saints throughout the centuries to see one's possessions as gifts of God that are
intended to serve human need and not to be selfishly hoarded. Seeking structural change does not, in other words, mean wealthy Christians are therefore
"off the hook" when it comes to caring for the poor out of their own material
resources. But there is also no reason to assume that personal examination and
repentance of material idolatry is the best or only way to address inadequacies
in how a society connects work to the distribution of goods.

There are several further difficulties with an approach that places primary
responsibility on individuals or the church. Most obviously, even with substantial public assistance we continue to have profound needs that are not being
met by individuals or by Christian organizations. Given this reality, it is hard to
imagine that a massive and longstanding wave of generosity would accompany
the elimination of government programs. Many proponents of this approach
also appeal to the principle of subsidiarity, which says that human needs are best
met by those who are closest to a situation and have the greatest knowledge of
the circumstances. This sounds great in theory, but we live in a society that is
highly segregated along racial and economic lines. In this situation subsidiarity
begins to look suspiciously evasive. When is a wealthy person, the one with
the most means to help, ever going to be the closest to the situation of need?
As Mary Hirschfeld notes, persons in insular wealthy communities are likely
to develop a distorted sense of what standard of living is truly appropriate and
how much excess they are therefore able to give away.[64] Relying on only the
local community and extended family networks therefore risks perpetuating
the historical injustices that have impoverished poorer communities to begin

64. Hirschfeld, *Aquinas and the Market*, 182.

with. Finally, a "charity only" approach risks a distorted vision of love, where one group of people is always in the position to give and another always the one in need. At times this may be the unfortunate reality, but if we are content to remain here, we risk cultivating a sense of superiority and pride on the part of the giver and a sense of diminished dignity and agency in the receiver.

Objection 4. If we prioritize economic efficiency and productivity rather than intervene in markets through mechanisms like a minimum wage or required sick days or paid parental leave, overall growth will increase, and everyone will be better off.

This objection is, in part, a matter of economic expertise, so I will note in response that there is substantial debate on this question among economists. Many argue that a narrow focus on efficiency and shareholder value actually harms overall productivity and growth.[65] For example, there might be a long-term economic cost when "efficient" employment practices destabilize families and prevent parents from providing adequate care to their children. Or when a substantial portion of the population has stagnant wages and thus limited purchasing power. Or when millions of preschool-age children miss out on critical early-learning opportunities because their parents cannot afford quality preschool. But even setting these arguments aside, as a theologian I must insist that there are moral limits to the productivity argument. Even if companies were always more efficient and productive by not offering sick days to employees, that would not change the fact that human beings are creatures with bodies that get sick. It would not change the reality that human life is a gift from God, is given dignity and value by God, and is meant *for* God and not for whatever productivity can be squeezed out of people when they have no other options to provide for their bodily needs. Various economic circumstances might produce a change in what practical options are available in a given context, but we cannot establish as a general principle that whatever makes for the most economic growth automatically trumps all other concerns.

In this section I have sought to address ideological and theological objections to structural changes in work and the distribution of material goods associated with work. I have not advocated specific policies, largely because doing so would involve engaging much more empirical literature to assess the efficacy of different approaches and might be better undertaken by scholars with expertise in fields other than theology. Indeed, many scholars are already doing this

65. For one example, see Heather Boushey, *Unbound: How Inequality Constricts Our Economy and What We Can Do about It* (Cambridge, MA: Harvard University Press, 2019).

work well.[66] I do, however, want to discuss briefly the kinds of approaches that might be most consistent with a vision of the human person as established in grace and sustained in interdependent community. First, changes that increase social support and resources for an entire community, and do not serve just impoverished populations, can reinforce a sense of human interdependence and decrease unnecessary stigma associated with receiving "help." All people receive assistance of many different kinds. It is good to make this assistance visible and to reinforce a sense of community benefit. Public education has been one prominent example of this approach in the United States, and proposals for universal prekindergarten would be a natural expansion. Approaches that see health care as a community good provided for the benefit of all would also fall within this category, as would child allowances if these were not only available to lower-income households. A child allowance would also recognize that raising children is work in the broadest sense and would create flexibility for parents to do that work well for the benefit of everyone. Finally, proposals that increase the capacity of workers to use collective bargaining to advocate for humane schedules, better working conditions, and higher pay are consistent with the theological vision developed here because these things highlight the agency and dignity workers deserve no matter what type of work they do. On a practical level, collective bargaining also seems preferable to attempts to broadly legislate restrictions on scheduling and working conditions because collective bargaining can be tailored to the specific contexts of different industries.

Work and Christian Social Ethics: The Role of Civil Society and Personal Choice

Structural changes to work and its relationship to the distribution of goods should emphasize human interdependence, the dignity of all human agency, and the fact that humanity is made for loving relationship rather than for productivity. These structures, however, are not limited to the large and admittedly impersonal bureaucracy of the federal government—or government at any level. Civic institutions, especially churches, and corporations can also think about how to structure work with these values in mind. To give one example, Hope College, where I am on faculty, has set the ambitious goal of offering tuition-free education to all students so that they will be unencumbered by debt

66. Boushey, *Unbound*; Avent, *Wealth of Humans*; Michael Tanner, *The Inclusive Economy: How to Bring Wealth to America's Poor* (Washington, DC: Cato Institute, 2018); Jonathan Rothwell, *A Republic of Equals: A Manifesto for a Just Society* (Princeton: Princeton University Press, 2019); Desmond, *Poverty*; McMullen and Otteson, *Should Wealth be Redistributed?*

and will see education as a gift that enables all students to pursue work that contributes to the good of society. Many public libraries have now expanded offerings to include a "library of things," in which they circulate items like tools, sewing machines, telescopes, and cotton-candy machines that families might want to use only occasionally. These libraries are thus extending a sense of shared ownership and communal use of goods. Churches could easily do something similar, maintaining lists of items that parishioners are willing to lend to others. Although doing so is admittedly difficult because existing legal and financial structures push corporations to value efficiency above all else, employers could also think about how to structure employment for human and social welfare, resisting models that treat human beings like any other algorithmic input.

The tensions between contemporary work and a theology of grace call for personal and cultural responses as well as structural ones. Part of the current cultural sickness with respect to work is a mutually reinforcing relationship whereby certain forms of work are seen as less worthy of dignity and respect and certain workers are treated in ways that violate human dignity and purpose. And, of course, people who for various reasons are not actively working in the paid economy or who receive government assistance that is exclusively for the poor are often treated with the least dignity or respect. At the level of personal response, it is crucial to break these entrenched patterns of thinking, speaking, and acting. As we saw in chapter 4 in our study of the apostle Paul, this kind of moral exhortation is deeply rooted in Christian thought. Paul is particularly adamant in his letters that the grace of Christ should overcome and abolish human distinctions of status and worth. In Christ, no one can boast. Christians today, similarly, should cling to and internalize the gospel message in its vast social implications. If human goodness and worth originate in divine gift, and if all alike are born in sin and are freely rescued through the work of Christ and the Spirit, then the all-too-human tendency to establish hierarchies of worth is an afront to the good news. We might, quite reasonably, prefer individuals with particular skills for particular tasks; if someone has cancer, they will highly value an oncologist, and if they have a burst pipe, they will seek out a plumber over an electrician. Yet we must constantly resist the impulse to convert these practical judgments into deeper assessments of ultimate worth. The COVID-19 quarantines of 2020 exposed considerable hypocrisy on this score. Many of those whose received low pay and had low social status were revealed to be crucial to the functioning of society, while many well-paid and highly educated workers saw day-to-day life proceed just fine without their labor. But these lessons are perhaps too few and too easily forgotten. Part of the Christian calling, for both the individual and the local church, is to regularly bring these truths to mind and internalize them and to identify and repent of a tendency to value human beings based on what they can produce through their work. For low-skilled workers, a theological affirmation that one's worth and identity are found in Christ and not in human productivity might provide resources to reject the constant messages a meritocratic culture sends them and to advocate for the recognition and protection of their dignity.

As discussed above, various forces have combined to make an idol of certain forms of work. Work has become a kind of religion, especially for many highly educated and ambitious workers in the professional class. These workers look to work as a primary, or *the* primary, source of meaning and self-worth, and they therefore dedicate more and more of themselves to work. For many Christians, the language of "vocation" and the traditional esteem for hard work have melded with these other cultural trends to create a distinctly Christian version of this idolatry. In many cases work has been spiritualized to such an extent that it has replaced discipleship as a form of dedication to God and has replaced other responsibilities and other forms of participation in human community, including involvement in the local church. Work, however, is an insatiable master. There is always more to be done. And without a proper sense of God's grace in establishing and enabling human work, there is a risk that the worker will feel that it is fundamentally up to them, that without their action evil will triumph, and the goodness of creation will remain unrealized. Yet at the same time, one meets the profound needs of creation and humanity at every point: poverty, gun violence, deaths of despair, climate crisis, and on and on. What, in this context, is an appropriate ethic of work?

For Christians, any moral reflection on work must occur within the recognition that discipleship—learning to live into one's purpose of loving God and neighbor—is the true human vocation. This, indeed, was a genuine insight of the Reformation; discipleship was a vocation open to all Christians, not just those who entered ordained ministry or vowed religious life, and it was the same calling for all. Christian communities today would be better off emphasizing this singular and unifying vocation—especially during the critical ages of late adolescence and early adulthood—rather than insisting that young people discern a special call to one kind of paid labor. Certainly, young adults should be encouraged to train for some form of work and to seek something that they think they will be good at and that will make some genuine contribution to society. But we should not encourage the notion that this is their singular purpose in life or that this activity is why they matter.

In a culture that teaches people that work is the source of value and encourages them to dedicate themselves completely to work, an important means of resistance is the establishment of limits to the claims of work. Christians and Jews have done this for millennia through the observance of the Sabbath.[67] Setting aside a day for rest, for the things of eternity, for joy in the divine presence and the life God has given, is not a way of dividing life into different spheres and giving each its due: "This much for mammon but no more." On the contrary, the Sabbath is a reminder that the whole of life is for God and that work is for the sake of authentic humanity. It is a discipline of remembering that the work of creation and redemption is always God's work—in which we are graciously empowered to participate. When we must stop our working on the Sabbath, we are forced to confront this reality: God's work goes on without us and does not ultimately depend on us. Embracing limits is not, however, an invitation to apathy regarding the needs of others or the redemption of creation. It is, rather, an invitation to trust and ultimately to prayer. The Sabbath is about learning to be a finite creature in the midst of the longings for eternal restoration and healing.

Limits to paid employment, however, should not be confined to the observance of a day of worship. Part of the analysis of this chapter has highlighted the fact that labor within the formal economy can crowd out other forms of work, like caring for children, preparing a meal for a sick neighbor, or teaching Sunday school. In many cases unpaid labor of this kind is actually a greater expression of human purpose than what one does for a living. This is especially the case when one's career primarily involves serving the ego by establishing a sense of personal success and superiority. In this context, and to the extent that one's social location allows it, "observing the Sabbath" might mean setting limits on the paid labor one does during the work week and thereby creating space for one to offer labor as a gift.

Of course, many laborers do not have the option of choosing these kinds of limits to paid employment. Whether they work multiple jobs to survive or have no choice in their work schedule, rest for many workers depends on the choices of others. Proper observance of the Sabbath, therefore, also involves pausing the demands one makes on the labor of others. In the Mosaic law even animals are exempt from work on the Sabbath. For those who are in a position to establish the labor requirements of other people, this aspect is particularly important. Authentic Sabbath observance means recognizing that other human beings are also not created for the sake of productive labor—whether that labor is performed on Sunday or any other day. They are created for life with God. When

67. Jewish and Christian theologians have provided several deep reflections on the meaning of the Sabbath in industrialized society. The reflections here are indebted to Abraham Heschel, *The Sabbath: Its Meaning for Modern Man* (New York: Farrar, Straus & Giroux, 2005); Karl Barth, *Church Dogmatics*, III/4, *The Doctrine of Creation*, ed. T. F. Torrance, trans. Geoffrey W. Bromiley (Edinburgh: T&T Clark, 1956–1975); Norman Wirzba, *Living the Sabbath: Discovering the Rhythms of Rest and Delight* (Grand Rapids: Brazos, 2006); Walter Brueggemann, *Sabbath as Resistance: Saying No to the Culture of Now* (Louisville: Westminster John Knox, 2014).

undercover journalist Emily Guendelsberger was working at McDonald's, she joined a local church choir. This activity reminded her of the positive church experiences of her teen years and was one of the few activities that brought her joy while she was in San Francisco. Unfortunately, she had to quit the choir—her work schedule was just too unpredictable.[68] Like so many low-wage workers, Guendelsberger had no choice. But many others do. Using this power responsibly means that employers must see employees as gifts, as having been created by God for their own purpose and not simply to be exploited for others' ends.

Finally, a personal response to the dilemmas of work and distribution today surely must include reflection on personal wealth. Recognizing a limit to our work also means recognizing a limit to our own needs and the material goods that should remain in our care. Just as we do not establish our worth through our working, we also do not show our value by possessing an ever-growing quantity of goods. And regardless of what market structures may tell us, we do not deserve, in a moral sense, unlimited possession of whatever our work produces. A Christian social ethic will thus always involve discerning these limits by returning to the "difficult passages" of Scripture, the passages that encourage dispossession of material goods, radical generosity, and daily trust in the goodness of God.

Conclusion

This chapter has examined the US culture and practice of work and has found it to be in profound contradiction to a Christian understanding of the human person as beginning in gift and being redeemed by God's grace. Work does matter. After all, God made human beings to be agents—specifically to be lovers—and work is often the way in which people care for creation and love their neighbor. But work is not the source of people's life or value. In response I have argued that a theology of grace requires us to resist this cultural system. It calls us to self-examination and repentance. It also calls us to seek ways of embodying a different approach to work, one that serves human dignity and purpose and that respects the goods of creation as gifts of God that are intended for the flourishing of creation as a whole. The astute reader may have noticed that the theology of this chapter focuses heavily on the grace of creation—human beings are made by God and given worth by God, and creation as a whole is a gift to be directed toward God's purposes of fellowship and love. In the next chapter, we will follow the narrative of Christian grace and focus more on what happens when this vision goes badly, when it is disrupted by sin and humans stand in need of forgiveness and transformation.

68. Guendelsberger, *On the Clock*, 255–56.

CHAPTER 6

CRIMINAL JUSTICE

The American preference for thinking in terms of what individuals deserve based on their actions is not limited to economics. At the popular level, our approach to crime and punishment is much the same. People who commit crimes must "pay their debt to society." Sending someone to prison is connected to making sure that justice is served, that a person gets what is due to them. As with the world of work, assigning human value based on one's actions is also relevant in the arena of criminal justice. As we will see, persons entangled in the criminal-justice system, especially poor people and persons of color, are often treated as though they have forfeited their humanity. Their actions—or their alleged actions, when they are detained prior to any conviction—have made them "deserving" of debasement and degradation. Certainly, there is no recognition in this system as a whole that all people are sinners who will, at times, hurt others and who stand in need of forgiveness and reconciliation. When most people think of Christian grace, it is this emphasis on forgiveness of sins that comes most readily to mind. Yet where one would most expect Christian understandings of sin, repentance, and forgiveness to infiltrate public life— the realm of criminal justice—the response in the United States over the past half century has been predominantly one of harsh punishment. This attitude toward wrongdoing is not limited to crime; it is also visible in cancel culture and the social-media shaming that have become regular features of American public discourse. We have a deeply instilled cultural belief that when someone acts wrongly, punishment is deserved. Punishment exists in the realm of secular justice and is necessary. Grace is a strictly religious category and is optional.

Perhaps these attitudes and practices should not be surprising. Forgiveness of sin might be a paradigmatic expression of grace, but this very familiarity obscures forgiveness's radical, shocking, and offensive claims. That someone could seriously hurt others—rape or torture or kill—and be welcomed back into God's family is scandalous. Throughout most of Christian history God's forgiveness has not been understood to apply without qualification in human societies. God forgives through Jesus's death and resurrection, but human societies must still punish. In this chapter I will challenge this notion. In interdependent community, and given the reality of sin, we must have practices and institutions to respond to wrongdoing and support the social fabric. But are such practices best construed in terms of punishment? For Christians, a theological understanding of sin, repentance, and forgiveness in Christ cannot be neatly separated from the public legal responses to crime that are considered appropriate, even in a secular society. By examining our current criminal-justice system in the context of a Christian theology of sin and forgiveness, we will find that much of our current approach rests on assumptions that are fundamentally at odds with a human nature that is always established and upheld by grace.

Sin, Original Sin, and the Universal Need for Grace

Sin, in Christian theology, is a condition. It is a distortion of personhood as much as it is a discrete set of behaviors. There have been many ways of describing this core distortion. Often, Christians have characterized sin fundamentally as pride—putting oneself in the place of God or in the center of choice and action. In chapter 1, I argued that sin can be seen as a refusal of gift. Sin is when people think they do not depend on God, that they can and must fulfill all needs for themselves, that they must be enough without the gifts of God and others. This approach to life leads to fearful and desperate striving—the need to accumulate goods and power, the willingness to exploit others, the insistence that others must also provide for themselves, that they must be enough on their own. Ultimately, the refusal of gift means violence: I must protect myself at all costs, and when I withhold support, solidarity, and care from others, they must do whatever it takes to ensure their own survival as well.

This is not the full story, of course. The grace of God, which has never been absent from creation, has also enabled genuine acts of love, glimmers or signs of our true personhood, to shine through. It is this grace that alerts us to the fact that we are not well. I use the pronoun "we" here quite intentionally because in Christian thought this is very much a shared condition. If sin is a disease, as it is so often depicted, it infects us all. This concept of "original sin" involves several quite controversial and interlocking claims. Human beings are born into sin. The condition is inherited rather than something any of us individually cause or choose for ourselves. We did not bring it about through our own agency. Yet we are still responsible. We are still blameworthy. And crucially, we are incapable of escaping this condition on our own. In Pauline terms, it has enslaved us (Rom. 6:6, 16, 20).

A thorough discussion and defense of this doctrine, which has been quite controversial, goes beyond the scope of this chapter, but I want to briefly discuss some of these more controversial features, particularly the inherited nature of sin and the insistence that inherited sin is blameworthy.[1] These aspects are counterintuitive for many today, but they are also, on deeper reflection, tremendously important. In a culture that values individual agency and self-sufficiency, it goes against the grain to say that sinful dispositions could be inherited and thus not chosen. Yet when we stop to reflect on our own deepest character flaws, this notion can capture human experience quite well. Parents who regularly yell at their children, despite wanting to have positive and loving interactions, probably never consciously chose to be so prone to anger. It is also quite likely that these patterns of interaction existed in the parent's childhood family dynamics. Similarly, it makes sense when we observe that an elderly white relative who grew up in the South makes racist comments. We could multiply examples here. The idea that we inherit or receive sinful dispositions is actually not so strange. In fact, it is thoroughly consistent with the notion of human interdependence that has been woven throughout this book.

If people do not choose their deepest failings and flaws, if these failings and flaws are, in many respects, beyond individual control, one might wonder why we should be blamed for them. Again, this question calls for a much lengthier treatment than I can provide here. For our purposes, the important question to ask in response is, What is the alternative? If we are not to be blamed for inherited flaws, then it seems we must largely abandon the idea that humans have moral agency. Even if we wanted to do so, however, our psychology rebels against the effort. In our evil desires and actions, we are not like animals acting purely on instinct. We are not like the lion who cannot help but kill and eat the zebra, causing the zebra to suffer in the process. Rather, we are creatures who are capable of reflection, before and especially after we act. We are capable of putting ourselves in the place of others and considering how our actions affect them. We have quite pronounced moral emotions, so much so that our

1. For a thorough defense of inherited sin and blameworthiness along these lines, see Jesse Couenhoven, *Stricken by Sin, Cured by Christ: Agency, Necessity, and Culpability in Augustinian Theology* (Oxford: Oxford University Press, 2013).

lives can be destroyed by guilt. Seeing ourselves as amoral seems not to be an option for us. Given the depths of our moral failures, this is truly a miserable condition to be in, and that is perhaps why so many of us utilize psychological mechanisms of self-enhancement and self-protection. This sense of the misery of our condition is precisely what the notion of original sin is meant to capture. Insisting on the legitimacy of blame and responsibility in this context is a way of recognizing this conflicted but real moral agency. It is, perhaps counterintuitively, a way of respecting the dignity of the human person. This insistence is also an essential part of any process of transformation. By assigning blame and asking people to take responsibility, we are holding out hope that a better character and a better way of life can be attained, though the Christian would be quick to add that such hope depends on divine grace.

Original sin—specifically the idea of inherited sin—thus allows for a very nuanced account of human agency that fits lived experience well. When it comes to human evil, we both are and are not at fault. Ultimately, this complexity should lead to profound compassion, especially since we discover that we are all in this predicament together. The specifics may vary, but none of us escapes the misery of a flawed character, of desires or inclinations we despise but find we cannot get rid of.

But how is it that this condition is inherited, and why can we not get rid of it? Much of the Christian tradition has defined sin as distorted desire (pride or idolatry) and has closely associated it with biological drives for food or sex or physical security. As a result, it made sense, traditionally, to think of sin as transmitted biologically, through sexual reproduction. More recent generations of theologians, out of a reluctance to pathologize sexual desire and out of a greater awareness of human reproduction and biological inheritance, have hesitated to speak of sin's transmission in these ways. More and more, the shared condition of sin and its unavoidable transmission from one generation to the next have come to be understood as a feature of human sociality.[2] We are not individuals first and then people in community with others. We become the people we are through our complex web of culture and social relationships. We reproduce sin from one generation to the next through a destructive and warped social existence. Crucially, it is worth remembering from our study of human evolution that emerging scientific understandings of human sociality

2. Couenhoven, *Stricken by Sin*, 208–13; Joseph Ratzinger, *'In the Beginning . . .': A Catholic Understanding of the Story of Creation and the Fall* (Grand Rapids: Eerdmans, 1986), 72–74. It should be noted that this conception, while increasingly common, would have been regarded by earlier generations of Augustinian theologians, including Luther and Calvin, as Pelagian. While I believe the following discussion will address concerns about Pelagianism, this is an area where I do not follow the Reformers.

do not separate the cultural and biological. Our bodily existence is formed in distinct ways in and through our social environment. And lest one think, like Jean-Jacques Rousseau, that we can simply separate a young child from a corrupt society and thereby "fix" human nature, there is no surviving apart from human community, and there is no "pure" group of people with whom one could begin again.

There are several advantages to this way of thinking about the transmission of original sin. It is consistent with widely accepted scientific understandings of the human species. It corrects a distorted individualism that has, in the modern West, tended to ignore biblical language of communal sin and repentance. It helps make sense of Pauline language associating sin with "powers" and "authorities"—mysterious forces transcending human agency that have humanity in their grasp. And it helps explain sin as a shared condition that individuals cannot escape on their own. At the same time, one need not think that a social understanding of sin is somehow a superficial one. As we saw in our study of human evolution, the social niche forms the species holistically, even having an influence on the physical body and the wiring of the brain. Thus, all aspects of the human person, including natural or biological desires, are understood to be shaped by and captive to sin when persons exist in a social context that is captive to the power of sin. Because the person is made for dependence on God in interdependent human community, when humanity is alienated from God, people's relationships with one another are inevitably subject to a twisting that is tragically self-perpetuating.

At this point the reader may wonder why I am including a discussion of Sin 101 in a chapter on criminal justice. Sin and crime are not identical categories, but they are certainly related. On the surface it may seem reasonable to think of crime as a subset of sin: not all sins are written into the legal system of a particular society, but some kinds of sin are, and violating these laws is crime. The typical assumption is that criminal acts are the most socially destructive behaviors, and this is why society finds it important to regulate them. More careful reflection complicates this assumption, however. Some behaviors are criminal even though they have no inherent moral significance. Traffic regulations, for instance, often fall in this category. Other crimes might actually be virtuous behaviors that a society has prohibited. These crimes are not sinful, and in fact, it might be a sin to conform to such unjust laws. Still other laws might simply be tools of the state used to render certain groups of people "criminal." These ways in which crime and sin diverge are quite important in understanding the American criminal-justice system and will appear at various times throughout this chapter even though they are not the primary focus. In this chapter I primarily want to wrestle with the theoretical question of how human community should respond to the category of wrongdoing that *is* genuinely socially destructive. Many crimes, especially violent crimes, are also sinful because they cause serious harm to others or to the broader community. How should a community that is (whether it realizes this or not) rooted in gift respond to this type of crime?

Given the complex connection between sin and crime, it is reasonable to expect that Christian thinking about the former would have implications for the latter. One crucial point is the leveling effect of original sin. In public discussion of crime there is a common tendency to resort to terminology like "good guys" and "bad guys." The concept of original sin, however, does not allow for "good guys." Christian teaching does not allow people to put themselves in a category of those who have not acted destructively, who do not stand in need of forgiveness and transformation. Even acknowledging this, one might still be tempted to put crime in a special category of particularly bad action, but this distinction quickly falls apart. Not only are some crimes not particularly harmful, even if one would still say they are sins, but many lawful actions can be truly devastating. Compare, for example, a minor property theft with the emotional abuse of a spouse.

In addition to troubling the distinctions between "criminal" and "law-abiding citizen," the common condition of sin also means the same complex claims about agency and responsibility that apply to sin in general apply also to crimes that are sins. Of the person who commits a serious crime, Christian theology says, on the one hand, that this person is held captive by forces of evil that go beyond their control. This belief should invite compassion for the person in such an unfortunate state. On the other hand, the person who has committed this crime is also in some degree responsible and must be held accountable. Holding them accountable is a recognition of the dignity of the person and their agency. A Christian response to crime must not ignore evil as if it does not matter, as if the people involved, victims and perpetrators, do not matter. Finally, just as no person escapes the condition of sin, in Christian teaching no human being is without hope for redemption and restoration. This claim should push against any assumption that someone who has committed a crime is irreversibly entrenched in evil behavior.

In addition to these important implications of original sin for thinking about criminal justice, I want to address one frequent claim that is actually *not* a necessary conclusion of the doctrine. In the context of criminal justice, it is quite common to hear Christians say that because crime, like sin, is a "heart problem," the response to crime need not bother with other types of analysis into causes. The solution can only be conversion—what people need is Jesus. Now, I certainly do not want to suggest that people do not need Jesus! Those who experience the dehumanizing conditions of American prisons might especially need to hear a message of God's unconditional love in Christ. At the same time, the notion of inherited sin does not require one to choose between "spiritual" causes and other explanations for crime or, by extension, between spiritual and natural responses to it. Consider how we think about another facet of divine and human action, the creation of the human person. I can claim that God has created me and made me the unique person I am, and I can also tell a very specific story about how I came to be this person in my life narrative, including the influences of specific people and of broader cultural contexts. Similarly, I can use the language of original sin to describe my corrupt character while also telling a very specific story about my character flaws and how they came to be. I might even be especially sensitive to this in my parenting, as I hope to help my children avoid these same flaws. Doing so in no way suggests that I think my children can get by without God's forgiving and transforming grace in Christ.

If original sin were the only worthwhile explanation of crime, we would expect crime to be universal or at least evenly distributed. As we will soon see, however, this is not the case. Crime has a geography. We can recognize that many crimes are sinful and also investigate the specific conditions that seem to lead to concentrations of crime or, conversely, make crime less likely. In fact, the picture of the human person I have presented throughout this book provides important tools for doing so. If human beings are inherently interdependent, if we rely on the gifts of others to be our truest selves, to be whole, then understanding how we have failed one another can help us grasp how our characters have gone wrong. Understanding these patterns is all the more crucial for those who want to help bring about healing and redemption. If humans mediate the gifts of God to one another, as discussed in chapter 4, it should not be at all surprising that we are also to be involved, in very specific and targeted ways, in the grace of redemption. To say this is by no means to deny that the work of redemption is always, at the same time, Christ's.[3]

Crime and a Theology of Grace

As the previous point highlights, by focusing the theological analysis of this chapter on the category of sin we are not leaving behind the foundational

3. I have elsewhere developed a more specific account of how one might think about grace, and particularly the work of Christ and the Spirit, together with natural processes of formation. See Angela Carpenter, *Responsive Becoming: Moral Formation in Theological, Evolutionary, and Developmental Perspective* (London: T&T Clark, 2019).

principles of grace that are guiding our practical reflection on social ethics. The social explanation for original sin as a shared condition that passes from one generation to the next is consistent with human interdependence. That we receive our being as a gift and are thus made for giving and receiving in human community means that we cannot think about sin or crime strictly in terms of individual actions and individual responsibility. We are deeply enmeshed in this life together.

The universal destination of God's gifts of creation, which featured so prominently in our discussion of work and its relationship to the material goods needed to sustain life, may at first glance seem irrelevant for questions of crime and justice. On closer examination, however, we will find that crime is closely connected with material lack. Regular and systematic exclusion from the resources that allow for a legal participation in the common life of a society pressures people to access these goods by illegal means. This is not to say that all crime is a result of prior social injustice or oppression, nor does it excuse the profound harm that some crime causes. We cannot, however, allow a desire for nice and tidy determinations of blame and guilt to obscure such complexities.

In our study of the contemporary criminal-justice system, we will encounter sobering realities regarding the dehumanization of incarcerated persons. In this context it is crucial to remember our third principle from chapter 4: that human worth is given by God. Because human worth and acceptance by God does not arise from human action, it is not diminished by the reality of sin. A shocking claim of the Gospels is that Jesus most values those who are lost or discarded by society. Yet accountability for wrongdoing, whether criminal or not, is not ruled out by a recognition of human value. When carried out well and with wisdom, the insistence on accountability is actually an insistence on human worth—both the worth of victims and the worth of offenders.

Finally, the incarcerated person, like all persons, is made for the gift of fellowship with God and neighbor. The "jailhouse" conversion is often belittled, but a Christian ethic of grace cannot succumb to this cynicism. Any restoration of a person to fellowship with God is cause for rejoicing. In order to affirm this vocation consistently, however, a Christian ethic of grace must also care about the restoration of offenders to the broader community.

Two basic arguments will take shape in the remainder of this chapter. First, a social perspective on original sin suggests that the conditions that lead to a high occurrence of crime are themselves sinful—and that those whom society labels as "criminals" are also the victims of the sins of others. A response to criminal justice cannot ignore the conditions by which we reproduce fallenness in our fellow human beings, and an understanding of redemption cannot avoid taking responsibility for these conditions and seeking to change them. Second, an anthropology of grace, particularly one informed by God's reconciliation of sinful humanity in Christ, will resist any assumption that we can bring about temporal justice through punishment. I will present these arguments first by seeking to understand crime in the United States and the criminal-justice system and then by reflecting theologically on the assumptions and commitments that are embedded in current practice.

Crime in the Contemporary United States

The late twentieth-century American preoccupation with crime was not unwarranted. In the United States, violent crime, including murder, began to rise dramatically in the 1960s and continued to rise until the mid-1990s. At this point it began a decline that continued through the early 2000s.[4] Crime levels then stabilized until 2021, when the nation saw a rise during the COVID-19 pandemic. Although it is too soon to tell for certain, this rise appears to be temporary, as levels of violent crime in most areas declined in 2022 and again in 2023.[5]

Naturally, criminologists are eager to identify factors that contribute to the prevalence of crime in various contexts. Along with the ordinary difficulties in the social sciences of separating correlation from causality, researchers acknowledge that the subject itself is immensely complex. Causes and effects are bidirectional and woven together in vicious cycles of violence, poverty, social distrust, inadequate education, joblessness, family breakdown, and discrimination. Nevertheless, criminologists working in the US context have identified broad areas of consensus. One of the most commonly recognized factors is economic distress. Though scholars continue to debate whether absolute deprivation (poverty) or relative deprivation (inequality) is more important, virtually no one working in the field denies that crime is related to depressed economic circumstances.[6] This is not to say that poverty or inequality *necessarily*

4. Michael Tonry and David P. Farrington, "Punishment and Crime across Space and Time," *Crime and Justice* 33 (2005): 1–39.

5. David Lauter, "Killings in the U.S. Are Dropping at a Historic Rate. Will Anyone Notice?," *Los Angeles Times*, October 20, 2023, https://www.latimes.com/politics/newsletter/2023-10-20/killings-in-the-u-s-are-dropping-at-an-historic-rate-will-anyone-notice-essential-politics; Lindsay Whitehurst, "US Violent Crime Decreased in 2023, Continuing to Reverse Pandemic-Era Spike, FBI Data Shows," AP News, March 20, 2024, https://apnews.com/article/crime-fbi-violence-murder-8f47df4e8cf1917e6d8032e19dc1b4c9.

6. Ching-Chi Hsieh and M. D. Pugh, "Poverty, Income Inequality, and Violent Crime: A Meta-Analysis of Recent Aggregate Data Studies," *Criminal Justice Review* 18, no. 2 (1998): 182–202; Benoît De Courson and Daniel Nettle, "Why Do Inequality and Deprivation Produce High Crime and Low Trust?," *Scientific Reports* 11, no. 1 (2021): 1937.

leads to crime. Plenty of counterexamples can be marshaled to resist this sort of oversimplification.[7] But it is the case that those who commit crimes are overwhelmingly disadvantaged economically. A 2015 study by the Prison Policy Initiative found that 57 percent of incarcerated men had annual incomes less than $22,500 prior to incarceration. Only 22 percent had incomes greater than $37,000.[8] This data is consistent with estimates that 80 percent of criminal defendants cannot afford to hire an attorney.[9] Some theorists speculate that the absence of good jobs in a community or the lack of reasonable transportation to employment opportunities is a potential mediating factor.[10]

Another variable disproportionately associated with persons accused of crime is a history of trauma. In one large sample survey of incarcerated persons, over half of respondents reported having faced physical abuse as children. Ten percent of men and 47 percent of women also reported childhood sexual abuse. The numbers for traumatic experience more broadly are substantially higher, between 70 percent and 99 percent, depending on the study.[11] A third variable associated with crime is demographic: the ratio of young men to the broader population. This factor is particularly helpful in explaining the crime increase in the 1960s, an increase that occurred in other Western nations as well and that coincided with the coming-of-age of baby boomers.[12] Other factors frequently appearing in the literature include unemployment, education quality and quantity, and family stability.

One of the most important findings related to crime is that it has a geography. Crime, along with other metrics of disadvantage, is concentrated in certain areas and among certain communities. Sociologist Robert Sampson's extensive study of Chicago, for example, identified geographic "hot spots" of various metrics of compromised health, including a high prevalence of crime, that were durable over time.[13] For Sampson, the fact that seemingly

7. Barry Latzer, "Poverty and Violent Crime *Don't* Go Hand in Hand," *City Journal*, May 25, 2022.

8. Bernadette Rabuy and Daniel Kopf, "Prisons of Poverty: Uncovering the Pre-incarceration Incomes of the Imprisoned," Prison Policy Initiative, July 9, 2015, https://www.prisonpolicy.org /reports/income.html.

9. Richard A. Oppel Jr. and Jugal K. Patel, "One Lawyer, 194 Felony Cases, and No Time," *New York Times*, January 31, 2019.

10. William Julius Wilson, *When Work Disappears: The World of the New Urban Poor* (New York: Vintage Books, 1997).

11. Nancy Wolff et al., "Trauma Exposure and Posttraumatic Stress Disorder among Incarcerated Men," *Journal of Urban Health* 91, no. 4 (2014): 707–19; Carrie A. Pettus, "Trauma and Prospects for Reentry," *Annual Review of Criminology* 6 (2023): 423–46.

12. Theodore N. Ferdinand, "Demographic Shifts and Criminality: An Inquiry," *British Journal of Criminology* 10, no. 2 (April 1970): 169–75.

13. Robert J. Sampson, *Great American City: Chicago and the Enduring Neighborhood Effect* (Chicago: University of Chicago Press, 2012).

unrelated things like low birth weight correlated strongly with high levels of violence in a neighborhood suggests that neighborhoods can be sources of disadvantage broadly conceived, where many complexly interwoven factors combine to entrench disadvantage across time, even with high levels of mobility among the neighborhoods' inhabitants. These findings are consistent with Raj Chetty's work on child development, which suggests that the best way to improve a child's health outcomes is relocation to a better neighborhood.[14] One important implication of Sampson's research is the complexity of crime. It does not lend itself to simple approaches to prevention, whether conservative (increase marriage rates) or progressive (provide a basic income). Instead, it suggests a need for broad interventions targeting multiple sets of issues simultaneously.

Given the theological identification of interdependence as constitutive of human personhood, it makes sense that one's neighborhood would exert this kind of influence. In their recent study of disadvantaged places, poverty researchers Kathryn Edin, Luke Shaefer, and Timothy Nelson identified violence as one of the distinguishing features of the most disadvantaged places in the country. Strikingly, these places were largely rural. While rural areas have fewer people and thus fewer occurrences of violence than other areas do, the per capita rates of violence in disadvantaged rural places, especially in Appalachia and the Cotton Belt, are among the highest in the nation. In their efforts to identify why some places experienced heightened levels of violence, they found a few strong predictors. First, places of high violence were those that had a *history* of violence, particularly a history in which violence was used to enforce existing power structures. Violence begets violence. Second, high-violence places were those with the lowest intergenerational mobility.[15] Edin, Shaefer, and Nelson saw these factors as interrelated. They theorized that lack of opportunity had the potential to spark violence—that the absence of hope for something better left young people especially vulnerable to patterns of violence. They also theorized that barriers to opportunity were themselves a legacy of longstanding exploitation of particular populations. In other words, areas trapped in generational cycles of violence do not occur arbitrarily. According to Edin and her colleagues, they are made.

In his book *The Color of Law*, Richard Rothstein provides a historical account of the creation of some of these neighborhoods, which came about through legalized race-based housing discrimination at national, state, and

14. Raj Chetty and Nathaniel Hendren, "The Effects of Neighborhoods on Intergenerational Mobility I: Childhood Exposure Effects," *Quarterly Journal of Economics* 133, no. 3 (2018): 1107–62.
15. Kathryn Edin, H. Luke Shaefer, and Timothy J. Nelson, *The Injustice of Place: Uncovering the Legacy of Poverty in America* (New York: Mariner Books, 2023), 118.

local levels of government.[16] Beginning in the early twentieth century, the federal government responded to a housing crisis by constructing housing that either excluded black families or segregated them into units of poorer quality.[17] After World War II, the government-backed financing that made home ownership possible for the middle class also discriminated against black families by refusing to approve loans in neighborhoods with black people. Further, the federal government financed the building of new subdivisions on the condition that the homes be sold only to white families. These methods of legal segregation were then sustained by racial sales clauses in neighborhood associations that prevented the subsequent sale of white homes to black buyers.[18] Since black families could not qualify for the government-backed mortgage loans, the ones who did manage to purchase a house in a mixed or black neighborhood had to pay much higher interest rates and accept terms that did not allow them to accrue equity and threatened eviction should they miss a single payment. Throughout this period of racial segregation, many churches and other civic institutions acted to maintain segregation and protect the interests of white homeowners. Multiple churches financed legal battles to prevent black families from purchasing homes in white neighborhoods.[19] It is hardly surprising, especially in view of the education and employment discrimination that black Americans experienced during these same decades, that black neighborhoods deteriorated further and were more susceptible to crime.[20] By the time there were legal remedies for housing discrimination, most black Americans had fallen further behind white America economically and were effectively priced out of safe and desirable housing.

What should we make of this multigenerational history of racist housing policies that established communities that experience profound disadvantage, communities that are much more susceptible to cycles of violence and crime? As I have argued throughout this book, human beings are meant to live by the gifts of others, depending in a deep and all-encompassing way on the gifts of divine love and giving and receiving in community with others. No one is totally self-sufficient, nor can people earn all that they receive before

16. Richard Rothstein, *The Color of Law: A Forgotten History of How Our Government Segregated America* (New York: Liveright, 2017).

17. Rothstein, *Color of Law*, 22.

18. Rothstein, *Color of Law*, 70.

19. Rothstein, *Color of Law*, 102–5.

20. On the specific connection between segregation and homicide rates, see Anita Knopov et al., "The Role of Racial Residential Segregation in Black-White Disparities in Firearm Homicide at the State Level in the United States, 1991–2015," *Journal of the National Medical Association* 111, no. 1 (February 2019): 62–75.

receiving it. The history of US housing provides a striking demonstration of this point. White Americans throughout the twentieth century were housed through government programs and interventions that were, properly speaking, gifts. Massive investment of federal money went into the creation of housing for middle-class white America. These gifts then enabled many who received them to rise further in their standard of living. Black Americans were systematically and legally excluded from these gifts. Due to the pervasive sin of racism, they were denied the support that white Americans received. The result was the creation of geographic communities of disadvantage that were prone to a host of social ills and that became entrenched over a period of generations.

This tragic history is a profound illustration of original sin. It is the story of how sin is reproduced through dense networks of interconnected humanity. It is a story of how people are born into a warped world that proceeds to warp them, trapping them in patterns of fear, suspicion, selfishness, and anger—in other words, directing them into acts that destroy the self and others. One might recall here that Pauline scholar John Barclay interprets Paul's language of sin and "the flesh" as external forces that commandeer or bind the person, forces from which the person must be liberated by the Spirit.[21] When one looks at crime in America and sees only concentrations of violent crime in particular neighborhoods as "the problem" instead of seeing the legacy of sin that has created these circumstances, one is working with a partial and distorted picture. And when this person doing the seeing is someone who has benefited from exploitation, what this person is unlikely to see is their own entanglement in sin and need for repentance and the liberating work of the Spirit.

While I have focused on the sin of racism and the exploitation of black Americans, I should emphasize that economic exploitation among white Americans is also associated with geographically higher crime rates, as Kathryn Edin and colleagues discuss with respect to the Appalachian communities in their study. While black Americans are disproportionately represented in the prison population, the most recent data indicates that the overall number of incarcerated white Americans is slightly higher than the number of incarcerated black Americans.[22] Crime is by no means a problem restricted to black neighborhoods, and many sins, in addition to racism, reproduce conditions in which crime flourishes.

---

21. John Barclay, *Paul and the Gift* (Grand Rapids: Eerdmans, 2015), 425–28, 508.

22. Brennan Klein et al., "COVID-19 Amplified Racial Disparities in the US Criminal Legal System," *Nature* 617 (2023): 344–50.

American Responses to Crime

As is now widely recognized, policymakers in the United States chose to respond to crime largely through a punitive approach instead of seeking to identify and ameliorate its causes. According to the Sentencing Project, in 1972 the total incarcerated population was 196,092. In 2009, at its zenith, the number of incarcerated persons had risen to 1,553,570. Despite the decline in crime, by 2020 that number had declined only to 1,182,170.[23] During this same period other Western nations also experienced rises in crime, but they generally did not respond with increased incarceration. Not only does the United States incarcerate persons at a higher rate than any other country, but among developed nations with similar crime rates, no one even comes close. The United States incarcerates at a rate of 664 per 100,000, and the United Kingdom at a rate of 129. The lowest rate in an American state, Massachusetts, is higher than that of South Africa (275 versus 248 per 100,000).[24] The role of race in these numbers is particularly troubling. According to the most recent data, black Americans are imprisoned at almost five times the rate of white Americans, and this is a number that represents a substantial decline in the racial disparity.[25] Given that many countries with similar crime rates have far lower rates of incarceration, the United States's overall high incarceration numbers cannot be attributed to high crime. Instead, they indicate that the nation has chosen to respond to crime with high incarceration. Why did the United States choose this particular path?

According to most analysts, the shift to mass incarceration arose from the relationship between public opinion and the structure of criminal justice. Prior to the rise in crime in the 1960s, the dominant theoretical approach to criminal justice in the United States was rehabilitation: the goal in responding to crime was to rehabilitate offenders so that they would be restored to society. As crime rose in the 1960s, public opinion and criminal-justice policy began to shift. Americans were increasingly concerned about urban crime, particularly in the midst of the broader unrest of the civil-rights era and race-related riots in multiple cities. Politicians, experiencing pressure from their constituents to act on crime, responded to these concerns by shifting the overall approach

23. "Prison Population over Time," Sentencing Project, https://www.sentencingproject.org/re search/.

24. "States of Incarceration: The Global Context 2021," Prison Policy Initiative, September 2021, https://www.prisonpolicy.org/global/2021.html.

25. This disparity has actually decreased over the past two decades. Ashley Nellis, "The Color of Justice: Racial and Ethnic Disparity in State Prisons," Sentencing Project, October 13, 2021, https:// www.sentencingproject.org/reports/the-color-of-justice-racial-and-ethnic-disparity-in-state-prisons -the-sentencing-project/.

from one of rehabilitation to one of punishment and deterrence. During the mass expansion of the criminal-justice system, both conservative and liberal politicians participated in this shift and were eager to pass "tough on crime" legislation. Crucially, it was not just those writing the laws who felt political pressure to adopt a punitive approach. Judges and prosecutors were also often elected to office. Prosecutors were especially important, since they had wide latitude in deciding whether to charge a person for a crime and what crime to charge them with.[26] This dynamic created a feedback loop in which public fear of crime affected those running for office, who then subsequently used public fear of crime, and their own tough-on-crime actions in office, to distinguish themselves from their political competitors.

This attention to public opinion and political dynamics constitutes a departure from what has become the standard narrative regarding causes of mass incarceration. In the standard version, many commentators have focused on the war on drugs and incarceration for nonviolent offenses as factors driving up incarceration. While these factors are important, we must acknowledge that even after setting aside all persons incarcerated for drug convictions and nonviolent offenses, the United States would still have incarceration levels that are unseen in other countries.[27] Furthermore, while the system disproportionately incarcerates black Americans by a wide margin, mass incarceration would still exist if all demographic groups were incarcerated at the current level of white Americans.[28] Mass incarceration is a complex phenomenon driven by multiple factors, including racism, the war on drugs, fear of crime, and a system with very little buffer between public pressure and policy choices.

As incarceration rates increased in the twentieth century, Christians, and evangelical Christians in particular, played an important role in shaping the public discourse and calling for harsh punitive measures. Historian Aaron Griffith notes that a mid-twentieth-century evangelical approach to crime that focused on conversion and personal transformation gradually shifted in the 1960s, as crime was rising, to an emphasis on upholding the law and punishing lawbreakers.[29] Prior to the rise in crime, Christians had, for decades, already been worried that an increasing secularism in the broader society would lead

26. On the overall importance of prosecutors in the shift to mass incarceration, see John F. Pfaff, *Locked In: The True Causes of Mass Incarceration and How to Achieve Real Reform* (New York: Basic Books, 2017).

27. Pfaff, *Locked In*, 11.

28. Marie Gottschalk, *Caught: The Prison State and the Lockdown of American Politics* (Princeton: Princeton University Press, 2015), 4.

29. Aaron Griffith, *God's Law and Order: The Politics of Punishment in Evangelical America* (Cambridge, MA: Harvard University Press, 2020).

to rising crime. By the 1960s, when the rise in crime was a reality, "more law
and order, not the spiritual redemption of criminals, became the primary
evangelical answer to lawlessness."[30] This approach was evident in editorials
and letters to the editor in popular Christian publications like *Christianity
Today*. The magazine published an op-ed on youth crime by none other than
J. Edgar Hoover.[31] Another *Christianity Today* opinion piece even suggested
that the use of capital punishment for adultery and pornography might be
wise in the current depraved conditions.[32]

These punitive approaches stood in sharp contrast to the Lyndon B. John-
son administration's Commission on Law Enforcement and Administration
of Justice (known as the Katzenbach Commission), which located the rise
of crime in the broader failure of society and recommended a holistic approach: improving conditions of high-crime neighborhoods and providing
better education and jobs.[33] The following year the Kerner report similarly
pointed to deep social inequality and racism in its analysis of civil unrest and
suggested heavy financial investment directed toward the undoing of housing
segregation. Evangelicals, however, largely rejected this sort of analysis. By
the time the Moral Majority rose to prominence in the 1980s, the punitive
approach to crime among evangelicals was part of a broader narrative about
secularization, social decline, and the need for a return to law and order and
family values.

In light of the discussion earlier in this chapter on original sin and the
need for conversion instead of other forms of social action to combat crime,
it is worth noting here that both the evangelical approach and the Katzenbach recommendations presumed that crime could be reduced by public
and social action. The tough-on-crime response, which was subsequently
combined with a call for renewed family values, assumed that a combination of punishment for crime and support for family values could reduce
crime. These approaches operate on a different logic than one that says only
conversion can heal the heart and turn a person away from sin. The choice
for evangelicals in this era was not between spiritual conversion and social
action. It was between an individualistic logic that attributed crime solely to
individual choice and a more communal outlook that allowed for broader
social and structural influence.

30. Griffith, *God's Law and Order*, 101.
31. J. Edgar Hoover, "The Challenge of the Future," *Christianity Today*, May 26, 1958, in Griffith,
God's Law and Order, 106.
32. Gordon Clark, "Capital Punishment and the Bible," *Christianity Today*, February 1, 1960, in
Griffith, *God's Law and Order*, 111.
33. Griffith, *God's Law and Order*, 118.

Human Dignity in the Criminal-Justice System

While the primary policy response to crime was one of mass incarceration, it was not simply the number of prisoners that characterized the "toughness" of the approach. At every stage the system was harsh for those enmeshed within it, often in ways that denied the basic dignity of those accused or convicted of crimes. Policing practices, the first point of contact with the legal system, became increasingly intrusive, violent, and even militaristic. In *Rise of the Warrior Cop*, journalist Radley Balko portrays the war on drugs as not merely a symbolic war but, rather, a campaign that increasingly employed military equipment, personnel, training, and tactics, especially in the rise of SWAT teams across the country.[34] One of the defining features of this trend was the use of SWAT raids, where teams of heavily armed police would enter homes without warning, deploy flash grenades, violently detain residents, and search homes for drugs or drug paraphernalia. Raids would be conducted on the basis of little evidence, sometimes only an anonymous tip, and judges regularly rubber-stamped warrants without scrutiny. Unsurprisingly, residents often responded violently, not realizing that the individuals entering their home were police. Balko recounts instance after instance of civilian and police casualties. The story of the proliferation of SWAT teams, even in small-town America, is told in numbers. By 1995, 77 percent of all US cities with a population greater than twenty-five thousand had a SWAT team.[35] In 1980 the country saw three thousand paramilitary raids; in 2005 that number had risen to forty-five thousand.[36]

SWAT raids are only one aspect of an approach to policing that has relied heavily on violence toward citizens suspected of crime. From "stop and frisk" practices, to traffic stops resulting in the death of unarmed people, to the abuse of suspects being detained and arrested, to the use of excessive force on nonviolent protesters, the methods of policing seem to assume that any suspicion of crime—even based on the flimsiest pretext—justifies an intrusive or violent response. To be clear, this is both a problem of racial prejudice and a problem of police violence. People of color, especially black Americans, are disproportionately victims of these tactics, but the tactics themselves, even if they were deployed in a racially neutral manner, are cause for concern. The fear of crime is such that police have been empowered to use extreme methods regardless of the collateral damage. And when something goes wrong, as it so

---

34. Radley Balko, *Rise of the Warrior Cop: The Militarization of America's Police Forces* (New York: PublicAffairs, 2014).

35. Balko, *Rise of the Warrior Cop*, 207.

36. Balko, *Rise of the Warrior Cop*, 237.

often does, police are usually cleared of wrongdoing and the tactics determined to have been appropriate. Recent high-profile instances of these tactics, such as the 2020 killings of George Floyd and Breonna Taylor, have begun to dampen public support for a militarized police force, but the problems persist.

Treatment of those suspected or accused of crime remains problematic at the stage of arrest and prosecution. While the defendant in American jurisprudence is technically "innocent until proven guilty," over 60 percent of those arrested remain in local jails, not because they are a perceived flight risk or a danger to the public but simply because they are unable to afford bail.[37] These individuals, whose freedom is restricted without due process, are unable, while incarcerated, to advocate for the best outcome to their case. Quite the contrary—the threat of a lengthy pretrial confinement is simply another piece of leverage that prosecutors can use against them. Prosecutors are also able to take advantage of the extreme sentencing guidelines enacted in the tough-on-crime legislation from the 1980s and 1990s.[38] In the current system, very few criminal defendants actually go to trial. Rather, the threat of extremely long sentences is used to pressure them into plea bargains. Because little money, relative to that spent on prosecution, is dedicated to public defense, most defendants spend only a miniscule amount of time with an extremely overworked public defender.[39] It is quite easy to imagine that innocent defendants look at the lack of resources for defense and the risk of a brutally long sentence and choose to plead guilty to a lesser charge. Given the volume of people moving through the justice system and the slow pace of trials, the system would be unsustainable without recourse to this sort of plea arrangement. As one human-rights activist puts it, "It is better to be rich and guilty than poor and innocent" in the current legal system.[40]

As the number of prisoners has dramatically increased in the last half century, so has the need to house them and provide for basic needs. Unsurprisingly, this rapid shift has presented numerous challenges and has been accompanied by worsening conditions for incarcerated persons. The norm for prisons and jails at federal, state, and local levels has been dangerous overcrowding. Already by 1992, well before the apex of the prison population, forty state prison systems were under legal orders to reduce overcrowding, and the population of federal prisons was at 165 percent.[41] Overcrowding is not merely an inconvenience.

37. The US Commission on Civil Rights, "The Civil Rights Implications of Cash Bail," January 20, 2022, https://www.usccr.gov/reports/2021/civil-rights-implications-cash-bail.
38. For a description of the dynamics of prosecutorial decision making, see Pfaff, *Locked In*, 127–59.
39. Pfaff, *Locked In*, 137.
40. Stephen Bright of the Southern Center for Human Rights, quoted in Gottschalk, *Caught*, 9.
41. Craig Haney, "Riding the Punishment Wave: On the Origins of Our Devolving Standards of Decency," *Hastings Women's Law Journal* 9, no. 1 (1998): 29.

It radically alters the conditions in an institution, particularly the degree of safety inmates feel and the corresponding level of conflict and violence. Violence and trauma within prisons are common, as the campaign to eliminate prison rape has illustrated.[42]

The increasing volume of prisoners, and the ensuing financial burden, has led to other changes in the quality of life inside these institutions. As criminal-justice philosophy shifted from rehabilitation to deterrence, many states began to cut back on programs or services that were intended to rehabilitate offenders. These shifts were encouraged by federal funding. The 1994 Violent Crime Control and Law Enforcement Act excluded persons in federal or state prisons from receiving Pell Grant funding, leading to a decline from 350 to 8 programs offering a college degree.[43] This period also saw cuts for other educational programming and for addiction treatment and job training.[44] States searched for cost savings at the level of basic provisions—food, medical care, and sanitation supplies. Institutions sought to regain money from the people they housed by charging hefty amounts for phone calls or video calls and even charging room-and-board fees that would follow inmates as debt after they were released.[45] The failure to meet basic needs has become the norm in many US prisons.

The most outrageous aspect of prison conditions, however, is the regular degradation of incarcerated persons that goes beyond routine policies—like institutional clothing, restricted personal possessions, and intrusive body-cavity searches—to include neglect and abuse. During the extreme heat waves that hit Texas in the summer of 2023, more than forty-one incarcerated persons died of heart-related or undetermined causes in a state where the majority of penal institutions have no air conditioning.[46] Texas is hardly alone in failing to attend to the basic health needs of its prison occupants. From the infamous

42. Nneka Jones Tapia, "Holistic Safety at the Center of Incarceration," in *Parsimony and Other Radical Ideas about Justice*, ed. Jeremy Travis and Bruce Western (New York: New Press, 2023), 182.

43. Ben Austen, *Correction: Parole, Prison, and the Possibility of Change* (New York: Flatiron Books, 2023), 17. The number of college programs has since increased, and federal legislation has since restored access to Pell Grants, though implementation is slow. See Sara Weissman, "Reinstating Pell Grants in Prisons Moves Slowly After 26-Year Ban," Inside Higher Ed, November 17, 2023, https://www.insidehighered.com/news/governance/state-oversight/2023/11/17/after-26-year-ban-reinstating-pell-prisons-moves-slowly.

44. Craig Haney, "Counting Casualties in the War on Prisoners," *University of San Francisco Law Review* 43, no. 1 (2008): 87–138.

45. Lauren-Brooke Eisen, "America's Dystopian Incarceration System of Pay to Stay behind Bars," Brennan Center, April 19, 2023, https://www.brennancenter.org/our-work/analysis-opinion/americas-dystopian-incarceration-system-pay-stay-behind-bars.

46. Jodie McCullough, "As the Death Toll in Stifling Texas Prisons Climbs, Congressional Democrats Ask for Investigation," *Texas Tribune*, August 21, 2023, https://www.texastribune.org/2023/08/21/texas-prison-heat-deaths.

"tent cities" of Sheriff Joe Arpaio in Arizona to a New York jail lacking in heat and electricity, such neglect is all too common.[47] A staff shortage in Waupun, Wisconsin, has led to a months-long lockdown where inmates have been kept in their cells for nearly twenty-four hours a day since March 2023 (as of the time of writing it has been going on for eighth months, during which time three prisoners have died).[48]

Mistreatment and degradation are not limited to neglect but also include episodes of intentional abuse. The scholarly and journalistic literature on this phenomenon is sadly robust, but I will limit the discussion here to a few incidents.[49] A 2020 investigation by the Marshall Project of abuse in New York prisons identified 290 cases between 2010 and 2020 in which the state attempted to fire correctional officers for involvement in the abuse of inmates. They also reported over 160 documented cases of lawsuits against the state for severe injuries of inmates, culminating in $18.5 million in settlement costs. Investigators noted that these numbers were likely underrepresenting the incidents of abuse, since many prisoners were reluctant to file reports of abuse out of fear of retaliation.[50] In his 2021 study of "ethically troubling" jobs, journalist Eyal Press documents the murder of Darren Rainey, an inmate convicted of cocaine possession who was also diagnosed with schizophrenia. After defecating in his cell in the Dade Correctional Institute in Florida City, Florida, Rainey was placed in a shower and subjected to a steady stream of 180-degree water. He suffered burns on 90 percent of his body and was pronounced dead shortly thereafter.[51] Rainey's murder is part of a broader pattern of mistreatment of mentally ill inmates in US prisons. Human Rights Watch found excessive measures against mentally ill persons to be routine, including the use of chemical sprays and stun guns and the practice of solitary confinement.[52]

47. Haney, "Riding the Punishment Wave," 32; Annie Correal and Joseph Goldstein, "It's Cold as Hell: Inside a Brooklyn Jail's Weeklong Collapse," *New York Times*, February 9, 2019, https://www.nytimes.com/2019/02/09/nyregion/brooklyn-jail-no-heat-inmates.html.

48. Drake Bentley, "Here's What You Need to Know about the Waupun Prison Lockdown, Now in Its Eighth Month," *Milwaukee Journal Sentinel*, November 2, 2023.

49. Graham Rayman and Reuven Blau, *Rikers: An Oral History* (New York: Random House, 2023); Shane Bauer, *American Prison: A Reporter's Undercover Journey into the Business of Punishment* (New York: Penguin Books, 2018); Nell Bernstein, *Burning Down the House: The End of Juvenile Prison* (New York: New Press, 2014); Alisa Roth, *Insane: America's Criminal Treatment of Mental Illness* (New York: Basic Books, 2018); Eyal Press, *Dirty Work: Essential Jobs and the Hidden Toll of Inequality in America* (New York: Farrar, Straus & Giroux, 2021).

50. Alysia Santo, Joseph Neff, and Tom Meagher, "Guards Brutally Beat Prisoners and Lied about It. They Weren't Fired," *New York Times*, May 19, 2023, updated May 25, 2023, https://www.nytimes.com/2023/05/19/nyregion/ny-prison-guards-brutality-fired.html.

51. Press, *Dirty Work*, 26–30.

52. Press, *Dirty Work*, 31.

It should be noted that in discussing these incidents the point is not to vilify correctional officers. The nature of their job includes constant stress. They are instructed to enforce order in overcrowded and often understaffed prisons and told that their charges are inherently dangerous. It should come as no surprise that these circumstances create an environment that encourages violence and desensitizes officers to the use of force and to the humanity of inmates.[53] Their job requires levels of vigilance that cultivate universal suspicion of incarcerated persons at best and universal demonization at worst. Corrections officers often experience trauma in their job, and they have a shockingly low life expectancy relative to the general population. These jobs are low status and often low wage, the kind of necessary "dirty work" that middle- and upper-class Americans rely on but largely prefer not to think about. The incidents of abuse that I relay here should be read as an indictment of a system of human value that dehumanizes incarcerated persons and correctional officers alike. As Craig Haney has noted, the shift in objectives from rehabilitation to deterrence and punishment has normalized the mistreatment of incarcerated persons: prison is supposed to be painful, so there is little incentive to sort through what kinds of inflicted pain go beyond the pale.[54]

I could go on. The scholarly and journalistic literature detailing the evils of mass incarceration is immense, and I have not even treated the obstacles that formerly incarcerated persons face on reentering society, where they continue to be excluded from many forms of employment, housing, and civic participation and are often at risk of returning to prison for minor parole infractions. Such practices presume that the offense of crime should be a permanent marker and forever shape the way a person experiences belonging in the broader society. Obviously, this system has negative effects on incarcerated persons. Those who enter a prison without exposure to trauma and violence will certainly leave with such exposure. Furthermore, the social costs of prisons extend beyond offenders and correctional officers and include families and communities who have lost so many young people, especially black men, in the prime of life. Children of offenders are especially victimized by this system.[55] The resources that have gone to constructing, staffing, and running prisons could also be put to far better use. In considering these costs it must also be noted that crime rates have declined and that they have done so in the United States more than in peer nations that have not responded with higher incarceration. According

53. Craig Haney, "A Culture of Harm: Taming the Dynamics of Cruelty in Supermax Prisons," *Criminal Justice and Behavior* 35, no. 8 (August 2008): 956–84.

54. Haney, "Counting Casualties," 100–101.

55. For a thorough discussion, see James Logan, *Good Punishment? Christian Moral Practice and U.S. Imprisonment* (Grand Rapids: Eerdmans, 2008), 65–99.

to most experts, even those who are critics of the current system, this decline is at least partially due to mass incarceration.[56] But was it worth this enormous toll? And were there no better options that could also have reduced crime?

Grace and Responding to Crime

The current system of mass incarceration is a gaping wound on contemporary American society. As we turn to a theological analysis, there are a few points from the foregoing description that we should keep in mind. First, the current system overwhelmingly penalizes those who are already disadvantaged by society: the incarcerated are almost universally poor and victims of prior abuse or trauma, and minority populations are disproportionately represented. Second, it is a system that denies the inherent worth of people at every stage of their involvement. Finally, this loss of dignity and associated mistreatment is understood to be in some sense deserved or merited. The degradation of the person is accepted because it is thought to be directed toward the objective of justice. In the following reflection, which is based on a theology of grace, particularly one rooted in original sin and redemption through Christ's death and resurrection, some practical conclusions will strike the reader as fairly obvious and expected, and others will potentially be more controversial.

Universal Sin, Universal Need for Grace

As discussed at the beginning of the chapter, the common Christian belief in the West is that all people are subject to a condition of sinfulness that they did not personally create (though all are involved in reproducing it) and for which they are blameworthy and responsible. What, then, do the shared condition of sinfulness and the shared need for grace mean in the current context of mass incarceration? I indicated at the beginning of the chapter that they encourage compassion for the person who has committed a crime. Now that we have observed the extent to which this system intentionally withholds compassion, this point bears repeating. Most incarcerated persons were themselves wounded long before they wounded others. Without excusing violent or destructive actions, we can recognize that those who commit them are, like everyone, at the mercy of inclinations and habits they did not choose for themselves and can-

---

56. Patrick Sharkey, *Uneasy Peace: The Great Crime Decline, the Renewal of City Life, and the Next War on Violence* (New York: Norton, 2018), 49. Sharkey notes that the reduction in crime is most likely due to incapacitation.

not eradicate. At the very least, such compassion should disrupt and moderate Christian calls for harsh responses to crime.

The doctrine of original sin also encourages us to look at the specifics of this wounding: What are the particular ways that sin is being reproduced in the contemporary context such that violence proliferates? I am not claiming that in so doing we can eliminate original sin. But understanding something of the specific ways we participate in it and reproduce the conditions of sin can give us insight into our particular need for grace and the actions that will promote healing. I have suggested, for instance, that we reproduce sin when we withhold the gifts that others need in their interdependence with us: the unconditional love that children need in order to develop their agency, access to basic provisions and services or the means to secure them, education that prepares people to contribute to the good of society, inclusion in the cultural and civic life of the community, and so on. How should we respond, not to the sin of crime but to the sin that leads to crime? We have seen in this chapter that sustained housing-segregation policies created neighborhoods of disadvantage that are susceptible to violence. How should Christians today respond to the legacy of racism, much of it perpetrated by ancestors who are no longer with us but from whom many white Christians continue to benefit?

Acknowledging sin can be difficult and painful. In chapter 3 we saw the extreme lengths to which humans will often go to avoid recognizing anything about the self that might be seen as an imperfection. We lie to ourselves. We focus on the flaws of others. We think about the good things we have done and forget the bad. These strategies might keep us from experiencing the negative effects of low self-esteem, but they do not do much to heal us or heal the damage we have caused. The Christian message of repentance and forgiveness of sins in Jesus offers a more complex way of configuring the self and coming to grips with sin. From a Christian perspective, the self who is the perpetrator of sin must be seen, acknowledged, and dealt with. But the Christian good news is that this sinful self remains of immense value to God and is loved by God. Jesus's parables about lost things—the shepherd going after lost sheep (Luke 15:3–7), the woman searching for the lost coin (Luke 15:8–10), and, of course, the prodigal son (Luke 15:11–32)—all point to this reality. Knowing that people are loved in the midst of sin and that Jesus is ready to forgive and welcome the sinner back into fellowship with God should give individuals the courage to honestly examine themselves and acknowledge sin. Moreover, the presence of the Spirit of Jesus with each one of us creates the possibility of a new self, a self who is becoming like Jesus. While we cannot simply undo the legacy of racism, we can and should imagine steps we might take as we walk in the Spirit.

One of the most important is educating our children about this legacy of sin and the ways we are still enmeshed in it. As Richard Rothstein points out, most public-school history textbooks say very little about the legal discriminatory practices that created segregated neighborhoods characterized by high crime.[57] In today's political climate, in which many oppose the teaching of the history of racism, even this tiny amount of instruction is controversial. Concerned parents and politicians worry that learning about this history will make white children feel guilty and bad about themselves. From a secular perspective, one could see how these concerns might arise. If one only has the categories of "good" and "evil" to assign to people, learning about how one has benefited from a history of oppression can indeed threaten one's identity. Christians, however, have the advantage of more complex categories that can help their children grapple with the realities of evil and their relationship to this evil. We have a theology of sin and grace. Given these theological resources, it is all the more lamentable and painful that, in many cases, Christians are among those who are opposed to the teaching of this history and who feel threatened by the exposure of the truth.

When he first encountered Jesus, the tax collector Zacchaeus did not simply acknowledge his sin; he volunteered to make restitution for the exploitation he had engaged in as a tax collector. This restitution was not just the initial amount overcharged but was four times that amount (Luke 19:8). The text does not tell us why Zacchaeus chose to pay so much, but I find the amount suggestive, because exploitation of other people can cause ripple effects of destruction far beyond the initial harm. In the contemporary US context, the harm caused by generations of housing segregation has caused ripple effects, including poor education, lost equity, joblessness, and involvement, both as a victim and as a perpetrator, in violent crime. Recent research, however, also indicates that investing in these neighborhoods can help ameliorate conditions associated with high crime.[58] Patrick Sharkey, one of the foremost criminologists studying the great crime decline of the late 1990s and early 2000s, has concluded that while higher incarceration did contribute to reduced crime, so too did the work and investment of many civic organizations in high-crime communities.[59] One way to continue this work is simply to support these organizations which are already present and working with deep knowledge of their specific contexts and challenges.

While personal choices to invest in communities can contribute to their revitalization, undoing housing segregation and the harm it has caused is not

57. Rothstein, *Color of Law*, 199.

58. Hanna Love, "Want to Reduce Violence? Invest in Place," Brookings, November 16, 2021, https://www.brookings.edu/articles/want-to-reduce-violence-invest-in-place/.

59. Sharkey, *Uneasy Peace*, 50–60.

likely to happen through individual action alone. It will require systemic change. But individuals can and must support this change to make it politically feasible. One logical place to start is by undoing zoning restrictions that make it impossible for middle- and low-income families to live in desirable neighborhoods. Other steps might include changing the mortgage-interest tax deduction to incentivize neighborhood integration by income.[60] More radically, and in the interest of greater justice, policies of redistribution that disproportionately benefit black families could help restore some of the lost wealth that these families have not been able to build. Which specific policies will best help restore neighborhoods devastated by crime is a matter for public debate. Whether we as a society take steps to restore justice to these communities should not be.

What I am arguing here is that the doctrine of original sin should instruct us that, in responding to crime, we must think bigger than the individual. We must resist the temptation to divide people into the categories of "good guys" and "bad guys." Our theology tells us that we are all good guys *and* bad guys: we are created good and fallen. We should not be surprised to find that our own sins reverberate outward and help create conditions for sinfulness in others. Responding to crime under the conditions of original sin means attending to and repenting of the specific ways each of us contributes to the conditions where crime proliferates.

Human Worth as a Gift

In addition to addressing the ways that those who have not committed crimes are still implicated in its proliferation, a theology of grace must stand in staunch opposition to the degradation of humanity in the current criminal-justice system. In 2004, when the world was outraged to learn the details of how the US military had conducted torture in Abu Ghraib prison, a number of commentators observed that similar treatment was a regular feature of American prisons.[61] I suspect the difficulty is not that most Americans consciously believe that incarcerated persons deserve to be stripped of their dignity and treated inhumanely. Rather, the problem is that we just do not care enough to be outraged. On a deeper level we have bought into the broader cultural message that worth as a human being is derived from a person's actions, and we assign lesser value accordingly—to low-wage workers, to mentally ill or disabled persons, and certainly to those convicted of crimes. It does not

60. Rothstein, *Color of Law*, 204–11.
61. Bob Herbert, "America's Abu Ghraibs," *New York Times*, May 31, 2004, https://www.nytimes.com/2004/05/31/opinion/america-s-abu-ghraibs.html?searchResultPosition=3.

help that conditions in US prisons are largely hidden from view, except to those who go looking for information. Most Christians would agree that sin does not erase the God-given value of a person. Indeed, the heart of Christian theology, God's action to become human and suffer and die in order to rescue humanity, contradicts any such assumption. We know this. But we are much more comfortable not paying attention. We would rather not know how many persons died in Texas prisons in last summer's extreme heat. We prefer not to think about the abuse and violence endemic in prisons.

When Rich Ray, a former co-director of the Hope-Western Prison Education Program, comes to talk to my classes about the joint effort of Hope College and Western Seminary to provide a liberal-arts education to inmates at Muskegon Correctional Facility, he goes to great lengths to impress upon students the humanity and worth of incarcerated persons. Ray invites students to think back to their own birth, to imagine themselves in a plastic hospital bassinet, wrapped up tightly in a hospital blanket, with a knitted hat on their heads, all lined up in rows with other tiny newborn infants. The students at Muskegon, Ray observes, started out just like that too: in a plastic bassinet, wrapped up tightly, with a hat on their heads. The baptismal liturgy for infants in the Reformed Church in America invokes a similar image of the given value of the child. During the baptism the minister proclaims, "For you Jesus Christ came into the world; for you he died and for you he conquered death; all this he did for you, little one, though you know nothing of it as yet. We love because God first loved us."[62] We all of us begin in gift, being utterly loved by God.

Contrast these images with the one provided by Nell Bernstein in her book on juvenile prison. Bernstein asks readers to imagine that a child they love has committed a crime. "Picture your child, this child whom you love, being called to account for the thing he has done. Do you see him kneeling, cuffed, in a pool of his own urine, denied all but one meal a day and a few hours of sleep? Does the picture include your child being raped or beaten—perhaps both—by the very staff entrusted with her rehabilitation? Can you hold this image as day after day passes? Can you hold it for months? Can you live with it for years?"[63]

The mind revolts, but those of us who have little exposure to the criminal-justice system, those of us who are too comfortable not knowing, need these images. We need to remember the sacredness of human life and be outraged

---

62. "Order for the Sacrament of Baptism," Reformed Church in America, accessed May 13, 2024, https://www.rca.org/liturgy/order-for-the-sacrament-of-baptism.

63. Bernstein, *Burning Down the House*, 14.

when it is betrayed. I confess I do not believe a system so massive, so hidden in its workings, so removed from any public accountability can simply be reformed. I suspect that meaningful change will be possible only with far, far fewer incarcerated persons.

Redemption, Forgiveness, and Christian Approaches to Crime

In addition to making basic claims about human dignity in the midst of sin, Christians also believe that "in Christ God was reconciling the world to himself" (2 Cor. 5:19). While the theological explanations vary, Christians broadly attest that forgiveness of sins and acceptance into God's family come as a gift through Jesus's death and resurrection. God, knowing the human plight, has acted decisively in Jesus to forgive, heal, and restore. It is in Christ that people are liberated from sin and in Christ that God defeats sin and death and reconciles "all things" to himself (Col. 1:20). Furthermore, because this is God's action, not something humans accomplish for themselves, Christians are discouraged from making their own pronouncements about people and are instead encouraged to pray and hope that others will come to experience reconciliation. Does this central claim about grace in the divine response to sin have any implications for thinking about a social response to crime? A single chapter here does not afford the space for a fully developed theory of criminal justice and its relation to punishment. What I will argue here instead is that the understanding of grace I have developed in this book, and particularly the Christian belief in repentance and forgiveness, pushes against any system that includes punishment as an essential component of justice.

Before considering the specific implications of Christ's death and forgiveness of sin, I should note that given the description of sin I have provided here and given the role of an interdependent humanity in the theology of grace, there is good reason to be skeptical of the notion that human beings can calculate the demands of justice. Because of the profoundly interdependent nature of human life, questions of blame and responsibility are messy. How much blame should society assign to a person who commits a violent crime after suffering a life of trauma and abuse? How can human beings begin to determine specific punishments that equal the amount of harm a person caused? Furthermore, the punishment inflicted on one individual reverberates to others, to families and the broader community, who are not guilty of crime. There is inevitably a deeply arbitrary aspect to human punishment, as our own system so vividly illustrates, reinforcing the broader Christian belief that true justice can ultimately be established only through the one who himself suffers the violence of humanity and overcomes that violence in resurrection.

While Christian understandings of the manner in which Jesus's death and resurrection provide forgiveness have been many and varied, some formulations of Christ's atonement, especially the conceptions that were prominent in twentieth-century American evangelicalism, center on the notion of punishment: sinful human beings deserve punishment from God, but Jesus, as a substitute, undergoes that punishment on behalf of sinful humanity. While I am not arguing for this understanding of atonement, it is particularly worth discussing because of its prominence in Reformation theologies, its centrality to American Christianity, and the fact that it suggests punishment for sin is legitimate and necessary. Does a penal-substitution theory of atonement, as many have suggested, call for the kind of harsh criminal punishment the United States currently employs?[64] One cannot rule out the possibility that a popular spirituality centered on penal substitution might encourage a human thirst for punishment, but the logic of the doctrine itself pushes against the idea that human punishment of crime or sin is a necessary part of justice. The whole point of substitutionary atonement is that finite, sinful humanity cannot, through its own suffering, restore itself to justice with God. In this conception, only Jesus, the God-man, can undergo the death due to sinful humanity and satisfy God's justice. Given this claim, it would make no sense to insist that human-inflicted punishment for crime is required in order to satisfy the demands of justice. Indeed, the entire witness of the New Testament calls for precisely the opposite conclusion in the frequent requirement, stated throughout the Gospels and Epistles, that followers of Christ must forgive others and leave judgment and the establishment of justice to God.

This is not to suggest that Christian theologians throughout history have resisted civil punishment of human behavior. But the overall rationale involved in this history is instructive. Alex Tuckness and John Parrish have surveyed the broad history of Christian approaches to mercy and punishment.[65] They note that early in the post-Constantinian church, Christian bishops saw themselves as advocates for mercy, regularly petitioning Roman authorities for leniency toward criminal offenders. Augustine likewise believed that always requesting leniency was a role of the church, but he also argued that civil authorities had their own obligation to respond to wrongdoing with punishment for the sake of public safety and for the ultimate good of offenders—to keep them from future sin. In Tuckness and Parrish's

---

64. Andrew Skotnicki, *Conversion and the Rehabilitation of the Penal System: A Theological Rereading of Criminal Justice* (Oxford: Oxford University Press, 2019), 47. Skotnicki himself suggests this and references the work of several other theologians.

65. Alex Tuckness and John M. Parrish, *The Decline of Mercy in Public Life* (Cambridge: Cambridge University Press, 2014), 87–137.

reading, Augustine's justification for punishment is not that it establishes justice. Punishment, for him, serves the goals of public order and correction, not justice. In the Reformation era, Martin Luther and John Calvin both maintained that Christians, in their personal lives, should forgive rather than seek vengeance or punishment, but like Augustine they held that the civil magistrate had a duty to punish. Here again, however, the goal was the good of society and the offender, not the satisfaction of an abstract standard of justice. This position, one that seems to have been held rather consistently since Augustine, does not require punishment in the sense of externally inflicting pain on someone who is guilty of wrongdoing in order to satisfy demands of justice. Rather, what these theologians believed civil authorities had to do was consider what would best achieve a degree of public order and safety while also attending to the well-being of the person who committed the crime. It presumes both empirical standards (What will actually lead to a safer society and the common good?) and determinations of value (What is a good outcome for someone who has committed a crime? What constitutes "good" for the community?)

I should note here that these questions can also be answered—and have historically been answered—in deeply problematic ways. Proponents of the current system of mass incarceration have often defended it on the grounds of public order and safety. And the desire to reform offenders by making them "penitent" was influential at the very origins of the system.[66] Simply shifting the conversation from punishment and retributive justice to the common good or restoration of social relationships does not inherently produce a system consistent with the theological claim that human beings are made by and for gift. Specific proposals must be analyzed for what they assume and communicate about the human person. At the same time, God's reconciling work in Jesus to forgive sins and reconcile creation to himself sits uncomfortably with any Christian argument that we should seek to establish justice through earthly punishment. Instead, and in keeping with the intuitions and advocacy of the early church, those who have themselves received God's mercy should argue for the extension of mercy. Christians should endeavor to temper the punitive impulses of the state and the public thirst for vengeance. We should regularly remind ourselves and our neighbors of our common humanity, of a shared giftedness and shared sinfulness that does not allow for tidy divisions between "good guys" and "bad guys" and does not allow us to relegate any person to the trash heap of society.

66. Muriel Schmid, "The Eye of God: Religious Beliefs and Punishment in Early Nineteenth-Century Prison Reform," *Theology Today* 59, no. 4 (January 2003): 546–58.

Reducing Incarceration

Given the thoroughly dehumanizing character of the current system, the most urgent task for those who share these beliefs is to reduce the size of the prison population through radical decarceration. To say this, however, is not to claim that it is the responsibility of every Christian to solve the problem of mass incarceration. Determination of the best practices will require the input of many, including those with experience in various aspects of the legal system, scholars in relevant fields, and those whose lives have been most directly impacted—currently and formerly incarcerated persons and their families. Christians who do not fit any of these categories, however, can participate in this process through their ordinary political action as citizens. Because a public that was eager for punishment enabled mass incarceration, Christians can resist it simply by critiquing and rejecting a harshly punitive approach that contradicts the understanding of humanity as constituted by grace. Christian institutions can likewise play a role by abandoning their prior support for mass incarceration and by elevating alternatives in the public imagination. In the past, evangelical Christians in particular have distinguished themselves in a positive way by "showing up" and caring about the spiritual well-being of incarcerated persons.[67] But evangelicals have been less willing to challenge the inhumanity of the broader system or to recognize the vast social costs of mass incarceration for the individuals, families, and communities most affected by it.

While I do not pretend to be an expert on the efficacy of alternative approaches, if we expect people to reject mass incarceration it is important to imagine and point to other options. Due to the complexity of the current system—which is actually many different systems in states and local governments—it is unlikely that a single response would allow us to unravel mass incarceration. With this complexity in mind, we should consider the range of options that most readily appear in the literature on decarceration. These suggestions relate to minimizing new entrants and would need to be combined with efforts like extensive pardons and commutations for those who have already received long sentences.

1. *Minimization of entry into the criminal-justice system.* The vast majority (80 percent) of cases in the criminal-justice system are misdemeanor offenses, and misdemeanors are often a person's first contact with the criminal-justice system.[68] In the past twenty years, policing practices

67. Griffith, *God's Law and Order*, 264.
68. Amanda Agan, Jennifer L. Doleac, and Anna Harvey, "Misdemeanor Prosecution," *Quarterly Journal of Economics* 138, no. 3 (2023): 1453–505.

have prioritized these types of offenses under the theory that doing so would reduce more serious crime.[69] A recent study, however, found that declining to prosecute nonviolent misdemeanors reduced the likelihood of a person having a later criminal complaint by 53 percent. Declining to arrest or prosecute persons for nonviolent misdemeanors could reduce the burden on the criminal-justice system and lessen the burden of aggressive policing on minority communities. Other approaches to minimizing entry into the system include decriminalization of some offenses, elimination of cash bail, and a shifting of policing resources toward solving more serious crime.[70]

2. *Diversion programs.* In the present era, during which the opioid crisis is ongoing and resources for mental-health care are limited, particularly for the poor, many people become involved in the criminal-justice system because of conditions that could be treated through public-health measures. Drug courts are one way of addressing this concern, though it would be even better if increased funding for addiction and mental-health treatment were also used preventatively rather than only after an arrest. Diversion programs for violent offenses have been less common, and experimentation in this area is greatly needed so that researchers can develop evidence-based approaches.[71] The Justice Reinvestment Initiative has assisted states in diverting funds from prisons to programs that improve public safety, although as legal scholar John Pfaff notes, these initiatives could be extended beyond the criminal-justice system to include mental-health and addiction treatment, job training and placement, and education.[72]

3. *Restorative justice.* Activists of diverse religious and ideological perspectives, especially from Indigenous communities, have long argued for an approach that provides a mediated process in which victims and offenders are heard and participate in decision making, with the ultimate goal of healing and restoration for the community.[73] Many Christians have

69. For a discussion of how these practices were implemented in New York City, see Sharkey, *Uneasy Peace*, 152–56.

70. The book *Ghettoside*, e.g., explores the low rate of closed cases for homicides in late twentieth-century Los Angeles. Jill Leovy, *Ghettoside: A True Story of Murder in America* (New York: Spiegel & Grau, 2015).

71. Pfaff, *Locked In*, 229.

72. Pfaff, *Locked In*, 226. Pfaff observes that these programs help local communities afford alternatives instead of pushing the cost of crime on to the state through incarceration.

73. For an overview of the various practices and theories that fall under the category of restorative justice, see Gerry Johnstone, "Introduction: Restorative Approaches to Criminal Justice," in *A Restorative Justice Reader: Texts, Sources, Context*, ed. Gerry Johnstone (Portland, OR: Willan, 2003), 1–18.

found this approach appealing because of its emphasis on accountability for action, restitution of harm, and reconciliation of the offender to the community. A number of diversionary programs throughout the country employ aspects of a restorative-justice model, though the vast majority of these programs are used in cases of nonviolent offenses.[74]

4. *Prosecutorial and defense reforms.* Because so much in the US legal system is left to prosecuting attorneys, any reform will need to address this stage of the process. Pfaff recommends sentencing guidelines that have a clear decarceratory impact by restricting threats prosecutors could make in the plea process and instructing prosecutors what to charge in particular situations, especially when there are mitigating factors.[75] As a corollary, adequately funding indigent defense could lessen the likelihood that those charged with crimes will be unfairly moved through the system and could help keep the power of the state in check.

When and How Should We Incarcerate?

The alternatives to incarceration must not be seen as options for only the nonviolent offender. Although such an approach often seems most palatable to the public, it ignores the difficult truth that many incarcerated persons today are in prison for violent crimes.[76] Reducing mass incarceration will mean coming to grips with the idea that even many violent offenders should not be incarcerated. At the same time, as the above list indicates, providing alternatives to incarceration does not mean that we must abandon accountability; rather, those advocating these reforms want to envision new forms of accountability, forms that respect human dignity and interdependence. These approaches reject the premise that those who commit crimes have somehow forfeited their worth as a person, and they seek to acknowledge that offenders are members of a community—dependent on the gifts of others and in relationship with people who depend on them.

Yet we must also recognize that some people will commit crimes that suggest they pose an ongoing threat to the broader public and that some will commit

74. See, e.g., the Cook County Restorative Justice Program. Joanna Hernandez, "Cook County Restorative Justice Program Is Giving People a Second Chance," WTTW News, November 16, 2023, https://news.wttw.com/2023/11/16/cook-county-restorative-justice-program-giving-people-second-chance.

75. Pfaff, *Locked In*, 210–11.

76. In state-prison populations, violent offenders constitute 58 percent of the population, though sometimes the classification of "violent offense" is deceptive. Vincent Schiraldi et al., "Mercy and Forbearance: A Parsimonious Approach to Violent Crime," in *Parsimony and Other Radical Ideas about Justice*, ed. Jeremy Travis and Bruce Western (New York: New Press, 2023), 73–90.

crimes of such devastating harm that the social wound cannot be ignored and alternatives would seem to belittle the immense evil that has occurred.[77] Should we think of incarceration here as a punishment that inflicts pain and thereby achieves a modicum of "justice" for society? Much hinges here on a careful definition of terms, but even in these cases the intentional infliction of pain is not what advances healing and the broader public good.

There are two ways to think of punishment as a response to wrongdoing. The first and most common is the arbitrary infliction of pain, where "arbitrary" means that the pain inflicted is not conceptually linked to the act of wrongdoing. So, for example, if a child misbehaves in a restaurant and the parent spanks the child, the spanking is arbitrarily connected to the misbehavior. But a second type—it is perhaps best not called "punishment," but here we lack proper vocabulary—occurs when a person experiences naturally painful consequences of their action, without any invented pain being added to the equation. In this type of "punishment," a parent might respond to the unruly child by saying, "Unfortunately, because you are disturbing other people, we have to leave the restaurant and cannot enjoy this delicious food." Incarceration could be construed in these terms, but this type of incarceration would need to be vastly different from the type we currently have. In this construal, loss of freedom would be the unavoidable consequence of extremely violent behavior, both because the person might cause future harm and because their ongoing presence, as someone who has committed an atrocity, would be too painful and destructive for the broader community before it had time to undergo a process of reconciliation.

Can we imagine a version of incarceration that would not inflict pain beyond confinement itself? In several Scandinavian countries this imaginative endeavor is already underway.[78] Many of these facilities operate on a rationale that is remarkably consistent with the Reformation psychology of grace that

---

77. Daniel Philpott, *Just and Unjust Peace: An Ethic of Political Reconciliation* (Oxford: Oxford University Press, 2012), 223–24. In this chapter I have been reluctant to employ the language of "prison abolition" for these reasons. However, if prison abolition is understood to mean the eradication of prisons in their current form and the severe restriction of the need for confinement, then there would be considerable overlap between my approach and an abolitionist one. For a defense of the abolitionist approach, see Joshua Dubler and Vincent W. Lloyd, *Break Every Yoke: Religion, Justice, and the Abolition of Prisons* (Oxford: Oxford University Press, 2020).

78. Doran Larson, "Why Scandinavian Prisons Are Superior," *The Atlantic*, September 24, 2013, https://www.theatlantic.com/international/archive/2013/09/why-scandinavian-prisons-are-superior/279949/; Jessica Benko, "The Radical Humaneness of Norway's Halden Prison," *New York Times Magazine*, March 26, 2015, https://www.nytimes.com/2015/03/29/magazine/the-radical-humaneness -of-norways-halden-prison.html. At present, California is looking to these facilities as a model for reform; see Anita Chabria, "California Prison Guards Are Dying Too Young. How Norway (Yes, Norway) Can Help," *Los Angeles Times*, November 9, 2023, https://www.latimes.com/california/story /2023-11-09/how-do-you-reform-california-prisons-to-be-more-like-norway-hire-more-guards.

we explored in chapter 1. A foundational principle of these approaches is to make life in an institution as much like life outside it as possible. In Norway's Halden Fengsel, a maximum-security prison, inmates live in facilities that more closely resemble US college dormitories than US prisons. The inmates shop for groceries, cook their own meals, spend time in nature, engage in recreational activities, and attend therapy sessions. While US observers sometimes mock Fengsel as "luxury," the emphasis on normalcy has a psychological and philosophical rationale. Architects of these facilities not only want to create an environment where inmates and staff feel respected, sensing that their needs and safety matter, but also seek to avoid any unnecessary deprivation that would encourage an oppositional or defiant attitude in the inmates. When they do not sense an "enemy" in the state or the prison employees, when they are confronted at every turn with people who are seeking their genuine welfare, they are forced to confront their own role and responsibility in their situation. Notably, employees in these institutions, unlike correctional officers in the United States, report high job satisfaction and find the work rewarding.[79]

The logic here is quite similar to the Reformation psychology and particularly Calvin's approach to connecting repentance and sanctification to one's awareness of God as a loving parent. For Calvin, if one senses only divine wrath, believing that God is the enemy who will make a person suffer for sin, there is no space for repentance. One can only run from God in fear or deny one's sin. It is when a person experiences God's love, an act of pure grace, that this person can be secure in that love to confront sin, even though the process may be immensely painful. Calvin did not merely apply this psychology to the human relationship to God. He cautioned parents against disciplining children too harshly, and in the Genevan consistory he encouraged moderation and gentleness in matters of church discipline so that the goal could be repentance.[80] Calvin might not be moderate and gentle by our standards, and he did not consistently apply the logic of this psychology to questions of civil punishment, but in any case the logic, if worked out thoroughly, pushes against any notion that harsh punishment will lead to personal transformation.

Conclusion

For many Americans, the notions of individual responsibility and self-reliance are easy and familiar. Given this ethos, it makes sense that the United States,

79. Chabria, "California Prison Guards."
80. Jeffrey Watt, *The Consistory and Social Discipline in Calvin's Geneva* (Rochester: University of Rochester Press, 2020), 5.

of all countries, would develop a system of mass incarceration and punitive criminal justice. But the failures of this system are serious: people who go to prison have often themselves been victims of trauma and injustice. Incarceration causes harm to families and communities, and imprisonment often denies or denigrates basic human worth. These failures expose the weaknesses of the underlying ethos of independence and deservingness. Christians are called to a different ethos. We are called to recognize the ways all humans are meant to be linked together in networks of mutual belonging and care, and we are also to recognize that we are instead tragically linked together by our rebellion and sin and our need for grace. It is possible to think about crime and responses to crime in ways that acknowledge these truths and our universal need for grace. In this chapter I have tried to model such an approach by considering the sin that lies at the origin of crime-ridden communities and by proposing a gracious accountability that need not be punitive but can instead be extended in the hope of transformation. In this vision, any exclusion, which may be a painful necessity, can be enacted only toward the goal of eventual reincorporation. In this sense, sin does not alter the unconditionality of grace, which remains in the form of patient and hopeful expectation.

CHAPTER 7

GUN CONTROL

Throughout this book I have argued that Christian theologies of grace, particularly those stemming from the Protestant Reformation, do not undermine social ethics. Quite the contrary, they call for a particular social ethic. Grace is not simply a set of claims about what God has done for humanity. In addition to telling us something about God, grace also tells us something about humanity. To be human is to be constituted by grace all the way down, to be creatures whose very existence is the gift of God, who live by God's sustaining power, who are saved from sin by God's grace, and who were made to receive and live in the gift of Godself. And we are meant to *understand* this about ourselves, to know as thoroughly and deeply as we can that God is for us, that God *is* unending, overflowing, self-gift. I have also argued, perhaps more controversially, that we cannot be persons of deep dependence on God's grace if we think that in community with other people we must each be for ourselves, if we think we must create our value or must make our own way in life. To think in this way would mean that we were simultaneously two very different and ultimately contradictory sorts of creatures. Rather, in community with others we should mediate God's gifts in mutual love. We should support and enable one another's freedom and agency so we can all fulfill the human purpose of fellowship with God and neighbor.

Yet this same person who is constituted by gift must also be a vulnerable person, a finite person. These are two sides of the same coin. For how could we exist in a community of love if we did not have both agency and need? As Thomas Aquinas puts it, to be people who can experience friendship we must also be creatures "who may fare well or ill."[1] What meaning would our gifts to one another have if we were not creatures for whom things could go better or worse, if we were not, in other words, vulnerable and finite? Vulnerability is a condition for human love. But as we explored in chapter 1, it can also be an impediment to love. Because a person is vulnerable, there is always the risk that they will reject loving others in favor of self-protection or that their efforts to love others will really be an effort to get something from them—that they will exploit others in *their* vulnerability.

In the past two chapters I have considered the practical implications of a theology of grace focused first on creation and then on redemption. In this final chapter I will focus on eschatological grace, a grace of the "last things." In particular, this chapter will address how eschatological grace interacts with human finitude and vulnerability. Does God's grace meet the person in the context of vulnerability, finitude, and fear? As we proceed, I will analyze a particular aspect of contemporary American vulnerability and fear: our culture of gun violence. The proliferation of dangerous weapons among the civilian population is both a cause of and response to the particular American experience of vulnerability. In the midst of a dangerous world, guns offer an alluring promise: "You do not have to be vulnerable." I will ask if eschatological grace suggests a different way of being human in a dangerous world.

Finitude, Fear, and Despair

In Karl Barth we find one of the most robust Christian reflections on the goodness of our creaturely limitations. A core feature of human nature, for Barth, is that it has a natural limit, a beginning and an end. In fact, it is through this limited character that human nature is most clearly seen to be a gift of God.[2] By virtue of having a birth and death that are not in human control, human lives are seen for what they are: purely gratuitous. Without this signification of the person utterly arising from and depending on divine gift, "he would be blinded by the illusion that he can rely on many other things as well as God, and especially on himself."[3] Without a bounded nature, people would be tempted to imagine themselves to be God and would

---

1. Thomas Aquinas, *Summa Theologica*, trans. Fathers of the English Dominican Province (New York: Benziger, 1911–1965) Ia, q. 20, a. 2, https://www.newadvent.org/summa/1020.htm.

2. For a more thorough discussion of this theme, see Gerald McKenny, "Biotechnology and the Normative Significance of Human Nature: A Contribution from Theological Anthropology," *Studies in Christian Ethics* 23, no. 1 (February 2013): 29–34.

3. Barth, *Church Dogmatics* III/2, *The Doctrine of Creation*, ed. Thomas F. Torrance, trans. Geoffrey William Bromiley (Edinburgh: T&T Clark, 1956), 569.

miss their ultimate purpose of fellowship with the God who loves them and is for them.[4]

While an unbounded nature might lead the creature astray, Barth also recognizes that the vulnerability of finitude can be a source of fear and sinfulness if the person does not also acknowledge that Jesus meets the person in their finitude and limitation: "As the Crucified, He lives at the very point where our frontier is reached and our time runs out. He is the Victor there."[5] For the person who accepts and trusts this truth of God's grace, there can only be cause for rejoicing and hope when he contemplates reaching that limit. While Barth sees an awareness of grace as grounds for peace and joy, he thinks that most Christians do not actually accept and trust this truth about the God who is for them. As a result, they view this frontier with fear and anxiety, with the sense that at the end of the day all is lost and there is only nothingness. This generalized hopelessness is not always explicitly in mind, but it is a backdrop to human existence and propels all sorts of anxious striving. In what Barth categorizes as a form of sloth, either anxious people seek to avoid dangers that might bring them to the frontier of life, or they pursue other objectives that provide momentary satisfaction and distract them from life's impending end. Barth assigns the term "human care" to this combination of fear and desire that arises from not accepting the limit to our existence.[6]

The constant hum of anxiety and the stress of pursuing an endless string of distractions are such ordinary features of human life that it can be difficult to grasp why Barth finds "care" so destructive. Yes, we are anxious when contemplating mortality. How can Barth suggest that we should not be? Yes, we are driven to make a mark on the world or take temporary pleasure from life. Would he want us simply to fritter away our lives? When it comes to Christian ethics, many can easily see how pride leads people to trample on their neighbors, but anxiety—well, it is just so *normal*. We might even think it prudent to be a little anxious. Barth recognizes this. It is quite easy, he thinks, to dismiss care as "a regrettable human weakness or an occasional mistake."[7] Why, then, does he also call it "the root of all evil"?[8] The problem with our endless, insatiable anxieties is that they close off the kind of life we are meant to enjoy. Throughout this discussion Barth repeatedly mentions the absence of

4. As McKenny notes, Barth also sees this bounded nature as crucial for the existence of a particular person who can be in fellowship with God. An unbounded life would lack the specificity on which relationship depends. See McKenny, "Biotechnology," 34.

5. Barth, *Church Dogmatics* III/2, 468.

6. Barth, *Church Dogmatics* III/2, 468–70.

7. Barth, *Church Dogmatics* III/2, 472.

8. Barth, *Church Dogmatics* III/2, 468.

joy: "As man refuses to find joy and comfort in his end, it thrusts itself (in the form in which he sees it, and therefore without joy and comfort, but menacingly) into his present."[9] Anxiety is a deep and persistent dissatisfaction in the life that is actually a gift of God. Instead of freely making use of this gift for fellowship with God, the person is instead in bondage to his own need for security. Care exercises a power over the person such that belief in a hopeless end generates a "joyless present."[10]

One way to grasp this distinction of lived existence is to consider how the same ordinary good human activity—spending time with family—can appear dramatically different depending on whether a person trusts in the goodness of life's limit and the presence of Christ in the frontier of death. As I write this chapter, my oldest daughter is in her last year of high school, and I find myself often contemplating the upcoming change to our family life. Our time as the nuclear family we have known is bounded and will soon change dramatically. If I acknowledge this reality as an aspect of life's limit, as a gift of God and a means for me to know God's love, then I can recognize and be grateful for the gift of my daughter and the joy it has been to parent her. I can also particularly enjoy and savor these final months before everything changes. When I fail to see the boundedness of life, however, the good gifts, like parenting children, stand out to me only in their loss. I want them to continue forever, and since they cannot, even what I now have is tinged with the fear of its end. The truth is that when we grasp desperately at departing gifts, we become incapable of seeing the gifts for what they are and simply being grateful. This is human care as Barth understands it.

For our purposes it is particularly important to emphasize how "care" in Barth's construal produces alienation from God and from other people. With respect to God, at the very point where God has come closest and acted on humanity's behalf, the person of anxiety has, by definition, already turned away. The God this person sees is a phantasm, a shadow, not the God of Jesus Christ, who is utterly for them. Because of the desire to make something of their life or for self-protection, the God who has left them vulnerable to death and loss must be an opponent and not a friend.[11]

Human care also influences human relationships. While each person operates out of a basic dissatisfaction and longing, people also ignite and magnify specific fears in one another. In this respect Barth thinks that particular anxieties can be symptomatic of whole groups of people and descriptive of

9. Barth, *Church Dogmatics* III/2, 471.
10. Barth, *Church Dogmatics* III/2, 471.
11. Barth, *Church Dogmatics* III/2, 476.

"world-situations."[12] Even though we may share some of these anxieties, they do not necessarily bring us together in fellowship. In fact, Barth thinks they are much more likely to divide and isolate. Those who do not share our particular anxieties are likely to be the "other," the enemy, and there is a potential for hostility or violent outbreaks among us. One can see here how anxiety, like pride, leads to the trampling of the neighbor. And even among those who do share our anxieties, our concerns are still, at their core, individualized. We are each secretly concerned with how something will affect us personally, wanting others to help us rather than vice versa. "Care," Barth says, "dissolves and destroys and atomizes human society."[13]

Before examining the persuasiveness of this account as a description of contemporary human experience, I would like to address two concerns that Barth's analysis might raise. First, in this section Barth is describing a pattern of sin that he sees as universal for humans under the denial of God's grace. It is, however, worth making some distinctions in the lived experience of this condition, particularly regarding persons who have been subject to oppression or exploitation by others or to profound loss and suffering. The question of trust in God's grace is put to all vulnerable people, but while some observe human susceptibility to death from a distance, others have been traumatized by extreme suffering or violence. If this reality is not acknowledged, there is a risk that Barth's talk of sloth can come across as deeply insensitive. Yet as liberation theologians like Gustavo Gutiérrez have reminded us, it is often these same wounded people who are most radically trusting and able to summon inexplicable hope.[14] This is a point to which we will return when we consider grace and spirituality in the epilogue.

Even apart from these specific concerns about the oppressed, one might challenge the sensitivity of Barth's account on its own terms. In saying the person who fears death is slothful, is Barth giving sufficient attention to ordinary finitude as an embodied experience of suffering? We might not all experience profound trauma or be part of an oppressed group of people, but we all suffer, and we all bear witness to profound suffering. What are we to tell ourselves when we believe and yet still fear? On the one hand, Barth appears to assume that faith should be immediately transformative of one's most habitual patterns of thinking and reacting as vulnerable, finite creatures. But this is simply not the case. Human response to bodily threat is deeply engrained in our biology and cannot simply be switched off. This potential gap between knowledge and

12. Barth, *Church Dogmatics* III/2, 471.
13. Barth, *Church Dogmatics* III/2, 477.
14. Gustavo Gutiérrez, *We Drink from Our Own Wells: The Spiritual Journey of a People*, trans. Matthew J. O'Connell (Maryknoll, NY: Orbis Books, 1984), 114–21.

practice will also call for reflection on a spirituality of grace. We will need to tell a story about how faith takes root deeply and how, over time, trust in God's goodness affords new possibilities for response to our embodied vulnerabilities. On the other hand, when Barth claims that human care is the root of all evil, he is hardly alone in this conclusion. Plenty of thinkers, both Christian and non-Christian, have thought that the human inability to come to terms with finitude and the tendency to deny death are deeply problematic.[15]

The second area of concern in Barth's account of human care is that he seems to call into question all action that seeks to address a particular "fear" or "anxiety." But would this category not include most human action in pursuit of social justice? Barth speaks in this passage of the activist who plunges himself into work "so that something is actually achieved for himself and others by the fact that he is anxious."[16] Does he thereby dismiss any efforts to improve the concrete lives of humans, including the efforts of oppressed people to work for liberation, as simply another form of sloth? Again, this would seem to be quite insensitive to those whose lives are ground down in poverty or exploitation.

Barth's account of human care as sin also raises questions like those we observed in chapter 1 regarding the Reformation psychology of grace. If we say that activism arising from fear is sloth, does this lead to a kind of pious passivity where a person is hesitant to take positive action on behalf of a social good because he thinks such action might actually be sinful? Admittedly, we are considering only a small portion of Barth's work, but we will have to keep this concern in mind as we move ahead. One important point to make in the context of Barth's analysis, however, is that activism does come with the risk of descending into despair. At the end of the day, the activist is limited by his own finitude. No matter how much good he is able to achieve, there will always be more to do. And for many who labor for justice, their fight can seem to face insurmountable odds that no human person could possibly overcome. In the face of social problems like worker exploitation or mass incarceration, the person who wants to do good is always at risk of despair. As we move ahead, we will find that Barth's comments on the source of human care still have something to teach us.

While we will need to keep these difficulties in mind, it is also worth asking whether Barth's account of human care is a recognizable feature of human society as we experience it. A brief survey of contemporary American politics suggests that indeed it is. What are the prominent features of our political experience today? The rise of white-nationalist groups and the increasing strength of

15. See Ernest Becker, *The Denial of Death* (New York: Free Press, 1973).
16. Becker, *Denial of Death*, 473.

Christian nationalism seem to be driven by anxiety over a rapidly changing society. These fears are stoked when politicians draw attention to "migrant caravans" approaching the southern border or when news commentators talk about asylum seekers as "military-aged men." The 2017 Charlottesville white-supremacist rally both emerged from these anxieties and triggered corresponding anxieties among other segments of the population. Actress Tina Fey brilliantly satirized these fears in a comedy sketch on *Saturday Night Live* when she encouraged anxious women like herself to buy a sheet cake from a local minority bakery and "just eat it" while screaming their fears into the cake.[17]

More recently, the COVID-19 pandemic highlighted all sorts of fear-based action, including months-long school closures and widespread vaccine resistance. As the pandemic waned, fear-based politics on the right has shifted to "don't say gay" laws and the movement to sanitize the history of racism from public-school curricula. On the left, it can likewise be seen in reactions to these political movements and the constant level of social-media outrage, which, incidentally, seems to be roughly as effective as shouting into a cake.[18]

In drawing attention to these examples, I am not intending to comment on the legitimacy of any particular fear. Instead, I wish to highlight the role of anxiety in public life and what it means for communal flourishing. In keeping with Barth's analysis, anxieties have spread socially like wildfire and have become tools for gaining and wielding political power. We are a society marked by divisions, resentments, animosities, and no small potential for violence. In the midst of our individual fears, with their varying degrees of legitimacy, those with opposing views become our enemies.

This fear-based approach to politics has become especially salient for many Protestant Christians in the Trump era. In a recent book, journalist Tim Alberta, himself an evangelical Christian, explores the intersection of faith and politics in congregations across the country.[19] One memorable chapter describes a ministry on the "furthest fringes" of the evangelical movement, Greg Locke's Global Vision Bible Church in Mt. Juliet, Tennessee. In a large tent in which many churchgoers openly carried guns, Alberta observed Locke speak about the latest hot-button issues in the culture wars, like vaccines, celebrity pedophiles, and the "stolen" 2020 election. A celebrity guest warned of threats to the country and the potential need to "take it back." As Alberta concedes,

17. *Saturday Night Live*, "Weekend Update," NBC, August 17, 2017, https://www.nbc.com/saturday-night-live/video/weekend-update-tina-fey-on-protesting-after-charlottesville/3570730.

18. See Helen Lewis, "The Left Can't Afford to Go Mad," *The Atlantic*, December 8, 2023, https://www.theatlantic.com/magazine/archive/2024/01/trump-biden-democratic-left-opposition/676141/.

19. Tim Alberta, *The Kingdom, the Power, and the Glory: American Evangelicals in an Age of Extremism* (New York: HaperCollins, 2023).

Locke's ministry is clearly extreme, but what surprised him, after visiting scores of churches across the country, were the similarities. "How many pastors," he wonders, "at smaller conservative churches . . . would have felt uncomfortable sitting inside this tent listening to Locke? The answer, I suspected, was very few."[20]

Perhaps, however, we can attribute these public fears to the particular toxicities of our media culture and political structures. What about human care at the personal level? Several months ago my daughters and I were stuck in our car behind a very long and slow-moving train. As my frustration increased, I observed, "I could walk faster than this train." After a few seconds, my eldest daughter replied, "I like being stuck behind trains; it's a good reminder that we are not in control." Wise words. I was reminded of them a few months later when I finally caught COVID-19 and spent a week languishing in bed. Being sick is a lesson in finitude. There was so much I wanted to accomplish, and so many emails about upcoming tasks continued to populate my inbox, but in my fevered haze I could only let time pass. I was not in control. Such experiences expose the default setting most of us operate on: thinking that it *is* all up to us, that we *can* orchestrate the desired outcome. We alternate between momentary fears of that which might harm us (Should I be worried about this new and seemingly random health ailment? Is it safe for my teenager to drive in this weather?) and the determination to accomplish things (I *will* finish this book by Christmas!). When we encounter things that are truly frightening and beyond our control, we are thrust into panic. I have not screamed into a sheet cake yet, but I am quite familiar with doomscrolling. I doubt any of us are strangers to these patterns of fear and desire.

Contemporary US Christians more broadly are not immune to this personal level of human care. Theologian J. Todd Billings reflects on the tendency for Christians facing a terminal diagnosis to pursue "heroic measures"—aggressive treatments that are unlikely to be successful. Billings, himself a cancer patient, notes that in the medical literature and in his anecdotal experience, Christians are much more likely than non-Christians to pursue such options, a difference he attributes to Christian faith in a God who heals and revives. As Christians in American culture approach the end of life, this dominant narrative of healing cannot accommodate the unexpected fracturing of one's life story. "There is no role in it for a dying disciple of Jesus."[21] The dominant messages that Christians receive in discipleship, worship, and Christian culture do not prepare them

---

20. Alberta, *Kingdom*, 230.

21. J. Todd Billings, *The End of the Christian Life: How Embracing Our Mortality Frees Us to Truly Live* (Grand Rapids: Brazos, 2020), 123.

to approach the limit or frontier of death with trust that God loves them and is for them even in their death. They do not prepare Christians to resist the power that fear of death has over their lives.

Grace and Eschatology

For Christian theology, this reflection on the end of life and the ultimate defeat of death falls within the scope of eschatology, the study of the "last things." In chapter 5 much of our discussion drew on Christian theologies of grace in creation: the gifts of creation are intended for all, and the human person was created for fellowship with God and neighbor. In chapter 6 we considered the grace of forgiveness and redemption, grace as a response to human sin. In this chapter we will devote special attention to the fulfillment of grace, the grace of the last things. I will focus on two aspects of Christian eschatology: first, how the "ultimate" or "last" things are, according to Reformation theologies, brought forward into the present through the person's union with Christ and, second, how the final restoration of God's kingdom is an act of radical grace that is brought about through divine action alone.

As we saw in chapter 1, in Martin Luther's account of justification the person of faith is forgiven and restored to right relationship with God solely on the basis of what Christ has done and not on the basis of his own actions. In terms of eschatology, what Luther does in this theological maneuver is to wrench the final judgment of the believer from the end of time and bring it forward into the present. In Luther's justification, the person knows the final verdict already: righteous and forgiven. This declaration of "righteous" applies to the still-sinful person when that person is united to Christ by faith. Luther describes this relationship as a marriage in which the person experiences communion with Christ and also benefits from the intermingling of possessions that occurs in marriage. The Christian receives all the benefits that Christ possesses—righteousness, life, and salvation—and Christ takes all that is negative and destructive of the human person—sin and death and hell—and overcomes them.[22]

The implications of this "great exchange," according to Luther, are profound. Because the person receives the fullness of life in Christ, he is radically liberated to perform acts of sacrificial love for his neighbor. Luther writes, for example, "Therefore he should be guided in all his works by this thought and contemplate this one thing alone, that he may serve and benefit others

---

22. Martin Luther, *The Freedom of a Christian*, in *Martin Luther's Basic Theological Writings*, ed. Timothy Lull (Minneapolis: Fortress, 1989), 603–4.

in all that he does, considering nothing except the need and advantage of his neighbor."[23] Later he says, "Here faith is truly active through love (Gal. 5:6), that is, it finds expression in works of the freest service, cheerfully and lovingly done, with which a man willingly serves another without hope of reward; and for himself he is satisfied with the fullness and wealth of his faith."[24] Describing the inner psychology of the Christian, Luther writes, "I will do nothing in this life except what I see is necessary, profitable, and salutary to my neighbor, since through faith I have an abundance of all good things in Christ."[25] Particularly noteworthy here is the way Luther thinks the great exchange transforms the human heart in the face of earthly evil.

> If the knowledge of sin or the fear of death should break in upon it, it is ready to hope in the Lord. It does not grow afraid when it hears tidings of evil. It is not disturbed when it sees its enemies. This is so because it believes that the righteousness of Christ is its own and that its sin is not its own, but Christ's. . . . Death is swallowed up not only in the victory of Christ but also by our victory, because through faith his victory has become ours and in that faith we also are conquerors.[26]

When one reads *On the Freedom of a Christian*, it can seem as though Luther expects a mere change in cognition to result in an astonishing transformation of life. His more pastoral writing affords a fuller picture of human struggle in which he recognizes the way that fear of death, aided by the scheming of the devil, can torment the soul. In his "Sermon on Preparing to Die," for instance, Luther notes the power that death holds over the person when the heart "constantly fixes its gaze on it."[27] He observes that the narrowness of death makes this life appear expansive and makes whatever is to come beyond death seem small and confined by comparison. The devil seizes on and encourages this fear "while cultivating a love and concern for life," causing the person to forget God and abhor death.[28] The proper way to approach these anxieties, for Luther, is not to attempt to abolish all thought of death but to instead "familiarize ourselves with death during our lifetime, inviting death into our presence when it is still at a distance and not on the move."[29] One should consider the

23. Luther, *Freedom of a Christian*, 617.
24. Luther, *Freedom of a Christian*, 617.
25. Luther, *Freedom of a Christian*, 619.
26. Luther, *Freedom of a Christian*, 609–10.
27. Martin Luther, "Sermon on Preparing to Die," in *Martin Luther's Basic Theological Writings*, 640, 393.
28. Luther, "Sermon on Preparing to Die," 393.
29. Luther, "Sermon on Preparing to Die," 394.

significance of death in the course of one's ordinary life and should particularly look at it from the perspective of Christ and God's grace, with the aid of the sacraments. From this perspective it will not appear terrifying, "for Christ is nothing other than sheer life."[30]

Luther had the occasion to apply his pastoral reflections on death to real circumstances of earthly terror when the Black Death returned to Wittenberg in 1527. Here he did not reject the inclinations of ordinary Christians to preserve their lives by fleeing danger—one should not, Luther thought, neglect the preservation of body and life. But he insisted, in keeping with his earlier analysis of grace and Christian freedom, that the priority in one's decision should always be care of neighbor. And in encouraging Christians to care for their sick neighbors, he directed them to God's promises as a source of comfort in the midst of danger and risk: "Again, what harm could overtake you if the whole world were to desert you and no physician would remain with you, but God would abide with you with his assurance?"[31]

The grace of the last things that are brought forward into the present is a source of resistance to the ways in which human care distorts and diminishes the loves of finite and vulnerable creatures. In the context of a divisive culture of fear, such grace should expand the horizon of human concern. Instead of encouraging each person to baptize their own fears and special areas of interest so they can claim them as central to the divine will, this grace reminds them that their needs are ultimately within God's care without denying the legitimacy of human action to preserve one's own life in the present. The difference is that such actions do not need to be given priority over the needs of the neighbor. Christians can instead sacrificially care for others and entrust their lives and well-being to God.

At the same time, this grace also speaks to the particular fears and vulnerabilities of those who have suffered injustice, oppression, or trauma. Howard Thurman, a spiritual leader for many civil-rights activists, argues that material and physical oppression have negative consequences for identity and personhood beyond the injustice itself. They degrade people and assault their sense of self-respect, leading to a paralyzing sense of inferiority. Recall here our study of social psychology in chapter 3 and the evidence connecting a negative sense of one's personal efficacy with depression and failure to act. In response to this debilitating loss of self, Thurman argues that the religion of Jesus is capable of stabilizing the egos of oppressed people by giving them assurance

---

30. Luther, "Sermon on Preparing to Die," 395.
31. Martin Luther, *Whether One May Flee from a Deadly Plague,* in *Martin Luther's Basic Theological Writings,* 746.

that they are children of God, which can then enable an honest assessment of their abilities.[32] For Thurman, the power of this knowledge can meet a person in the face of bodily harm or even death: "And he cares for me! To be assured of this becomes the answer to the threat of violence—yea, to violence itself."[33]

This all sounds promising for our reflection on eschatology and social action, but what are we to make of the *very* last things, those which are not "brought forward" but remain stubbornly in the eschatological horizon, to be fulfilled when Christ returns and restores all things? Does not such perpetual deferment undermine social action and create a sense of resignation with the current fallen state of affairs? As I noted in chapter 4, many readers of Luther have suspected that his two-kingdoms theology leaves little space for Christians to strive for God's kingdom in contemporary and temporal circumstances. While I am not entirely pessimistic regarding the potential for a socially engaged two-kingdoms theology, I find that several liberation theologians of the late twentieth century are more consistent than Luther, and John Calvin too, in applying the Reformation theology of grace to questions of eschatology.[34] Take, for example, Gustavo Gutiérrez's discussion of eschatology and "temporal progress." For Gutiérrez, as for most Christian theologians, the promises of God await an eschatological fulfillment that will come as a gift at the end of history. Yet Gutiérrez refuses to separate spiritual liberation from sin (or from one's alienation from God) and liberation from material oppression. Indeed, he insists that these forms of liberation are inherently intertwined because material oppression is itself a manifestation of human sinfulness. Sin is "the breach of friendship with God and with other persons."[35] To suggest that someone could experience spiritual liberation and not care about the liberation of the oppressed would be to say that one could be set free from sin and yet not need to resist sin and its consequences. "Misery and social injustice reveal 'a sinful situation,' a disintegration of fellowship and communion; by freeing us from sin, Jesus attacks the roots of an unjust order."[36] This means that liberatory events within history, while not the complete coming of the kingdom "which is above all a gift," are part of the growth of the kingdom.[37] In his discussions of liberation and spirituality, Gutiérrez makes clear that such liberatory efforts within history are propelled by an awareness of God's grace that is expressed

32. Howard Thurman, *Jesus and the Disinherited* (Boston: Beacon, 1996), 43.

33. Thurman, *Jesus and the Disinherited*, 46.

34. For one approach using Calvin's political theology, see Matthew J. Tuininga, *Calvin's Political Theology and the Public Engagement of the Church: Christ's Two Kingdoms* (Cambridge: Cambridge University Press, 2017).

35. Gutiérrez, *We Drink from Our Own Wells*, 103.

36. Gutiérrez, *We Drink from Our Own Wells*, 134.

37. Gutiérrez, *We Drink from Our Own Wells*, 104.

in language quite similar to that of Luther and Calvin. He writes, "But the knowledge that at the root of our personal and community existence lies the gift of the self-communication of God, the grace of God's friendship, fills our life with gratitude. It allows us to see our encounters with others, our loves, everything that happens in our life as a gift. There is a real love only when there is free giving—without conditions or coercion. Only gratuitous love goes to our very roots and elicits true love."[38]

If Gutiérrez is correct here, the recognition that one's actions on behalf of liberation do not bring about the ultimate restoration of creation is not cause for abandoning them. These actions are the grateful response to God's transforming love in Christ. James Cone, a liberation theologian in the black American context, also affirms that full liberation awaits an eschatological completion, and for Cone, this future completion is essential to the sustaining of liberative action. Cone sees the traditional emphasis on heaven in African American spirituality not as endorsing a passive escape from this-worldly suffering but as supporting the black struggle in the midst of profound suffering. The promise of heaven means both that God does, in fact, desire freedom and liberation for black people and that for those in the midst of oppression, their suffering is not the final word. Without this promise the oppressed within history are simply left to the brutal forces that deny their dignity. With it, the knowledge that God is for them affirms their true being as God's children and provides strength for the present struggle. It also signals the possibility that God's future will "break into" the present social existence.[39] If one acts in faith that Christ is also present and active, the person has the opportunity to experience a success that exceeds human striving and thereby points to the reality of God's gifts in an especially vivid way.

In short, the grace of the last things, in both its "already" and "not yet" manifestations, speaks to the human condition of finitude and vulnerability. The promises of God, already made true in Christ's resurrection, encourage finite people to trust that they too will share in new life—indeed, that they already share in this life. This confidence gives them the freedom to prioritize the needs of their neighbors, entrusting their own lives and comfort to God, and in particular to struggle on behalf of those who bear the oppressive weight of human sin and injustice. When they themselves are oppressed, these promises remind them that exploitation and bondage are not God's will, that they are part of the old order, which is already passing away. But what, we might ask, does trust in such promises look like in circumstances of actual

38. Gutiérrez, *We Drink from Our Own Wells*, 119.
39. See James Cone, *God of the Oppressed*, rev. ed. (New York: Maryknoll, 1997), 129, 134, 145–49.

vulnerability and fear? In the remainder of the chapter, I consider this question from the perspective of the US epidemic of gun violence. For virtually all of those invested in this issue, fear of death and loss are a defining feature and propel human action.

Contemporary Gun Violence

In June 2023, sixteen-year-old Ralph Yarl accidentally knocked on the wrong door in Kansas City, Missouri, to pick up his twin brothers. The homeowner, an eighty-four-year-old white man, thought Yarl, who is black, was trying to break into his house. He shot Yarl within seconds of opening the door. Earlier that year, Kaylin Gillis was shot and killed in upstate New York when she turned into the wrong driveway while looking for a friend's house. That same month Payton Washington, a Texas cheerleader, was shot in a parking lot after her friend accidentally tried to enter the wrong vehicle. What is so striking about these incidents, all occurring in the span of just a few months, is the way fear and distrust can turn an ordinary human error into a tragedy. Examples like these could be multiplied. In 2022 someone in the United States was shot in a road-rage incident approximately once every sixteen hours.[40] American gun violence sits right at the heart of human fear, isolation, and distrust.

As with low-wage work and mass incarceration, the data on gun violence is sobering.[41] In 2022 over forty-eight thousand people in the United States died from firearm violence. Approximately 56 percent of these deaths were suicides, and gun deaths were the number one killer of children and teens. Gun suicides increased by 1.6 percent from 2021, which was itself a record year. In 2022 there were 19,592 gun homicides. As we saw in chapter 6, interpersonal gun violence disproportionately impacts black communities.[42] These numbers

40. Sarah Burd-Sharps, Paige Tetens, and Jay Szkola, "Road Rage Shootings Are Continuing to Surge," Everytown for Gun Safety, March 20, 2023, https://everytownresearch.org/reports-of-road-rage-shootings-are-on-the-rise/.

41. Data from "Fast Facts: Firearm Violence and Prevention," Centers for Disease Control and Prevention, accessed December 19, 2023, https://www.cdc.gov/violenceprevention/firearms/fastfact.html; Katherine Schaeffer, "Key Facts about Americans and Guns," Pew Research Center, September 13, 2023, https://www.pewresearch.org/short-reads/2023/09/13/key-facts-about-americans-and-guns/; "CDC Provisional Data: Gun Suicides Reach All-Time High in 2022, Gun Homicides Down Slightly from 2021," Johns Hopkins Bloomberg School of Public Health (website), July 27, 2023, https://publichealth.jhu.edu/2023/cdc-provisional-data-gun-suicides-reach-all-time-high-in-2022-gun-homicides-down-slightly-from-2021.

42. "Invisible Wounds: Gun Violence and Community Trauma among Black Americans," Everytown for Gun Safety, May 27, 2021, updated February 27, 2023, https://everytownresearch.org/report/invisible-wounds-gun-violence-and-community-trauma-among-black-americans/.

reflect the large quantity of firearms in US households relative to every other nation in the world. Roughly 40 percent of US adults live in a household with a gun, and the country boasts approximately 378 million guns in circulation. This means that, as is commonly reported, the country has more guns than people.[43] The fatality numbers, of course, do not capture the trauma of living in neighborhoods plagued by gun violence or the communal fear of mass shootings carried out in public places, shootings that are often motivated by animosity toward a specific group.

Two-thirds of gun owners cite personal protection as the primary reason for owning a gun, a number that has been gradually increasing in past decades as interest in owning guns for hunting and other sport use has declined.[44] About half of Americans who do not currently own a gun say they could see themselves doing so in the future. While most gun owners indicate that protection and safety—for themselves but also for others—is the main reason for owning a gun, guns also present significant safety risks.[45] According to one recent longitudinal study, handgun owners were four times more likely than nonowners to commit suicide.[46] Another study found that the overall fatality rate for suicide attempts was 8.5 percent but gun suicide attempts were fatal 90 percent of the time.[47] This high rate of fatality is incredibly significant given that 70 percent of people who survive a suicide attempt do not try again.[48] Unless they are stored safely, guns also present a risk of accidental death for children. Safe storage, however, decreases the accessibility of guns for self-protection, undermining the reason for owning one in the first place. A gun locked away in a gun safe, in a separate location from ammunition, is not going to be much help if there is a nighttime intruder. Debates about the frequency of protective gun use are notoriously fraught, and data is limited. Gun-rights activists will often cite telephone-survey research from the late 1990s suggesting that guns

43. Jennifer Mascia and Chip Brownlee, "How Many Guns Are Circulating in the U.S.?," *The Trace*, March 6, 2023, updated December 19, 2023, https://www.thetrace.org/2023/03/guns-america-data-atf-total/.

44. Nicholas Buttrick, "Protective Gun Ownership as a Coping Mechanism," *Perspectives on Psychological Science* 15, no. 4 (2020): 835–55.

45. For a summary of the academic research on safety, see Melinda Wenner Moyer, "Will Guns Keep Your Family Safe? Here's What the Evidence Says," *The Trace*, April 7, 2020, https://www.thetrace.org/2020/04/gun-safety-research-coronavirus-gun-sales/.

46. David M. Studdert et al., "Handgun Ownership and Suicide in California," *New England Journal of Medicine* 382 (2020): 2220–29.

47. Andrew Conner, Deborah Azrael, and Matthew Miller, "Suicide Case-Fatality Rates in the United States, 2007 to 2014: A Nationwide Population-Based Study," *Annals of Internal Medicine* 171, no. 12 (December 2019): 885–95.

48. "Gun Suicide across the States," Brady Campaign (website), https://www.bradyunited.org/fact-sheets/gun-suicide-across-the-states.

are used defensively 2.5 million times a year. Meanwhile, a recent analysis of
the National Crime Victimization Survey indicated that among crimes occurring in the presence of a victim between 2007 and 2011, guns were used for
self-defense in only about 1 percent of cases and that the use of a gun did not
result in a lower rate of injury.[49]

Americans have responded to the steady increase in firearm violence, and especially to highly publicized mass shootings, with a modest increase in support
for policy changes meant to curb gun violence. According to Gallup polling,
57 percent of Americans support making the laws covering the sale of firearms
stricter, up from a low of 44 percent in 2010. When asked about specific measures, like universal background checks, Americans support many policies at
even higher levels, raising questions about how well informed Americans are
as a whole regarding current laws. According to the most recent survey data,
92 percent favor universal background checks, 81 percent support red-flag
laws, 77 percent support a thirty-day waiting period for gun purchases, and
depending on the survey, anywhere from 46 percent to 60 percent support
a ban on new assault-weapon purchases.[50] Even among gun owners, support
for specific restrictions is high. In one large national survey, 75 percent of
gun owners supported universal background checks, 67 percent supported a
required safety course, and a substantial minority of 41 percent supported an
assault-weapon ban.[51]

Gun Culture and Gun Enthusiasm

As these numbers indicate, not all gun owners fit the broader cultural stereotypes of "gun culture." Behaviors like participation in the National Rifle
Association (NRA), opposition to any gun-control legislation, regular practice
of concealed carry, and frequent attendance of events like gun shows play
a substantial role in the perception of gun owners among the non-owning
population, but in the academic literature this subculture represents a minority

49. D. Hemenway and S. J. Solnick, "The Epidemiology of Self-Defense Gun Use: Evidence from
the National Crime Victimization Surveys 2007–2011," *Preventative Medicine* 29 (2015): 22–27.

50. Data from "Guns," Gallup, accessed December 19, 2023, https://news.gallup.com/poll/1645
/guns.aspx; "Drop in Assault Weapon Ban Support," Monmouth University (website), April 24, 2023,
https://www.monmouth.edu/polling-institute/reports/monmouthpoll_us_042423/; "Voters Favor
Gun Limits over Arming Citizens to Reduce Gun Violence," Fox News, April 27, 2023, https://
www.foxnews.com/official-polls/fox-news-poll-voters-favor-gun-limits-arming-citizens-reduce-gun
-violence.

51. Michael Siegel and Claire Boine, "The Meaning of Guns to Gun Owners in the U.S.: The
2019 National Lawful Use of Guns Survey," *American Journal of Preventive Medicine* 59, no. 5 (2020):
678–85.

of gun owners. Sociologists Claire Boine, Kevin Caffrey, and Michael Siegel classify this group of gun owners as "second amendment activists," and in their analysis, such people constitute 18 percent of gun owners.[52] Other researchers have classified this type of gun owner as a "gun enthusiast" or have sought to analyze such people according to the rubric of "gun empowerment," meaning that the owners have a high level of moral and emotional attachment to guns.[53]

Ethnographic studies of gun culture are particularly helpful in attending to the self-understanding of gun owners and the values they associate with owning or carrying a firearm. In her book *Citizen-Protectors*, sociologist Jennifer Carlson describes the motives and values of gun owners in Michigan who applied for concealed-carry licenses.[54] Carlson notes that her subjects, who were racially diverse and living in high-crime areas of Detroit and Flint, understood themselves to be fundamentally peaceful people who wanted to protect themselves, their families, and the broader public from a breakdown in public order. To this end, persons going through the process of acquiring a concealed-carry license had to take a training course, most of which were taught by NRA-certified instructors. As Carlson describes them, these courses were intended to cultivate a particular moral identity. Instructors asked students to reflect on the significance of taking another human life and made clear the gravity and horror that would be involved in doing so. For these instructors, carrying a gun was a commitment to a set of moral values, including civic duty, protection of the innocent, self-reliance, and, ultimately, the celebration of life. Carrying a gun was also a way to participate fully in one's citizenship by exercising a constitutional right. In order to inhabit this character well, students in the training courses were encouraged to think deeply about their own limits, to visualize danger scenarios, and to be actively aware of situations and potential threats while they were carrying. Carlson notes that her subjects were responding both to the threat of violent crime—she conducted her research in the midst of the economic recession, when crime rates in Detroit and

52. Claire Boine, Kevin Caffrey, and Michael Siegel, "Who Are Gun Owners in the United States? A Latent Class Analysis of the 2019 National Lawful Use of Guns Survey," *Sociological Perspectives* 65, no. 1 (February 2022): 35–57.

53. F. Carson Mencken and Paul Froese, "Gun Culture in Action," *Social Problems* 66 (2019): 3–27.

54. Jennifer Carlson, *Citizen-Protectors: The Everyday Politics of Guns in an Age of Decline* (Oxford: Oxford University Press, 2015). Carlson's research is not limited to the category of gun enthusiast or activist, but because many of her subjects are instructors for NRA training courses, there is considerable overlap between her subjects and the category descriptions of other researchers in the field. Boine and her colleagues locate Carlson's work with other scholarship that has focused "only on a fraction of gun owners who are the most active in gun rights activism." Boine, Caffrey, and Siegel, "Who Are Gun Owners," 36.

Flint remained high—and also to status threats. Many of her male subjects were experiencing economic hardship that prevented them from fulfilling the cultural role of family provider.[55]

Researchers using both survey and ethnographic methodologies make connections between personal identity and gun culture. In a number of studies racial resentment and a perceived threat to masculinity correlated with aspects of gun culture, such as opposing universal background checks, seeing guns as important to personal identity, or finding guns emotionally empowering.[56] Gun ownership and the desire to own a gun were also associated with economic and social anxieties.[57] Survey studies such as these cannot establish causation, but ethnographic work also supports the hypothesis that guns are being used as a source of security in the face of not only physical and material threats but also symbolic threats to personal identity.[58] Associating guns with one's sense of self, however, makes the stakes in public debate rise even higher. As Nicholas Buttrick observes in his analysis of gun ownership as a psychological coping mechanism, "One consequence of making guns a marker of identity is that arguments about gun control become arguments about identity."[59]

During the past few decades the NRA, the flagship organization for gun-rights support, has tried to instill a connection between gun ownership and personal identity in their communications with members by using positive language of virtuous citizenship to describe gun owners.[60] By connecting NRA members' identity and sense of belonging to gun rights and gun ownership, the organization is then able to use threats to these psychological needs (real or imagined) to mobilize their members for political activism against gun

55. Carlson, *Citizen-Protectors*, 31–56.

56. Kevin Drakulich and Brandon M. Craig, "How Intersectional Threat Shapes Views of Gun Policy: The John Wayne Solution," *Social Problems*, spac017 (2022), https://academic.oup.com/socpro /advance-article-abstract/doi/10.1093/socpro/spac017/6550556?redirectedFrom=fulltext; Tara D. Warner and Shawn Ratcliff, "What Guns Mean: Who Sees Guns as Important, Essential, and Empowering (and Why)?," *Sociological Inquiry* 91, no. 2 (May 2021): 313–45.

57. Tara D. Warner and Trent Steidley, "Some Fear, More Loathing? Threats and Anxieties Shaping Protective Gun Ownership and Gun Carry in the U.S.," *Journal of Crime Justice* 45, no. 4 (2022): 484–505.

58. Jennifer Carlson, "Mourning Mayberry: Guns, Masculinity, and Socioeconomic Decline," *Gender and Society* 29, no. 3 (June 2015): 386–409; Angela Stroud, *Good Guys with Guns: The Appeal and Consequences of Concealed Carry* (Chapel Hill: University of North Carolina Press, 2016); Scott Melzer, *Gun Crusaders: The NRA's Culture War* (New York: New York University Press, 2009).

59. Buttrick, "Protective Gun Ownership," 843.

60. Matthew J. Lacombe, "The Political Weaponization of Gun Owners: The National Rifle Association's Cultivation, Dissemination, and Use of a Group Social Identity," *Journal of Politics* 81, no. 4 (2019): 1342–56. See also Melzer, *Gun Crusaders*.

control.[61] As the history of US gun legislation shows, the NRA has been enormously successful in this effort. Many attribute this success to the power of money and political donations, but the NRA's real strength is the commitment of grassroots activists. To take just one example, after the 1999 shooting at the Columbine, Colorado, high school, the gun manufacturer Smith & Wesson, in conversation with the Clinton administration, agreed to several voluntary reforms, including child-safe triggers and the development of a "smart" gun that could be discharged only by the owner. In response the NRA criticized Smith & Wesson as a "sellout," and a massive grassroots campaign of boycotts and angry phone calls ensued, pressuring the company to abandon the reforms.[62] In his study of the NRA and its members, sociologist Scott Melzer observes that it is not love of guns that motivates these members; it is fear.[63] And the fact that NRA members are fearful is not an accident. The NRA maintains a sense of threat through frequent and derogatory references to enemies in their publications and events. While NRA members are described as moral, patriotic, and brave, the media and anti-gun activists are "liars," "devious," "extremists," "tyrannical," and so forth.[64]

The NRA has also made use of religious language and symbolism, tapping into its members' existing religious beliefs to construct a common identity for their grassroots political activism.[65] Beginning in the 2000s, NRA publications increasingly used the language of a "God-given right" to talk about gun ownership and the Second Amendment. During the NRA presidency of Charlton Heston, a professing Christian famous for playing Moses in the film *The Ten Commandments*, the organization made use of implicit religious symbolism. In speeches and writings Heston drew explicitly on religious language and biblical stories. The use of the category of "evil" also increased in the 2000s and referred not just to criminals or terrorists but also to those who wished to limit gun ownership. In NRA meetings, entertainment includes religious music, and speeches are peppered with religious platitudes.[66]

61. Melzer, *Gun Crusaders*, 73–109; Lacombe, "Political Weaponization of Gun Owners," 1352–53; Kevin Lewis O'Neill, "Armed Citizens and the Stories They Tell: The National Rifle Association's Achievement of Terror and Masculinity," *Men and Masculinities* 9, no. 4 (April 2007): 457–75.

62. Avi Selk, "A Gunmaker Once Tried to Reform Itself. The NRA Nearly Destroyed It," *Washington Post*, February 27, 2018, https://www.washingtonpost.com/news/retropolis/wp/2018/02/27/a-gunmaker-once-tried-to-reform-itself-the-nra-nearly-destroyed-it/

63. Melzer, *Gun Crusaders*, 1.

64. Lacombe, "Political Weaponization of Gun Owners," 1348.

65. Jessica Dawson, "Shall Not Be Infringed: How the NRA Used Religious Language to Transform the Meaning of the Second Amendment," *Palgrave Communications* 5, no. 1, article 58 (2019).

66. Melzer, *Gun Crusaders*, 3, 13–15.

Christians and Gun Enthusiasm

The NRA's regular use of religious language suggests that American Christianity is no stranger to enthusiastic gun culture, and plenty of popular-culture evidence can be marshaled to support this connection. At a 2022 Christian conference, Colorado congresswoman Lauren Boebert joked that if Jesus had possessed assault rifles, maybe his government would not have killed him. Attendees at the conference responded with tepid and awkward laughter, but the very fact that Boebert even made the comment is quite informative. It suggests a Christian subculture where allegiance to guns is so pervasive that an opportunist like Boebert would assume this could be an effective argument. In the past decade several churches have confirmed this impression by giving away assault rifles in order to lure visitors to church.[67] Given the plentiful images available online depicting Jesus holding an assault rifle, as well as prominent politicians' Christmas-card photos showing everyone in their family holding assault rifles, the existence of a gun-friendly Christian subculture would be difficult to deny.

These cultural markers are consistent with a broad overlap between conservative Protestantism, especially white conservative Protestantism, and gun culture in the sociological literature. In one recent nationally representative study, 36 percent of white evangelicals and 35 percent of white mainline Protestants said they personally owned a gun, whereas only 25 percent of the general population and 24 percent of black Protestants answered likewise.[68] In another study only 37 percent of evangelicals favored stricter gun-control laws, whereas 48 percent of mainline Protestants, 64 percent of Catholics, and 76 percent of black Protestants did. Evangelicals were also more likely to favor religious solutions to gun violence, like reintroducing prayer in public schools.[69] While these associations between gun ownership and Christian faith do exist, researchers have also discerned important nuances regarding the level of personal commitment to religion, gun ownership, and gun identity. One study found that while theological conservatism predicted handgun ownership, higher levels

---

67. "Troy Church Gives Away AR-15, but Not without Controversy," WRGB, June 29, 2020, https://cbs6albany.com/news/local/troy-church-gives-away-ar-15s; Andrew Wolfson, "Ky. Baptists Lure New Worshippers with Gun Giveaway," *Louisville Courier-Journal*, March 3, 2014, https://www.usatoday.com/story/news/nation/2014/03/03/churches-guns-giveaway/5967533/.

68. Diane Orcés, "The Gun Ownership Bubble: Gun Owners Are More Likely to Have Other Gun Owners as Close Friends," PRRI, June 10, 2022, https://www.prri.org/spotlight/the-gun-ownership-bubble-gun-owners-are-more-likely-to-have-other-gun-owners-as-close-friends/. See also David Yamane, "Awash in a Sea of Faith and Firearms: Rediscovering the Connection between Religion and Gun Ownership in America," *Journal for the Scientific Study of Religion* 55, no. 3 (2016): 622–36.

69. Stephen M. Merino, "God and Guns: Examining Religious Influences on Gun Control Attitudes in the United States, *Religions* 9 (2018): 189.

of religious involvement actually correlated with lower ownership.[70] Another study found that gun owners who self-identified as more religious reported less of what researchers termed "gun empowerment"—a sense of symbolic attachment to one's guns—than owners who were less religious.[71] A third study found that belief in an "engaged God" correlated with lower levels of gun empowerment.[72] Finally, researchers found that identification with Christian nationalism, rather than with identifiers like "evangelical" or "mainline," was a very strong predictor of opposition to gun-control legislation.[73] Findings like these, though limited in scope according to the particular variables in each study, point to greater complexity in the relationship between Christianity and guns than the popular stereotypes suggest.

The very limited ethnographic work on religion and gun ownership has likewise added nuance to the relationship between Christianity and gun culture. In one short qualitative study, ethnographers discerned that their Christian participants understood themselves to have several interlocking duties—to protect, to be diligent, and to defend—and that participants interpreted these duties as part of their Christian faith.[74] These interviewees affirmed the existence of evil as a motivating factor in their gun ownership, but they did not articulate distinctly Christian reasons and seemed to sense some tension with the teachings of Jesus or with the perceived wishes of their religious leaders. Religion scholar Michael Grigoni's more extensive ethnographic work with Christian handgun owners, however, provides a picture of a distinctly Christian approach to gun ownership.[75] Grigoni's interlocutors had often reflected deeply on the implications of their faith for their use of firearms and believed that their Christian commitment imposed limits. Grigoni documents that many of his research participants, despite not having formal theological training, employed traditional just-war criteria when thinking through legitimate and illegitimate uses of force in dangerous situations. This ethnographic work confirms the quantitative research suggesting a variety of approaches to gun

70. Yamane, "Awash in a Sea of Faith," 631.

71. F. Carson Mencken and Paul Froese, "Gun Culture in Action," *Social Problems* 66 (2019): 3–27.

72. Laura Upenieks, Terrence D. Hill, and James E. Robertson, "Pictures of You: God Images, Gun Ownership, and Empowerment in the United States," *Social Science Quarterly* 104 (2023): 92–109.

73. Andrew L. Whitehead, Landon Schnabel, and Samuel Perry, "Gun Control in the Crosshairs: Christian Nationalism and Opposition to Stricter Gun Laws," *Socius* 4 (2018): 1–13. The data set used for this study is from 2007. It would be interesting to see if the results from new data would be consistent or perhaps even stronger.

74. Abigail Vegter and Margaret Kelley, "The Protestant Ethic and the Spirit of Gun Ownership," *Journal for the Scientific Study of Religion* 59, no. 3 (2020): 526–40.

75. Michael R. Grigoni, "The Christian Handgun Owner and Just War," *Journal of Moral Theology* 12, no. 2 (2023): 108–32.

ownership and differing levels of participation in stereotypical gun culture. The participants in Grigoni's research certainly do not seem to be so cavalier about the implications of faith for owning and operating lethal weapons that they would pose in front of a Christmas tree with assault rifles.

Eschatological Grace and Gun Culture

Both those who own guns for personal protection and gun-control advocates can exemplify what Barth terms "human care," and I will take each of these in turn, beginning with gun ownership. My intent here is not to single out enthusiastic gun owners as extreme exemplars of human fear and anxiety in American culture. I agree with Barth that these phenomena are very nearly universal, and for whatever reason, they are especially intense in our cultural and historical moment. My objective is also not to reflect on Christian use of violence for self-defense or the protection of vulnerable people, although my comments here may ultimately be relevant for such a discussion. Instead, my objective is to shift from the question of what is permissible or prohibited based on Christian values and teaching (e.g., did Jesus prohibit his followers from making any recourse to violence?) to the question of what sort of life is possible for vulnerable and finite creatures if Jesus really has defeated sin and death. If we are to avoid practical atheism, a state in which we profess a radical-sounding belief in Christ that makes no actual difference in our lives, then this question is essential. It must actually matter that God's promises of ultimate restoration are brought forward into the present. How, then, does this matter when it comes to gun violence?

Here I submit that grace asks of the person, and calls them to, a life of trust, a life in which the vulnerable and finite person might not eliminate fear of death but can make peace with death and with the ordinary uncertainties of human existence. In short, grace enables and calls the person to be willing to be a creature and to affirm finite existence as good. If God is utterly and completely for a person, even in their death, then the constant hum of anxiety, however natural its embodied aspects may be and however understandable its presence may be, is in tension with this life of trust and joy. I say this, of course, knowing that I too am an anxious person.

Here it seems that those who regularly practice concealed carry might be formed toward an attentiveness to life's dangers and the need to be vigilant in self-protection. As we have seen, this attitude can be admirable and appealing, especially for those who undertake the practice with care and a sense of due diligence. It is a distinct moral stance. It is not, however, a particularly

Christian stance. It is important to be clear on this point: I am not claiming that regular concealed carry will invariably encourage a disposition of fear. We have already seen in Grigoni's ethnographic work that some Christian gun owners approach the moral questions with their faith fully engaged and with resources to resist a simplistic denial of human mortality. At the same time, it is not difficult to see how keeping a weapon on one's person could exert such a potent influence. In the absence of any specific threat, the rationale for carrying a concealed weapon is the simple presence of danger and evil in the world. In other words, the rationale is the ordinary experience of human vulnerability. Regular concealed carry suggests that the default response to vulnerability should be attentiveness to it. Danger is a constant possibility, and people should be prepared to respond *themselves*. As opposed to a circumstance where one is the target of a very specific threat and must discern—perhaps, for the Christian, in the context of prayer and communal discernment—whether the protection of a lethal weapon is appropriate to the specific good one is called to pursue, routine concealed carry presumes self-defense is always necessary.[76]

Just as Luther argued that extreme wealth could cultivate a disposition of self-sufficiency and a distrust in God, a practice like concealed carry has the potential to instill a sense of trust in a weapon and, ultimately, to generate trust in the self as the overriding source of security. The argument here is complicated because the Christian tradition has generally affirmed ordinary actions of self-preservation as congruent with the sort of creature we are before God. Thus, Christians do not, as a rule, reject medical care in favor of trusting God to heal. But treating concealed carry as a default setting seems less like receiving medical care for a serious illness or injury and more like calling one's doctor friend to inquire about every minor ailment. As a routine practice, concealed carry both reflects and reinforces a particular orientation to life, one that resists any reckoning with the inevitable end to one's present existence as part of God's grace rather than a contradiction of it. That all of this is physically represented and felt in the gun attached to one's person makes the gun a kind of antisacrament. Rather than a sign of God's grace, it is a sign of the need for self-protection and of the potential absence of God.

A similar distrust is manifest when guns become a central feature of personal identity. As we have seen, sociologists studying gun culture have focused on the way an identity as a family protector or a responsible conceal-carry citizen replaces a threatened sense of self-worth that is grounded in an

---

76. I am indebted here to Grigoni's insightful analysis of the Deacons for Defense and Justice, an armed group of black Americans that provided protection for civil-rights activists during the dangerous era of Jim Crow and lynchings. See Grigoni, "Christian Handgun Owner," 125–28.

economic or social status. In the context of a theology of grace, none of these identities is the true source of a person's worth. Rather, the primary identity of a child of God cannot be threatened by any human circumstances and is freely given without regard for prior status or identity. It is this identity that Howard Thurman claims can stabilize the ego and put a person "in a position to appraise his own intrinsic powers, gifts, talents, and abilities."[77] The security of God's love, brought into the present in one's communion with Christ, tells us we each have much to contribute to the flourishing of our neighbors and community and helps us see clearly what those contributions might be. The difficult thing about basing one's identity on heroic protection is that it requires a world of constant danger, even if this danger must be manufactured and even though the expectation of sudden peril can lead to phantom threats, with tragic consequences. Recall what I said earlier in the chapter about the trend of shootings carried out in response to perceived but untrue threats. There is no room for peace or for a flourishing community in the imagination of the person whose identity and worth comes from heroic violence.

As for gun culture, participating in it narrows a person's sphere of concern and divides and atomizes human community. Organizations like the NRA intentionally cultivate fear, anger, and enmity toward the "bad guys," a category that is problematically racialized in the US context, and toward anyone who opposes their political objectives. Participation in the NRA's political activism, with its polarizing rhetoric, privileges a narrow concern for the right to protect oneself and one's family over having a broader conversation about steps that might help reduce gun violence for the community as a whole. It is a posture that pays scant attention to who is actually harmed by most gun violence— the poor minority residents of high-crime neighborhoods and the people who are hurt by a gun in their own home, whether through an accident, domestic violence, or a suicide attempt.

When the defense of Second Amendment rights extends to the military-style rifles used in most mass shootings, the sphere of concern is narrower still. No reasonable person can insist that an AR-15 is necessary for self-defense or the protection of one's family. As Tyler Austin Harper, a gun owner and professor at Bates College, wrote after the shooting in his own town of Lewiston, Maine, "I'll let you in on the dirty secret that everyone knows in their heart of hearts: The AR-15 is America's best-selling rifle not because people need them for protection or because our country is full of aspiring militiamen or paranoid whack jobs waiting for civil war. People own AR-15s because they think they're

77. Thurman, *Jesus and the Disinherited*, 43.

sexy and cool and manly."[78] Here the primary concern is not even the lives of one's family members; it is personal pleasure. In my own classes I have taught students who were present during a school shooting or who personally knew victims of a mass shooting. Of course, I know about this only because the students mentioned the ongoing trauma associated with the events. The narrow focus on personal freedom for self-defense, or on the identity and enjoyment one derives from owning such weapons, prevents meaningful reflection about the broader communal risks associated with the increasing availability of guns. In the language of this book, it rejects human interdependence and mutual concern for the vulnerability of the other.

I have argued in this chapter that the grace of the last things calls a person to a life of trust and provides an alternative to a life filled with human care. As we saw above, a handful of studies suggest that greater commitment to Christian faith or practice is correlated with lower levels of involvement in some aspects of gun culture. This empirical evidence is too preliminary and too general to support any firm theological conclusions, but it does perhaps provide some ground for hope that American Christianity and gun culture are not inseparable. It suggests an opening for Christian pastors and leaders to reflect more specifically on the role of death and hope in Christian life and to challenge the efforts of those who wish to co-opt Christian language and manipulate ordinary believers. The widespread capitulations of Christians to the broader culture of fear, a culture that extends beyond the contentious issue of reducing gun violence, will not, however, be self-correcting. We have traveled very far down this path, and correcting our assumptions and habits of thought will take concerted effort. There is a serious need for a renewed language of eschatological grace and hope.

Human Care and Gun-Control Activism

If Christian pastors and leaders were to adopt such language, would it have anything constructive to say to the person who opposes the mass weaponization of American society? In a country with more guns than people, for what should this person hope? For this person, too, the presence of Jesus at the frontier, at the limit of temporal life, opposes an attitude of fear. With respect to support for gun control, an attitude of fear might be the source of either avoidance or of activism. When Christian anti-gun activist James Atwood convinced the Virginia state legislature to adopt a "Stop Gun Violence" license plate, he was

78. Tyler Austin Harper, "How Much Blood Is Your Fun Worth?," *The Atlantic*, October 26, 2023, https://www.theatlantic.com/ideas/archive/2023/10/lewiston-maine-mass-shooting-guns/675790/.

saddened to discover that several friends declined to purchase them out of fear of facing vandalism or violence.[79] Similarly, when I attended an anti-gun-violence lecture by Shane Claiborne at Hope College in 2023, an audience member asked him if he was afraid of becoming an object of gun violence himself on account of his anti-gun activism. On the other hand, if support for specific gun control is focused mainly on the horror of mass shootings, disregarding the larger number of deaths from gun homicide in cities and suicide in rural America, then it may be an activism that is too narrowly determined by one's own human care and not shaped enough by love of neighbor. As we saw in chapter 6, serious efforts to reduce gun violence in the highest-crime areas must contend with social issues like poverty and lack of economic opportunity. And although we have not investigated the issue in this book, the increasing "deaths of despair"—deaths that include not only rising numbers of suicides but also deaths from drug overdoses and alcohol abuse—likely involve a complex set of causes.[80] Genuine love of neighbor will call for an approach to reducing gun violence that is much more holistic than simple advocacy of an assault-weapon ban or of an increase to the minimum age for firearm purchases.

While efforts to restrict gun access can be expressions of fear and anxiety, I am hesitant, for reasons already discussed, to affirm Barth's association of activism with human care. Undoubtedly, activism of various kinds can function as a denial of human limitations and, like gun ownership for personal protection, can become a kind of identity by which a person seeks to establish their own value. But just as someone can own a gun without it being the symbolic center of their personal identity and worth, so too can one pursue social and political change without granting this pursuit ultimate personal significance. Given the extent of gun violence today, gun-control activism in particular can be part of a life that seeks to testify to the coming kingdom of God. Further, gun-control activists can benefit from the recognition of eschatological grace. Like gun owners, activists must resist the temptation to see their struggle as being against a human enemy. They must reject the atomization of society and seek to understand others even when deep disagreement is present. Like gun enthusiasts, gun-control activists have also been guilty of rhetorically targeting their political opponents and using demeaning language. The sociological research on gun owners provides some evidence that this sort of language has alienated many gun owners who are sympathetic to some gun-control and gun-safety regulations. Although a majority of gun owners in one study

79. James E. Atwood, *Collateral Damage: Changing the Conversation about Firearms and Faith* (Harrisonburg, VA: Harold, 2019), 71.
80. The term "deaths of despair" was coined by economists Anne Case and Angus Deaton in *Deaths of Despair and the Future of Capitalism* (Princeton: Princeton University Press, 2021).

supported some kind of gun-violence prevention, only 7 percent had ever expressed their support publicly. The most commonly offered reason for not speaking up was that they felt they were being blamed for violence by gun-control advocates.[81] Christian activists in particular should, in their activism, seek to understand the other.

The promise of a full restoration of God's kingdom, which will come as a gift through God's action, should protect activists from despairing at the size of the task before them or the inadequacy of their own efforts. What is the gun-control advocate to think when encountering a society with more guns than people? While the burden of absolute restoration does not rest on human action, we should not take this to mean that activists should be indifferent to the success of their efforts. It is by knowing that God will ultimately restore peace that proponents of gun control are convinced that peace does matter and is worth pursuing. This promise tells them that God is at work now too and that they should hope God's efforts will succeed beyond what they imagine human action is able to accomplish. As Gutiérrez writes, "Concern for effective action is a way of expressing love for the other. The gratuitousness of the gift of the kingdom does not do away with effective action but rather calls for it all the more."[82]

Conclusion

The horrors of American gun violence provide all-too-frequent occasions for fear and anxiety in the face of human finitude and mortality. The easy availability of personal firearms offers a tempting solution. By arming ourselves, we can feel safe and protect those closest to us. Eschatological grace, by contrast, invites the person to a deeper reckoning. God in Christ has already accomplished human salvation and God will bring about the fullness of that salvation. In theory, God's gracious action means that we can relinquish fear, that we can expand our sphere of concern in responding to the threat of gun violence by considering not just our own safety but also the flourishing of our neighbor and our broader community. "In theory," however, can sometimes feel like a far cry from reality. Can we, in these mortal bodies, ever truly relinquish fear? One might ask a similar question of grace and human action more broadly. I have argued throughout this book that a theology of grace calls for a particular form of social existence. But to what extent does receiving grace actually enable this existence? In the epilogue, I suggest that addressing this concern calls not only for a theology of grace, but also for a spirituality of grace.

81. Siegel and Boine, "Meaning of Guns," 680.
82. Guttiérrez, *We Drink from Our Own Wells*, 108.

EPILOGUE

A Spirituality for a Graced Identity

Can a Christian experience of grace nurture behavior that is consistent with grace? The question is reminiscent of the end of Stanley Hauerwas's classic primer in Christian ethics, where he offers a discussion of spirituality. Though he notes that it may seem like an odd way to end a book on ethics, he argues that not doing so "is to risk an abstractness that belies the seriousness of our claims."[1] What is the point of arguing that we should live a particular way in community with others if that life does not seem within our grasp? This issue is particularly salient for reflection on a Reformation account of grace because the argument of Luther and Calvin is that grace has a distinct psychology. By breaking into the present, grace makes possible a life that is not otherwise possible. With grace, the person need not be driven by fears and anxieties. Here it seems that the experiential aspect is crucial. For grace to have such an effect, people must really experience it as breaking in. When reading Luther on the freedom that grace affords, the psychological component can, at times, seem unrealistic. Does Luther really imagine that a changed belief can override human fear of death? Is it not, perhaps, more likely that fear will distort the psychology of grace and turn it into a freedom to disregard sin, to continue living as one has always lived, with the comforting promise that because of God's forgiveness human action does not matter? In this final reflection, we will return to the dynamic with which we began this book—the psychology of grace and the question of human agency. My contention is that this psychology

1. Stanley Hauerwas, *The Peaceable Kingdom* (Notre Dame, IN: University of Notre Dame Press, 1983), 149.

ultimately depends on a spirituality because the claims of grace cannot simply be assented to. In order to become central to our identity and to be a source of action, grace must be experiential. As Calvin says of God's promises of mercy, "We make them ours by inwardly embracing them."[2]

In chapter 1, we considered the common objection that a Reformation account of grace, in which the final verdict of "righteous" is brought forward into the present, would potentially undermine Christian ethics by rendering it irrelevant. I want to return to this objection from the perspective of an experiential account of grace. Why should I not just continue to sin, knowing that God forgives me? It is not at all difficult to see why this objection has persisted, and I have no interest in denying that human psychology can and does, at times, function this way. Complacency with sin is indeed a risk of grace. Rather than deny this, I suggest two complementary avenues of response, one theological in orientation and the other pastoral, rooted in a spirituality of grace.

The theological response is that it is crucial to observe, as Paul indeed does, that though this temptation is understandable from the present perspective, it is also an absurdity. The objection is indicative of a mindset that is still trapped in an economy of action and merit and has simply found a nifty shortcut. In this mindset "salvation" is the arbitrary reward that could, in theory, come as the result of living a perfect life but, because of the shortcut, comes as the result of "faith." There is no intrinsic connection between good action and salvation. Salvation is simply the reward *assigned to* good action. Such caricatures are a distortion of what Christian theology actually understands salvation to be. Christian salvation is the eternal bliss of fellowship with God in communion with others. But love of God and neighbor is also the very thing that constitutes Christian virtue or righteousness. Salvation thus means being rescued *from* sin, and sin itself simply is damnation. It would be absurd for someone to say they want to be saved and then plan to continue sinning with the vague notion that their eternal salvation is secure. It would be like the same person—let's call her Anne—happily agreeing to be friends with a recent acquaintance named Lily but then entirely ignoring this new friend. Any friendship they had would simply be a mirage; it is not really friendship.

The appropriate pastoral response to this problem is not to turn back to the psychology of right action and a desirable outcome that is earned by it. Thinking in this way moves us out of the realm of love. Rather, the pastoral response, if we want to get to the place of mutually caring relationship, is to hold out consistently, through spiritual practice, the genuine good that such

---

2. John Calvin, *Institutes of the Christian Religion* 3.2.16, ed. John T. McNeill, trans. Ford Lewis Battles (Philadelphia: Westminster, 1960), 561.

a relationship, in fact, *is*. It is to remind one another of the inherent goodness
and joy of fellowship with God. In the example of two friends, Anne cannot
earn friendship by spending time with Lily, but she also cannot experience
friendship without some forms of togetherness and without corresponding
actions that indicate she genuinely cares about Lily. Anne might be so deep
in the economy of earning and deserving that she cannot possibly understand
this. If Lily insists that they cannot be friends because Anne has ignored or
mistreated her, Anne may very well interpret this as a punishment for her actions. Similarly, if Lily invites her to lunch, Anne might think that Lily is trying
to lure her into being nice to her. No matter. If Lily is ever going to succeed
in being Anne's friend, something like this—holding Anne accountable for
her actions while also making overtures of friendship—is the course she must
take. Similarly, if we are to have any hope of disrupting the false psychology
of grace in ourselves and others, this disruption must come through remembering, contemplating, and experiencing the inherent beauty and desirability
of friendship with God. This is what Jesus means when he says, "Store up for
yourselves treasures in heaven" (Matt. 6:20), and what Paul means when he
says, "Set your minds on the things that are above, not on the things that are
on earth" (Col. 3:2).[3]

We tend to think of spiritual practices, like meditating on "things that are
above," as a discipline that trains the body and mind for something that seems
unnatural or even initially unpleasant to us. Given that the practices can require
effort, it is quite easy for us to fit them into an economy of earning and deserving and hard for us to see how they might relate to grace. But they do relate
to grace. In a culture that is as thoroughly grace denying as our own, we have
to strain paradoxically against it to create space for an experience of gratuity.
For Gustavo Gutiérrez, prayer functions in this way. "Like every dialogue of
love, prayer runs the risk of being interpreted as a 'useless activity,' whereas in
point of fact it is precisely an experience of a gratuitousness that creates new
forms of communication."[4] Prayer can seem like a task—the worst of all tasks,
because it is unproductive. But in prayer we invite an encounter with God, an
encounter that is not within our control. In prayer we are ultimately saying
that we can receive only what God chooses to give us.

At the end of a book on social ethics, many readers might feel that the
social issues we face are overwhelming and that any possible course of action
prompts a sense of inadequacy, hypocrisy, and failure. Others might eagerly

3. See James Alison, *The Joy of Being Wrong: Original Sin through Easter Eyes* (New York: Cross-
road, 1998), 211–36.
4. Gustavo Gutiérrez, *We Drink from Our Own Wells: The Spiritual Journey of a People*, trans.
Matthew J. O'Connell (Maryknoll, NY: Orbis Books, 1984), 111.

and imaginatively plan out action only to discover that beneath the flurry of
activity is the unacknowledged refrain, "I can deserve God's love." Yet Jesus
says his yoke is easy (Matt. 11:30) and calls his message "good news" (e.g.,
Mark 1:15). In either case—that of a person acting from weary and uninspired
duty or out of energetic frenzy—the life of grace is the life of prayer. "Prayer,"
Gutiérrez writes, "takes place in the love we know to be marked in its very
source by gratuitousness."[5] In prayer we cultivate a sense of God's love, empowering presence, and constant forgiveness. In prayer we open up to unexpected
opportunity, undeserved consolation, and incongruous hope. As Christians
we must *act*, and in the course of our action we may very well find that we act
with a sense of either burden or self-congratulation. But in prayer we open up
these attitudes to gratuitous transformation.

   Virtually all spiritual practices can be interpreted as this sort of openness to
grace. By observing the Sabbath and ceasing from productive labor, we create
space to remember and experience our primal dependence on God's gifts. By
joining with others in communal worship, we affirm that we must mediate
the gifts of God to one another and eschew a solitary dependence on God. In
the sacraments, we recognize, in material, tangible ways, our embodied need
to receive.

   Given the themes of this book, a few points are worth particular emphasis.
The first is the necessarily communal nature of a spirituality of grace. On the
one hand, I suspect that when spiritual practices are conducted in a solitary
manner, there is a strong temptation, especially in an individualistic cultural
context, to view them as personal accomplishments. They are, of course, always dependent on God, but does the divine not recede from view as we
find ourselves excelling in devotion? On the other hand, when we receive
from the hand of another—prayer, bread, the sign of peace—we confront
our need in a visceral way. And it is a genuine need. The actor Hank Azaria
writes about his friend the late Matthew Perry walking alongside him in the
path to recovery, telling the story of being overwhelmed at his first Alcoholics
Anonymous meeting. "It's very hard to imagine how going into a room like
that is somehow going to make you want to stop drinking or make you feel
better. And he looked at me and said in his Matthew, half-joking, very loving
way: 'It's something, isn't it? God is a bunch of drunks together in a room.'"[6]
Our foundational human interdependence means that, most of the time, we
experience God's love and acceptance by being accepted in community with

   5. Gutiérrez, *We Drink from Our Own Wells*, 111.
   6. Hank Azaria, "To Matthew Perry, God Was a Bunch of Drunks in a Room," *New York Times*,
November 9, 2023, https://www.nytimes.com/2023/11/09/opinion/matthew-perry-addiction.html.

others. This genuine, embodied acceptance by others can help quiet our fears. Life is less terrifying, and our struggles seem less insurmountable, when we are not alone. There is a reason why so much of Jesus's ministry was just about being with people. Psychologist Todd Hall argues that due to our inherently relational nature, we must envision Christian transformation as a relational process that necessarily involves other Christians.[7] If our attachment to God is, in part, shaped by human relationships of attachment, then it makes sense that a healing of the divine-human relationship would likewise come in and through loving human relationships.

The second point to address is the potential for grace to be inscribed experientially in situations of profound need or distress. At the beginning of chapter 7 I noted that Barth's characterization of "human care" as sloth could come across as dismissive of those who experience deep trauma and pain. I also relayed the insight from liberation theology that, often, the testimony of Christians in such situations is one of profound faith and hope. Theologian and peace scholar Janna Hunter-Bowman describes the tensions involved in an outsider making this sort of observation. Commenting on her experiences working with marginalized communities in Colombia, Hunter-Bowman writes, "For a long time, I found the villagers' vulnerability, born of their life circumstances paired with submission to a non-possessed God, truly terrifying. . . . But the communities taught me that to be insistent about a comprehensible God would inhibit what they might be able to expect in the interaction. When the villagers reach out in what they describe as 'unconditional surrender' to God, they position themselves as open and poised for the greatest possible response. They expect the Spirit to move in their midst."[8]

It seems that it is the experience of being at the end of one's own action, of being out of options, that creates the stunning and terrifying possibility of experiencing the grace of God. With Hunter-Bowman, I find myself immensely uncomfortable with the prospect of this kind of vulnerability. This is not only because I am an academic and am, therefore, most comfortable in the world of ideas that I can manipulate and figure out and then keep at a distance; it is also because my *life* is comfortable. Therefore, I am afraid. The kind of experience Hunter-Bowman is referring to is born of a risk and vulnerability that I simply do not want to experience.

In this fear I find that at the end of the day I am not so different, maybe not even at all different, from the gun enthusiast who embraces the identity

---

7. Todd W. Hall with M. Elizabeth Lewis Hall, *Relational Spirituality: A Psychological-Theological Paradigm for Transformation* (Downers Grove, IL: IVP Academic, 2021), 255.

8. Janna Hunter-Bowman, *Witnessing Peace: Becoming Agents under Duress in Columbia* (New York: Routledge, 2023), 110.

of the family protector. I too want to protect what is mine, and I shudder at the thought of dependency. As someone who has never held a gun, I worried when writing chapter 7 that I would be unfairly focusing on a group I could not possibly hope to understand. Indeed, this may still be the case. But in exploring gun culture I discovered my own fear, insecurity, and need for control reflected back to me. I discovered my own human care. In trying to remove the speck, I discovered the plank. I do not like to ask other people for help. I prefer self-sufficiency. I often keep others at a distance. And most of all, I hate not being in control. Where, then, does this leave me? In his book *The Joy of Being Wrong*, James Alison describes the transformation of desire with the metaphor of a parent trying to disentangle their child from an unruly group of children. Rather than threaten the child with the loss of ice cream, the parent instead awakens the child's desire for something good by taking the ice cream out and beginning to unwrap it in front of the child. Alison writes, "When we are called to 'set your mind on things that are above, not on things that are on earth' (Col. 3:2), what we are being exhorted to is to allow our imagination to be centered on the good things that are in store for us and toward which we are tending in our urgent hope, *since it is this that begins to enable us to desire these things.*"[9]

In other words, this realization of my own very deep human care leaves me in the ordinary space of Christian spirituality—praying and worshiping and acting and hoping. In prayer and worship we open ourselves up to the very goodness that Alison is evoking—the joy of communion with God. We are incapable, of course, of simply choosing to live without fear or anxiety; we must trust the Spirit's work. But as Luther suggested, we can remind ourselves of God's grace and avail ourselves of the sacraments, the Scriptures, and the communal life, which bring grace before us in tangible ways and help us reject a grace-denying culture. In the process we can also act, bestirring ourselves to ordinary works of love without excessive thought about how inadequate we feel to the task. In his discussion of spirituality Hauerwas talks about this sort of action as the grace of doing one thing. "I do not have to begin by trying to 'solve' the real problem," he claims. "Instead I can take the time to do one thing that might help lead myself and others to God's peace."[10] In the process of acting, we also hope. We hope that our work will bear fruit, that God will be acting in it beyond our imagination and striving.

9. Alison, *Joy of Being Wrong*, 227 (emphasis original).
10. Hauerwas, *Peaceable Kingdom*, 150.

INDEX